GW0674202

OLD LIGHT
ON NEW WORSHIP

MUSICAL INSTRUMENTS AND
THE WORSHIP OF GOD,
A THEOLOGICAL, HISTORICAL
AND PSYCHOLOGICAL STUDY

JOHN PRICE

WITH A FOREWORD BY EDWARD DONNELLY

SIMPSON
PUBLISHING COMPANY

John Price is a graduate of Trinity Ministerial Academy, Montville, New Jersey. He is currently the Pastor of Grace Baptist Church in Rochester, New York, where he has served since 1995. Pastor Price and his wife, Mary Jo, have two children.

Simpson Publishing Company
Post Office Box 100 · Avinger, Texas 75630 · U.S.A.
www.simpsonpublishing.com

Scripture taken from the New American Standard Bible,®
Copyright © 1960,1962,1963,1968,1971,1972,1973,1975,1977,1995
by The Lockman Foundation. Used by permission.

Scripture quotations marked "NKJV™" are taken from the New King James Version.® Copyright © 1982 by Thomas Nelson, Inc. Used by permission. All rights reserved.

Scripture quotations marked "KJV" are taken from the King James Version.

Library of Congress Cataloging-in-Publication Data

    Price, John (John Douglas), 1957-
      Old light on new worship : musical instruments and the worship of
    God, a theological, historical and psychological study / John Price ;
    with a foreword by Edward Donnelly.
      p. cm.
    Includes bibliographical references and index.
    ISBN 1-881095-01-0 (hardcover)
    1. Music in churches. 2. Musical instruments--Religious aspects
    --Christianity. I. Title.
    BV290.P75 2005
    264'.2--dc22

                                 2005026942

CONTENTS

CONTENTS

Foreword

I T IS a privilege to be invited to contribute a foreword to *Old Light on New Worship*, a book which I believe to be both important and timely. Important because it examines the relationship between two of the most intense experiences available to human beings. To worship God is the highest activity in which we can ever engage, the goal of our creation and redemption. Music is, in the words of Martin Luther, "a fair and lovely gift of God . . . next to the Word of God the mistress and governess of the feelings of the human heart." To consider the interplay between them is a matter of no small significance.

The timeliness of this volume springs from the fact that we are living through a worship revolution. Evangelical worship has changed as much in the last twenty years as in the previous two hundred. The process has been swift, pervasive and controversial, leading to the tragic emergence of what have been called "worship wars" in which brothers and sisters in Christ actually quarrel over how to worship their heavenly Father. These developments have not taken place in a context of spiritual renewal. They seem, rather, to be partly the product and partly the cause of an increasing shallowness and worldliness among the professing people of God. Reformed churches are not proving immune to the clamour for change. So it is useful to have before us a calm, reasoned discussion of one of the issues.

John Price is not here dealing with "old versus new" in Christian music. If we are disturbed by the current mania for what is new, we should realize that an equally potent enemy of God-glorifying worship can be a stubborn ultra-conservatism. Some Christians have absolutized their traditions, their personal music preferences, the tunes associated with their early years in the faith. These they consider to be reverent and appropriate, yet look with suspicion on anything contemporary. But the melodies we use are not inspired and we should allow for legitimate differences in this area. Music which seems revolutionary to one generation has often become traditional in the next. We need to bear with one another, to love and respect our fellow-believers enough to sacrifice from time to time our own preferences in the interests of their edification. Divergences in musical taste should strengthen and not threaten our oneness in Christ, of which unity in diversity is a distinguishing characteristic.

Old Light on New Worship focuses on a single issue. Is there a place for the use of musical instruments in the new covenant worship of God? In answering this question, the author deals with three damaging weaknesses in modern evangelicalism.

The first is a failure to apply the principle of *sola scriptura*, the conviction that the Bible is our supreme and sufficient guide and that, specifically, we are to worship God only in the way appointed in his Word. This perspective, once the common property of Reformed churches, is now so overlooked as to seem bizarre or fanatical to many, while others choose to exempt worship from its scope, as if God had little or nothing to say about that which most intimately concerns his glory.

Another weakness is a kind of historical blindness, the neglect of what previous generations have discovered from the Scriptures. It almost indicates contempt for the past, a careless dismissal of how God has over the years been guiding the church into a fuller understanding of truth. This "chronological snobbery," as C. S.

Lewis called it, can masquerade as a commitment to "Scripture alone." But it is at least curious that those who lay such stress on what the Spirit has taught them from the Bible are so little interested in what he has taught others. Those believers are self-impoverished who will not listen to their forefathers.

A third characteristic of today's church is a frightening naïveté. Like children playing with high explosive, too many Christians seem unaware of music's potential for harm as well as good. Closing their eyes and ears to the manifold evidence around them, they introduce musical innovations with little reflection or discernment, apparently oblivious to the risks they are running. It is a lemming-like rush towards the coarsening of worship and the trivialising of spiritual experience.

John Price addresses each of these weaknesses. He demonstrates, with an impressive accumulation of scriptural evidence, the absence of any reference to musical instruments in the worship of the early church and the silence of the New Testament on this matter. For their use in the public worshipping assemblies of new covenant saints there is not a shred of scriptural warrant. His overview of church history will surprise many, with its weight of evidence that the church has sung praise unaccompanied for the greater part of her history and that this has been the position of many of the greatest and wisest of her leaders. A penetrating analysis of the psychology of music points up its frequently deceptive effect upon the human emotions and the very real danger of confusing a merely sensual excitement with true worship.

In these pages we find a two-fold appeal. Where musical instruments are part of worship, pastors and churches are urged to think again, to examine the evidence and to change to a more biblical pattern. Such a change would admittedly be startling, a radical step. True reformation usually is. But if our repeated assertion that "the reformed church stands in constant need of reformation" is more than a cliché, we need to have the God-given boldness to do what is right, no matter what. And, as the very word "re-formation" implies, this often involves a return to a purer original. In this sense, to go back to the practice of the New Testament would be the most constructive and forward-looking step possible.

But perhaps more urgent is the plea not to change. For we find ourselves at a moment of crisis in reformed worship. Churches which have up to the present accompanied their singing with a single instrument are contemplating moving to multiple instruments. Perhaps they are being influenced more deeply than they realize by the surrounding evangelical culture. It may be that they feel that this is one way of retaining the loyalty of their young people, an argument which Robert L. Dabney describes as "the most unsound and perilous possible for a good man to adopt." They may genuinely believe that this would make their worship more biblical. But this book is a call to pause and reflect.

The only possible scriptural basis for the use of instruments in worship is to be found in the Old Testament passages where the worshippers are described as using them or commanded to use them. "Praise him with trumpet sound; praise him with lute and harp! Praise him with tambourine and dance; praise him with strings and pipe! Praise him with sounding cymbals! . . ." (Psalm 150:3ff). But the overwhelming consensus of the church has been that these instruments were an integral part of that ceremonial worship fulfilled and abrogated in Christ. We sing in the Psalms of the hyssop (51:7), the altar (43:4), the sack-cloth (69:11), the evening sacrifice (141:2), the goats and bulls (66:15), the cherubim (80:1), the ark (132:8) and the new moon (81:3). No one applies these with a wooden literalism to the church today. On what grounds, then, can we place the musical instruments of the temple in a different category than other ceremonial elements? We may not as clearly understand the typical significance of musical instruments, but that is no warrant for assuming that they had none. "Musical instruments," wrote Calvin, "in celebrating the praises of God would be no more suitable than the burning of incense, the lighting up of lamps, and the restoration of the other shadows of the law . . . . Music was useful as an elementary aid to the people of God in ancient times . . . . Now that Christ has appeared, and the Church has reached full age, it were only to bury the light of the Gospel, should we introduce the shadows of a departed dispensation."

How wise is it to introduce such a momentous change on such a slender and dubious basis? The controversies which may well arise will be the responsibility of the innovators. New Testament practice is against it. The majority verdict of the past is against it. The dangers are patent. If, as reformed Christians believe, the words of our praise must always be primary, how much can instruments add to the singing of those words? Will the trumpets, tambourines and cymbals which the Old Testament requires really enhance our appreciation of what is being sung? How will churches organize the dancing which is an integral element in such passages (Psalm 149:3; 150:4)? Is this a constructive, edifying course to adopt?

I write as one who, for a lifetime, has sung unaccompanied praise to God. It puts us on our mettle, makes us depend on each other, for there is no fallback — singing or silence! And it can be wonderful! No equipment needed, no obtrusion of human talents, no controversy, nothing to distract from the glorious words — just the voices of the redeemed harmoniously worshipping the Lord. It is my prayer that the following pages may persuade more of God's people to experience in Christ this liberating simplicity. "Through him then let us continually offer up a sacrifice of praise to God, that is, the fruit of lips that acknowledge his name" (Heb.13:15).

Edward Donnelly
Pastor, Trinity Reformed Presbyterian Church, Newtownabbey
Principal, Reformed Theological College, Belfast
Northern Ireland
August 2005

Preface

THERE is perhaps no aspect in the life of the Christian church more important than its corporate worship. There may be no more difficult or controversial issue regarding worship in our generation than the role of musical instruments. A proper understanding of the use of musical instruments in worship is not a matter of secondary or subordinate concern. It is of the highest importance to the purity and the peace of the church. Musical instruments have a most direct and powerful influence upon the human emotions. They have a most profound impact upon the whole nature and atmosphere of Christian worship. Their use in worship has been the occasion of much strife and division between brethren. The subject before us is not one that we can simply ignore and hope will go away. This book is written from a Reformed perspective with a commitment to the regulative principle of worship. The worship of the modern evangelical church, which is often dominated by musical instruments, calls upon us as Reformed Christians to consider this issue and to come to a thoroughly biblical understanding of their use in public worship.

For more than twenty years, I have worshipped in Reformed Baptist churches that have always had a high regard for the regulative principle of worship. The musical accompaniment used with congregational singing has almost always been that of a single instrument, usually the piano. I have frequently asked the questions: Why do we, as Reformed Christians, use only the piano while the modern evangelical church very often employs such a variety of musical instruments? Why do musical instruments play such a minor role in Reformed churches while they have such prominence in Christianity all around us?

During my training for the Christian ministry at the Trinity Ministerial Academy in Montville, New Jersey, I prepared two papers for the courses in Historical Theology. The first was entitled "The Worship of the Early Church" and the second "John Knox and the Regulative Principle." Both of these papers were efforts, at least in part, to answer the above questions concerning musical instruments in worship. The following book is a continuation of these previous studies.

A brief statement as to how this book came into being may be in order. More than three years ago, a study was conducted in a sister Reformed Baptist church with the conclusion that various musical instruments are warranted in New Testament worship. The audio tapes of this study came into the possession of one of the members of my congregation who then passed them on to me. I later became aware that these tapes were having a wider distribution with some influence among other Reformed Baptists. In listening to these tapes, I realized that further study was necessary on this subject. What began as a relatively brief study developed over time into this book.

I have come to this subject with the conviction that the Scripture alone should be our final guide in all matters of faith and practice. I believe there is such a thing as pure worship that is according to the will of God and it should be our goal to have such worship in the church. Our worship should be governed, not by our own personal desires or preferences, nor by the culture and society in which we live, but by the Word of God alone.

The focus of this book is on the issue of musical instruments in public worship. There are larger principles relating to worship that the reader may desire to be familiar with before directly approaching this specific concern. I will take this opportunity to recommend several other books that may be helpful background reading in three areas of study: First, with respect to the regulative principle of worship, consider *The Regulative Principle of the Church* by Samuel Waldron and *The Church of Christ* by James Bannerman (Vol. 1, p. 335–375). Second, a helpful analysis of contemporary worship is found in Peter Masters' *Worship in the Melting Pot*. Third, an excellent treatment of the relationship between Reformed theology and worship is given by D. G. Hart and John R. Muether in their book *With Reverence and Awe*.

This book has three basic approaches to the subject of musical instruments in worship. Chapter I is a theological study in which the regulative principle of worship is applied to the use of musical instruments in public worship in the Old and New Testaments. Chapter II is a survey of the use of musical instruments throughout the history of the church. Here we will discover how the church has viewed this issue and applied the regulative principle since the coming of Christ. This chapter will perhaps be the most surprising to the reader, as it was to me. Chapter III is a brief look at the psychology of music, and some of the effects of musical instruments upon the human emotions in relation to Christian worship are discussed. In Chapter IV, various arguments that are often made in favor of musical instruments in worship are considered. Various other subjects related to worship and musical instrumentation will be presented as seen in the table of contents.

This book contains perhaps more than an ordinary number of quotations from Christian leaders of the past. My purpose in using them is that we may read and understand the convictions of those who have gone before us. The issue of musical instruments in worship is not novel to the Christian church. It is an issue that the church has wrestled with throughout its history and come to very definite conclusions about, often with surprising agreement. I would ask the reader to look briefly at the Index of Names at the end of this book. All of these men have come to the same conclusions as presented in this study. Most of them are quoted and their views expressed in their own words. I hope that a glance at this index will entice the reader to take the pains to consider what lies before him. This book is, in a sense, a summary of what the church has thought upon musical instruments in worship. It will be seen that the convictions expressed here have been held by vast segments of the Christian church over the greater part of its history.

I am compelled to say a word about my desires for unity among the Reformed churches. The situation of the modern evangelical church regarding the use of musical instruments may be divided into three general categories as seen in the following diagram:

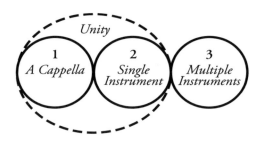

Group #1 are those churches that use no musical instruments in worship and whose congregational singing is *a cappella.*[1] These churches view musical instruments as a substantive addition to God's worship and, therefore, a violation of the regulative principle. The number of churches that fall into this category is relatively few in our generation. Group #2 are those churches that use only a single musical instrument, usually a piano, in accompanying the congregational singing. These churches often have a high regard for the regulative principle of worship. They believe that a piano is suf-

1. The term *a cappella* is from Italian meaning "in the style of the church." *The New Grove Dictionary of Music and Musicians*, ed. Stanley Sadie, (New York: MacMillan Publishers Limited, 1980), Vol. 1, 32.

ficient to aid the pitch and meter in singing. Since the piano is used only in a subordinate manner to aid the singing, its use is not seen as a substantive element or a violation of the regulative principle. Many Reformed churches, and other evangelical churches as well, fall into this category. Group #3 are those churches that use multiple musical instruments in any number of ways. Most of these churches can no longer legitimately claim that their use of instruments is a subordinate and non-substantive element in worship to merely aid the pitch and meter in singing. Their use of multiple instruments must serve other purposes. These churches have crossed a crucial boundary and entered into a clear and unacceptable violation of the regulative principle of worship. The vast majority of modern evangelical churches fall into this third category, and their numbers are rapidly increasing.

My primary purpose in publishing this book is to strengthen the convictions of those in Group #1 and to help those churches in Group #2, especially those that are Reformed in their theology. Many churches in Group #2 feel tremendous pressure in our day to accept multiple musical instruments into their worship and to move into Group #3. Some have already succumbed to this pressure, and I fear they may have done so without sufficient study and consideration. The subject before us is not one that can be handled in a light and cavalier manner. It is a concern with the most far-reaching ramifications and consequences, and one that is worthy of the most careful and diligent study. My hope is that this book will supply some of the materials that should be considered and that the above trend will be reversed. My desire is that those churches in Group #2 will feel constrained not to accept the use of multiple musical instruments into their worship. As will be seen in the following pages, the use of multiple instruments is a radical departure from biblical and Reformed worship. Such churches must by necessity become inventors in the worship of God. The use of multiple instruments seriously undermines any real commitment to the regulative principle, and, to one degree or another, it invites musical entertainment into worship.

As can be seen from the above diagram, I have drawn a circle of unity around Group #1 and Group #2. I have done so because I believe that unity and peace can and should exist between these churches. Those Reformed churches that exist within these two categories share the same theological convictions and a high regard for the regulative principle of worship. They generally both agree that the use of multiple instruments is an unacceptable violation of the regulative principle. The distinction between the use or nonuse of a single musical instrument is not an issue that should disrupt unity either within, or between, these churches. Any disunity between such brethren would be a greater violation of the will of Christ than the issue itself. It would be contrary to the intentions of this author, and a great grief, if this book were ever used for such a purpose.

As a result of this study, the church where I am pastor has moved from Group #2 into Group #1. We have become convinced that we should no longer use any musical instrument in accompanying our congregational singing. The reader will discover the compelling reasons why we have made this change in the pages that follow. While I would not be disappointed if other churches were persuaded to make this change as well, I have no desire to see any new faction formed among the Reformed Baptist churches. My purpose is to maintain unity and promote pure worship in our churches. While I have argued my case with force and conviction, my desire is to help us carefully think through the theological and historical issues involved in the use of musical instruments in worship.

I realize that some of my Reformed brethren will not come to the same conclusions presented here. I would not desire to harm fellowship with such brethren in any way. I will sincerely continue to hold them in high esteem though they may differ with me on this particular issue. I would have them to know that I do not believe that they are offering strange fire simply because they use a single musical instrument. My concern for unity is so strong that I have included an Appendix entitled, "An Exhortation to Unity," where this issue is furthered discussed.

As I have stated above, a proper understanding of the role of musical instruments in worship is of the highest importance to the worship of the church, especially in our generation. This is a subject worthy of the most diligent and careful study. I do hope that the efforts made in reading this book will not be unfruitful.

Introduction

THE central purpose of any congregation of God's people is to publicly gather to offer worship and praise to the living and true God. Our highest concern must be that our worship be acceptable and pleasing to God. The history of God's people, both in the biblical record and since the time of Christ, has shown that there is no area of the church's life which is more prone to corruption than its worship. Corruption in worship has often marked the beginning of the apostasy of God's people.

The Bible makes it clear that God has not left His worship open to the inventions and devices of men. God alone has the prerogative to determine how He will be worshipped. He alone has the right to decide what elements should be present in the public worship of His people. The central concern of worship should not be what men find desirable and pleasing, but what God desires. We may know His will only through His word. Only in bringing those elements commanded in the Scripture can we be certain that our worship is acceptable to Him.

This book assumes a basic understanding of the regulative principle of worship and makes no effort to provide the biblical support for it. That work has been very adequately done by others.[1]

1 J. Ligon Duncan III, "Does God Care How We Worship?" and "Foundations for Biblically Directed Worship" in *Give Praise to God*, eds. Philip Graham Ryken, Derek W. H. Thomas and J. Ligon Duncan, (Phillipsburg, NJ: P&R Publishing, 2003), 17–73. Samuel Waldron, *The Regulative Principle of the Church*, (Quezon City: Wisdom Publications, 1995). James Bannerman, *The Church of Christ*, (USA: Still Waters Revival Books), Vol.1, 335–375.

The view of John Calvin and the Puritans was that only what God has commanded in the Scripture is acceptable and all that is not commanded is forbidden. Only with clear biblical warrant for any element of worship can we believe that God is pleased with what we do. Any subtractions from or additions to God's commands in worship cannot be done with faith. (See Lev. 10:1–2; Deut. 12:30–32, 17:3; Josh. 1:7, 23:6–8; Matt. 15:3; 1 Cor. 14:37–38; Col. 2:20–23).

This view of the regulative principle of worship is expressed in Chapter 22, Paragraph 1 of the 1689 London Baptist Confession: "But the acceptable way of worshipping the true God, is instituted by Himself, and so limited by His own revealed will, that He may not be worshipped according to the imaginations and devices of men, nor the suggestions of Satan, under any visible representations, or any other way not prescribed in the Holy Scriptures."

As we approach this subject concerning the use of musical instruments in worship, we must do so with faith and confidence that God's word is sufficient and clear to guide us into His will (2 Tim. 3:16–17). We must make every effort to lay aside all of our own personal preferences and human reasoning and be committed to the great reformation doctrine of *sola scriptura*. We must be willing to submit our minds to the truth revealed in Scripture and to add nothing to it. "To the law and to the testimony! If they do not speak according to this word, it is because there is no light in them" (Isa. 8:20 NKJV).

Chapter I

The Regulative Principle Applied to Musical Instruments

ALL Christians recognize the prominence of musical instruments in the worship of the Temple under the Old Covenant. However, it is often assumed, even by those who hold to the regulative principle, that musical instruments somehow fall outside of the realm of God's authority. While God regulates every other element of His worship, somehow musical instruments are not recognized as coming under His regulation. Musical instruments are believed to be neither commanded nor forbidden, and, therefore, they are considered matters of indifference and liberty.

In this chapter we will see that God has always regulated His public worship even in regard to the specific musical instruments used. There is no record in Scripture of a musical instrument ever being used in public worship without an explicit divine command. We will then establish the following three basic theological principles of worship: (1) The Old Testament Temple worship in all of its outward ceremonies and rituals has been abolished; (2) We must look to Christ and His apostles alone for the worship of the church; and (3) With no command, example, or any indication whatsoever from the Lord Jesus that He desires musical instruments in His church, we have no warrant for their use. In Chapter II we will discover these same three principles over and over again throughout the history of the church. This is the way the vast majority of those who have held to a biblical and Reformed view of worship have applied the regulative principle of worship to the use of musical instruments. These three principles are the thread that is found in the Scripture and that runs throughout the history of the church.

Musical Instruments in the Old Testament

We begin with the Tabernacle in the days of Moses. The only musical instrument used in the public worship of the Tabernacle was the trumpet. As with every other element of the Tabernacle worship, musical instrumentation was regulated by specific divine command. We see the trumpet commanded in Numbers 10 and regulated in the following three ways: 1) The trumpet (including the number of them) was the only musical instrument authorized for use in the Tabernacle worship: Num. 10:1–2, "The LORD spoke further to Moses, saying, *'Make yourself two trumpets* of silver, of hammered work you shall make them. . . .'" 2) The priests were the only persons authorized to use the trumpets: Num. 10:8, "*The priestly sons of Aaron*, moreover, shall blow the trumpets; and this shall be for you a perpetual statute throughout your generations." 3) The occasions were specified when the trumpets could be used, including worship during the appointed feasts:

> Num. 10:10, "Also in the day of your gladness and *in your appointed feasts,* and on the first days of your months, you shall blow the trumpets over your burnt offerings, and over the sacrifices of your peace offerings, and they shall be as a reminder of you before your God. I am the LORD your God." (See also Lev. 23:24.)

These two trumpets were the only musical instruments used in public worship throughout the time of the Tabernacle in the wilderness.[1] It was not until after the occupation of Canaan and

---

1. The occasion of Miriam and the timbrel will be dealt with later in this chapter.

the entrance of the ark into Jerusalem in the days of David that any other musical instruments were added to the public worship of God. As with all the other elements of the Tabernacle worship, the use of musical instruments was regulated by divine command. God regulated not only the specific instrument that should be used but also the number of them, who could use them, and the occasions and purposes for which they could be used.

The ancient Egyptians were well known for their wide variety of musical instruments and their guilds of professional musicians. Musical instruments played a central role in the worship of the Egyptian gods.[2] As a man who was "educated in all the learning of the Egyptians" (Acts 7:20), Moses surely would have been familiar with these instruments and how they were used in Egyptian worship. However, Moses had no liberty to bring any of those instruments of Egypt into God's worship on his own. It was only under divine command that he was authorized to use the trumpet. We see the regulative principle of worship applied to musical instruments in the days of the Tabernacle. God regulates His worship even in regard to the use of musical instruments.

A distinctive change takes place in the history of God's worship in the days of King David. The people of God were no longer a wandering nation as they were during the time of Moses. They now possessed the land of Canaan, and the ark of the covenant was settled in Jerusalem. The Levites were no longer needed to transport the Tabernacle and all its furnishings. The time had come for their role in God's worship to be changed. David begins to use them as professional singers and musicians (1 Chron. 16:1–6, 23:1–5). David acknowledges, "The LORD God of Israel has given rest to His people, and He dwells in Jerusalem forever. And also, the Levites will no longer need to carry the tabernacle and all its utensils for its service" (1 Chron. 23:25–26).

2. H. M. Best; D. Hutter, "Music; Musical Instruments," in *The Zondervan Pictorial Encyclopedia of the Bible,* 5 Vol. (Grand Rapid: The Zondervan Corporation, 1976), Vol. 4, 312–314.

When we read through the historical narratives of 1 Chron.
13–16 and 1 Chron. 23–25, in which David brings the ark to
Jerusalem and orders the Temple worship, respectively, we are not
told why he brought the singers and the various musical instruments
into God's worship. We may be left with the impression that David
did so simply out of his own personal desires as a skilled musician.
Perhaps David believed it would enhance the experience of worship
and make it more festive and glorious. Perhaps the musical instruments had become more important in the culture of David's day
and the people found them appealing. We are not told why David
used them in the historical narrative.

We discover the reason why David brought musical instruments
into God's worship almost three hundred years later during the
reign of King Hezekiah. After many years of decay and neglect,
the Temple worship was restored by Hezekiah, and we read in
2 Chron. 29:25–27,

> He then stationed the Levites in the house of the LORD
> with cymbals, with harps, and with lyres, *according to
> the command of David* and of Gad the king's seer, and of
> Nathan the prophet; *for the command was from the LORD
> through His prophets.* And the Levites stood with *the musical
> instruments of David,* and the priests with the *trumpets.*
> Then Hezekiah gave the order to offer the burnt offering
> on the altar. When the burnt offering began, the song to
> the LORD also began with the *trumpets, accompanied by the
> instruments of David,* king of Israel.

When Hezekiah restored the Temple worship, he was faced
with the issue of how God should be worshipped. In regard to
musical instruments he needed to answer two questions. First,
should musical instruments be used at all in the house of the Lord?
And if they should be, what specific musical instruments should
be used? Hezekiah did not assume that he had any authority to

act in this matter apart from divine command. For both of these questions, he looked for divine authority in regard to the worship of the Temple. Hezekiah found that God had authorized only certain musical instruments for His worship. Trumpets and various other musical instruments had been brought into God's worship *"according to the command of David."* Hezekiah limited the musical instruments to only those divinely authorized through David. "And the Levites stood with *the musical instruments of David,* and the priests with *the trumpets,"* and all of this was done *"according to the command of David."*

Now we ask the question: where did this *"command of David"* to bring musical instruments into God's worship còme from? 2 Chron. 29:25 states clearly that David's command came from the Lord, *"for the command was from the LORD through His prophets."* Here is the reason why David instituted the Levitical singers and brought other musical instruments into God's worship. It was that they were commanded by God through His prophets Gad and Nathan. David's command was God's command. Even the great king and prophet David had no liberty to alter God's worship because of his own personal desires or musical inclinations. Neither could he make any additions because he believed they would enhance the experience of worship and make it more joyful and glorious. David could act only by divine authority. Just as in the days of the Tabernacle worship under Moses, God regulated His Temple worship under David, even in regard to musical instruments. Just as with Moses, He regulated the specific musical instruments to be used in His worship ("the instruments of David"), *"for the command was from the LORD through His prophets."*

A number of the biblical commentators share this same perspective on the divine regulation of musical instrumentation in the Temple worship. Keil and Delitzsch emphasize this point in their comments on 2 Chron. 29:25:

The Levites were appointed to sing, "according to the command of David," but this command was by interposition of Jahve, viz. given by His prophets. David had consequently made this arrangement at the divine suggestion, coming to him through the prophets.[3]

John Gill similarly explains, "This sort of music was not commanded by the law of Moses, but was directed to by David under a divine influence, and was approved of by the prophets of the Lord here mentioned."[4] Matthew Henry comments concerning these musical instruments that "God by His prophets had commanded the use of [them]."[5] Cotton Mather writes,

The instrumental musick used of the old church of Israel was an institution of God: it was (2 Chron. 29:25) the commandment of the Lord "by the prophets." And the instruments are called "God's instruments" (1 Chron. 16:42) and "instruments of the Lord" (2 Chron. 7:6).[6]

It is important for us, at this point, to understand what is included under this *command of David* since we will find it referred to in other passages as we proceed. We read of David's command in 1 Chron. 16:4–7, when the ark of God was brought into the tent in Jerusalem:

And he [David] appointed some of the Levites as ministers before the ark of the LORD, *even to celebrate and to thank and praise the LORD God of Israel*: Asaph the chief, and second to him Zechariah, then Jeiel, Shemiramoth, Jehiel, Mattithiah, Eliab, Benaiah, Obed-edom, and Jeiel, *with*

3. C. F. Keil and F. Delitzsch, *Commentary on the Old Testament*, (Peabody: Hendrickson Publishers, 1989), Vol. 3, 451.

4. John Gill, *Gill's Commentary*, (London: William Hill, 1852-1854; Reprint, Grand Rapids: Baker Book House, reprinted 1980), Vol. 2, 520.

5. Matthew Henry, *Matthew Henry's Commentary on the Whole Bible*, (Old Tappen, NJ: Fleming H. Revell Company), Vol. 2, 999.

6. Cotton Mather, *The Great Works of Christ in America*, (London: 1702; Reprint, Edinburgh: The Banner of Truth Trust, reprinted 1979), Vol. 2, 266.

musical instruments, harps, lyres; also Asaph played loud-sounding *cymbals*, and Benaiah and Jahaziel the priests blew *trumpets* continually before the ark of the covenant of God. Then on that day David first assigned Asaph and his relatives to give thanks to the Lord.

The *"command of David"* was his appointment of some of the Levites as ministers *"to celebrate and to thank and praise the LORD God of Israel" "with musical instruments, harps, lyres"* and *"cymbals"* and *"trumpets."*

David's commandment embraces the use of the trumpet first commanded through Moses, and to this was added the Levitical singing of praise with various other musical instruments. The musical instruments that David introduces are referred to above in 2 Chron. 29:26 and in other passages as *"the musical instruments of David."* We now have two sets of instruments in public worship: the trumpets that had been commanded through Moses and "the instruments of David." It was this commandment of David to which Hezekiah looked when reforming the Temple worship, and, in obedience to it, he instituted Levitical singing along with the trumpets and the musical instruments of David.

This command of David was not to be limited to the time in which the ark resided in the tent in Jerusalem, but it was to continue in the worship of the Temple that his son Solomon was to build. When David came to the end of his life and gave the throne to Solomon, he appointed the Levitical singers with his musical instruments to be used in the Temple worship. In 1 Chron. 23:1–5 we read,

So when David was old and full of days, he made his son Solomon king over Israel. And he gathered together all the leaders of Israel, with the priests and the Levites. Now the Levites were numbered from the age of thirty years and above; and the number of individual males was thirty-eight thousand. Of these, twenty-four thousand were to look after the work of the house of the LORD, six thousand were officers and judges, four thousand were gatekeepers, and four thousand praised the LORD with musical instruments, "which I made," said David, "for giving praise" (NKJV).[7]

The command of David here continues in the Temple with the Levitical singers accompanied by David's musical instruments.

We learn again of the divine authority in regard to the Temple and its worship, which came through David in 1 Chron. 28:11–13,19 (NKJV):

> Then David gave his son Solomon the plans for the vestibule, its houses, its treasuries, its upper chambers, its inner chambers, and the place of the mercy seat; and the plans for all that he had *by the Spirit,* of the courts of the house of the Lord, of all the chambers all around, of the treasuries of the house of God, and of the treasuries for the dedicated things; also for the division of the priests and the Levites, for all the work of the service of the house of the Lord, and for all the articles of service in the house of the Lord. . . . *"All this,"* said David, *"the Lord made me understand in writing, by His hand upon me, all the works of these plans."*

Everything concerning the construction of the Temple and all the utensils of its worship were given to David "by the Spirit" and "in writing, by His hand upon him." As we have seen, this divine inspiration regarding all the Temple worship included the use of musical instruments.

Just as Moses had received a divine revelation concerning all the details of the construction and the worship of the Tabernacle, so David received a divine revelation concerning all the details of the construction and the worship of the Temple. This revelation included the command to institute the Levitical singers with the

---

7. See also 1 Chron. 25:1–7.

various musical instruments of David and the trumpets. John L. Girardeau (1825–1898), a Presbyterian Professor at Columbia Theological Seminary, comments on the above passages:

> When the Temple was to be built, its order of worship to be instituted, David received a divine revelation in regard to it, just as Moses had concerning the tabernacle with its ordinances. . . . Instrumental music would not have been constituted an element in the Temple-worship, had not God expressly authorized it by his command.[8]

We have established several important truths concerning musical instruments in public worship from the Old Testament Scriptures. First, God has always regulated His worship even in regard to musical instruments in both the Tabernacle and the Temple. The use of musical instruments in worship has never been a matter of liberty for men to do as they please. The Lord has clearly placed instruments under His own authority in worship. Second, God has regulated even the specific instruments to be used: the trumpet in the Tabernacle and the trumpet with the instruments of David in the Temple. Third, the "command of David" concerning worship included the introduction of Levitical singers along with the trumpets of Moses and the various other musical instruments called "the instruments of David." As will be seen, there were no further additions to the instruments used in the Temple throughout the time of the Old Covenant.

We will now look at various passages in which it will be seen that musical instruments were always used in the Temple only under the divine authority that had come through David, the prophet or the man of God. On each of these occasions, we will see *"the com-*

---

8. John L. Girardeau, *Instrumental Music in the Public Worship of the Church,* (Richmond: Whittet & Shepperson, Printers, 1888), 31, http://www.fpcr.org/FreeEbooks.htm (accessed March 24, 2004). A controversy arose over the use of musical instruments in worship among the Southern Presbyterian Churches in the 19th century. Professor John L. Girardeau addressed this issue in this book.

mand of David" referred to as the authority under which musical instruments were brought into the Temple worship. As we have seen above, this command of David included the Levitical singing with the musical instruments of David and the trumpets.

We begin with the institution of Temple worship for the first time under Solomon's rule, and we find that it was all performed in accordance with God's command through David. When the ark was brought into the Temple, we read in 2 Chron. 5:11–13, "And when the priests came forth from the holy place . . . and all the Levitical singers . . . with cymbals, harps, and lyres . . . accompanied by trumpets and cymbals and instruments of music." In 2 Chron. 8:14, we see why Solomon instituted the Temple worship this way:

> Now *according to the ordinance of his father David*, he appointed the divisions of the priests for their service, and the Levites for their duties of praise and ministering before the priests *according to the daily rule*, and the gatekeepers by their divisions at every gate; *for David the man of God had so commanded.*

Solomon brought the trumpets and the instruments of music into the Temple worship because it was *"according to the ordinance of his father David . . . for David the man of God had so commanded."* Solomon found that the divine authority for musical instruments in worship had come from his father David, the man of God.

We will now witness this same pattern, repeating itself over and over again, throughout the history of the nation of Israel, in which men continually look back to *"the command of David"* as the divine authority under which musical instruments were to be used in the Temple worship. On each of these occasions, the Temple worship had been corrupted and needed to be reformed. The people of God were faced over and over again with the same question of how God should be worshipped. Should singing and musical instrumentation be brought into the house of the Lord? If so, what specific musical instruments had God approved to be used? On every occasion, they continued to look back to God's command through David many hundreds of years earlier.

About 170 years after David, we read of the reforms under Jehoiada the priest in 2 Chron. 23:18,

> Moreover, Jehoiada placed the offices of the house of the LORD under the authority of the Levitical priests, *whom David had assigned over the house of the LORD*, to offer the burnt offerings of the LORD, as it is written in the law of Moses—with rejoicing and singing *according to the order of David.*

About 380 years after David, King Josiah reformed the Temple worship. He commanded the Levites to look back to the writings of David for authority. In 2 Chron. 35:4, Josiah said, "prepare yourselves by your fathers' households in your divisions, *according to the writing of David king of Israel and according to the writing of his son Solomon.*" When the reforms were instituted, we read in 2 Chron. 35:15, "And the singers, the sons of Asaph, were in their places, *according to the command of David*, Asaph, Heman, and Jeduthun the king's seer."

After the return from the Babylonian captivity, 550 years after David, Zerubbabel the prince and Jeshua the priest instituted worship in the second Temple. We read in Ezra 3:10 (NKJV),

> When the builders laid the foundation of the Temple of the LORD, the priests stood in their apparel with trumpets, and the Levites, the sons of Asaph, with cymbals, to praise the LORD, *according to the ordinance of David* king of Israel.

Nearly 600 years after David, we read of the reforms under Nehemiah in Neh. 12:24,

And the heads of the Levites were Hashabiah, Sherebiah, and Jeshua the son of Kadmiel, with their brothers across from them, to praise and give thanks, group alternating with group, *according to the command of David the man of God.*

Nehemiah instituted the trumpets of Moses and the musical instruments of David in Neh. 12:35–36, "and some of the sons of the priests with *trumpets. . . .* and his kinsmen. . . . with *the musical instruments of David the man of God.*" A few verses later we read (45–46),

Both the singers and the gatekeepers kept the charge of their God and the charge of the purification, *according to the command of David* and Solomon his son. For in the days of David and Asaph of old there were chiefs of the singers, and songs of praise and thanksgiving to God.

As we read through the above verses, we notice that in each case of restoration of the Temple worship these men looked back to "*the command of David the man of God.*" They all recognized that the worship of the Temple had come by God's command through David. Although we do not find all the musical instruments mentioned in every case, we may assume that they were all present, for as we have seen, "the command of David" included Levitical singing and the instruments of David with the trumpets. God's commands for Temple worship came through David, as "*the man of God.*" David's command was God's command.

We have established an important biblical principle at this point in our study. The men of the Bible have always viewed musical instruments in public worship as under God's authority. Their use has never been seen as a matter of liberty so that men may do as they please. It is important for us to note that nothing throughout the remainder of the Bible will change this perspective. Musical instruments in worship have always been viewed by the people of God as under divine authority. Those who assume that instruments in worship are a matter of liberty have adopted a view that is contrary to the men of the Bible and finds no support in the Word of God.

In every situation described above, we see an application of the regulative principle of worship. We see this in regard to the particular musical instruments used in God's worship. The people of God continued to look back hundreds of years to what God had commanded through David in the Scripture, and they brought only those musical instruments into worship. They understood that God regulated His worship even in regard to the specific musical instruments. Nearly 600 years after David, in the days of Nehemiah, they limited the musical instruments to those which were approved by God: the *"trumpets"* and *"the musical instruments of David the man of God."* They never assumed they had authority to bring any other instruments into God's worship without clear divine command.[9]

John Girardeau writes in regard to the use of musical instruments in worship,

> In the Jewish dispensation God . . . kept the ordering of this part of his formal and instituted worship in his own hands. There is positive proof that it was never made an element of that worship except by his express command. Without his warrant it was excluded; only with it was it employed.[10]

Many who advocate the use of musical instruments in the church today claim that men may bring any instrument they desire

---

9. This same basic line of argument concerning God's authority over musical instruments in worship beginning with 2 Chron. 29:25–26 and continuing with some of the other verses listed here is outlined by Andrew Fuller, "On Instrumental Music in Christian Worship," in *The Complete Works of Andrew Fuller,* (London: Arthur Hall, Virtue, and Co., 1851), 859–861.

10. Girardeau, 27.

into worship. It is assumed that God has not specified or approved which musical instruments are acceptable to Him. This was clearly not the view of the men of the Bible. During the seventy years of captivity in Babylon, the people of God would have been exposed to a wide variety of new musical instruments (Dan. 3:5, 7). We may assume that their own personal preferences and musical desires, especially those of their children and grandchildren, changed during the long captivity. But when they returned to Israel, they laid aside their own personal preferences when it came to the worship of God. They were careful not to use any of the instruments of Babylon, but only those commanded by God through David. From the examples of Jeshua and Nehemiah, we see that their only concern was to restore the Temple with *"the musical instruments of David the man of God"* and to do all things *"according to the command of David"* (Neh. 12:36,45).

Many of the modern advocates of musical instruments claim that the church should bring the instruments of the contemporary culture into the house of God. They reason that as the musical tastes of every generation change, so must the musical instruments used in public worship. This was surely not the view of the men of the Bible. David first established his instruments of worship under divine direction about 1000 B.C. Hezekiah reestablished those very same instruments about 270 years later. Josiah, Jeshua and Nehemiah lived 350, 550, 570 years, respectively, after David. We may assume that cultural changes in musical instrumentation had taken place over the hundreds of years since King David, and especially after the Babylonian captivity. However, when these men restored the Temple worship, this was not at all their concern. They did not look to their contemporary culture for what musical instruments to use. Their only concern was to use those instruments God had commanded through David the prophet. More than 500 years after David, Jeshua had "the priests stand in their apparel with *trumpets,* and the Levites, the sons of Asaph, with *cymbals*, to praise the LORD, *according to the ordinance of David,*" and Nehemiah restored only *"the musical instruments of David the man of God," "according to the command of David."*

We have noted a recurring set of phrases on every occasion when the Temple worship was restored: *"according to the ordinance of David"* and *"according to the command of David the man of God."* We should also note another set of recurring phrases on each of these occasions having to do with the re-institution of the sacrificial system of Old Covenant worship. These phrases are "as it is written in the law of Moses, the man of God" (2 Chron. 23:18, 31:3; Ezra 3:2), or, "as it is written in the law of the LORD" (Neh. 8:14–15, 10:34–36, 13:1), and, "according to the word of the Lord by Moses" (2 Chron. 35:6, 12). Both sets of recurring phrases, those that have to do with the re-institution of sacrifices, and those that have to do with the re-institution of musical instruments, are remarkably similar. Just as these men looked back to Moses, the man of God, for authority concerning sacrifices, so they looked back to David, the man of God, for authority concerning the use of musical instruments in worship. The divine authority concerning musical instruments was no less than the divine authority concerning the sacrifices. Both had been revealed by the Lord through His prophets.

Our concern has been focused on musical instruments used in the public worship of God. In every case, we have seen that they were regulated by the divine command. There were other occasions in which musical instruments were used for private purposes in the Old Testament (Gen. 31:27; Judg. 11:34; 1 Sam. 18:6 and various passages in the Psalms), but these have no bearing on the concerns of public worship. Musical instruments were used in private without ever being used in the Tabernacle or Temple.

We also find musical instruments used for religious purposes other than public worship in the Old Testament. On these occasions we read of no explicit divine command for their use, but this does not mean one did not exist. On every such occasion when musical instruments were used for religious purposes, they were used by those who were divinely inspired. And being used by those who were divinely inspired, we may rightly assume that they were used under divine command. We read of the timbrel in Exod. 15:20, "And Miriam the prophetess, Aaron's sister, took the timbrel in her hand, and all the women went out after her with timbrels and with dancing." The timbrel does not appear to be used during the singing of the song of Moses, but only afterward. It is important for us to note that this is the only place in Scripture where Miriam is called a "prophetess." For what reason would she be so designated here other than to indicate that she used her timbrel under divine command? It was not just Miriam, but "Miriam the prophetess" who played the timbrel. In the same way, we find the use of musical instruments by the prophets in 1 Sam. 10:5, and 2 Kings 3:15. Though we read of no explicit command on these occasions, the fact that these men were under divine inspiration would indicate that the command existed. As prophets, they were acting under divine guidance even in regard to their use of musical instruments. This view is consistent with all that we have already seen concerning musical instruments throughout the Old Testament. The Spirit of God directed these prophets just as He directed Moses and David. Andrew Fuller makes this point:

> Though we read of no express appointment, but merely of things being ordered or done by men who were divinely inspired, yet the same thing is in many cases clearly to be understood. Thus, though the use of the psaltery, tabret, pipe, and harp, in sacred things, be not expressly commanded till the times of David, yet, being used before his time as the means of prophetic inspiration, their being Divinely appointed for the purpose cannot be denied.[11]

11. Fuller, 860

We recognize that God does not always need to express His command explicitly, but He may do so through the example of His prophets.

Furthermore, it should also be remembered that Israel was a theocracy, and, as such, there were times of civil celebration that were mingled with the praises of Jehovah. Occasions such as Miriam's use of the timbrel and David's return after killing Goliath (1 Sam. 18:6) would fall into this category, but they have no direct bearing on the concerns of formal and public worship. David's bringing of the ark into Jerusalem in 1 Chron. 13–15 may also be considered a civil celebration. It should also be noted that these were all unique occasions and none involved a continuing state of public worship for all the people of God. Each case is limited in terms of those involved and is only temporary in nature. Because the occasions do not involve a continuing state of public worship for all the people, we would not expect to find an explicit divine command. We have seen that the use of musical instruments in public worship was always under divine authority throughout the Old Testament, and none of the above occasions diminish the force of this argument at all.

We see above that the timbrel was used by the prophetess Miriam to celebrate the special deliverance of Israel from the Egyptians. We should note that Moses, who was present on that occasion, never instituted the timbrel in the Tabernacle worship but instituted the trumpet alone. Moses recognized that musical instruments could be used in worship only by divine command. John Girardeau reasons similarly:

> Why did not Moses, who was an accomplished psalmist, and who heard the thrilling sound of timbrels in the great rejoicing over the discomfited host of Pharaoh on the shore of the Red Sea, incorporate this kind of music as an accompaniment of singing into that worship? The

answer is, Because he had no divine warrant for such a measure.[12]

Many who hold strongly to the regulative principle of worship have assumed that musical instruments are somehow left outside the sphere of God's authority; while He specified, in the most minute details, every other element of His worship in both the Tabernacle and the Temple, somehow musical instruments were not under His command. However, here we find that this is not at all the case. The Lord has reached out His sovereign hand and taken musical instruments out of the hands of men and placed them under His authority alone in His worship. There is no scriptural record of musical instruments ever being used in public worship except by an explicit divine command. The regulative principle applies to musical instruments just as it does to every other element of God's worship. We have seen that, under the Old Covenant, even the specific instruments of worship, the trumpets of Moses and the instruments of David, were commanded by God. No musical instrument has ever been brought into God's public worship except by explicit divine command. Just as all the other elements of His worship were specified, so also were the musical instruments to be used. These are truths clearly established from the Old Testament Scriptures.

We are about to consider the issue of musical instruments in worship from the New Testament Scriptures, but before we do so, there is something that must be understood. There are many who claim that God no longer holds musical instruments under His authority in the New Testament. They say that He may have established His authority over them in the Old Testament but He has relinquished His authority in the New Testament. Those who make this claim must prove their case, not from human reasoning

12. Girardeau, 75.

and evasion of the truth, but by the Word of God alone. They must go to their Bibles, as the final authority in all faith and practice, and show, by clear and convincing evidence, that God has actually relinquished His authority over musical instruments. The burden of proof rests upon them to show that it is so. Apart from such evidence, we must leave musical instruments where God has placed them, under His authority, to be used by His command only.

The issue before us is really a matter of *sola scriptura*. Will we look to the Scripture alone to govern our thinking in regard to musical instruments in worship, or will we look to human reasoning? Once God has made His mind known on any subject in the Scripture, we have no right to think otherwise apart from further evidence from the Scripture. Once the truth has been established that God has placed musical instruments under His control, without further light from the Scripture we have no right to remove them from His control by human reasoning so that we may do as we please. The question is: what proof is there in the New Testament that God has relinquished His authority over musical instruments in worship? As we shall see, there is none.

Musical Instruments in the New Testament

When we come to the New Testament, we must again be guided by the regulative principle of worship. The God of the Bible has not changed, and He will still be regarded as holy by those who draw near to Him (Lev. 10:3; 1 Pet. 1:16). We must always ask the question: What has God commanded in His worship? Only by using those elements that are divinely instituted can we be certain that our worship is acceptable to Him (Matt. 15:3, 7–9; 1 Cor. 14:37; Col. 2:20–23; 1 Tim. 3:15; 2 Tim. 3:16–17).

When we come to the issue of musical instruments in worship, we must ask the same question as did Jehoiada, Hezekiah, Josiah, Jeshua, and Nehemiah. Should musical instruments be used in the worship of the church? If so, what specific musical instruments has

God commanded? We must look to the same authority as they did, to the writings of the Scripture. The difference with us in the New Testament is that we can no longer look back to Moses or David for authority in regard to the worship of the church. The New Testament clearly states that the Temple worship, in all of its outward ceremonies and rituals, has been abolished by the coming of Jesus Christ. This includes the Levitical priesthood and the musical instruments that were an inherent part of that priesthood. Having been abolished by Christ, there is no ceremony or ritual of that Temple worship that we may bring forward into New Testament worship. The Temple worship has been replaced by a new gospel worship instituted by Christ and His apostles.

We will now consider a number of verses which confirm that the Temple worship has been abolished in the New Covenant.[13] It is of the highest importance that this truth be grasped. Many errors in worship throughout the history of the church have resulted from assumptions that elements of the Temple worship are to continue under the New Testament.

The book of Hebrews presents the strongest case for the abrogation of the Temple worship in its entirety. John Owen states that one of the main arguments of Hebrews is "the total cessation of the first covenant"[14] and "the removal of the old covenant and all

13. It may be helpful to make a distinction at this point. From the creation of the world there have been what the Puritans called "moral" or "natural" elements of worship. These are the spoken word of God, prayer, and singing of praise with the human voice. As "moral" or "natural" elements, no command is needed to perform them. They are also permanent or perpetual and are meant to continue for all time. A second kind of worship was "ceremonial" or "typical" of the coming of Christ and the blessings of His salvation. These elements were instituted primarily in the Tabernacle and Temple in Jerusalem and added onto the "moral" elements. As "ceremonial" and "typical," they were only temporary, and meant to disappear with the coming of Christ. In our following argument regarding the abolition of the Temple worship, we are referring only to its "ceremonial" and "typical" elements, not to its "moral" elements, which were always in the background and meant to continue under the gospel. This distinction between "moral" and "ceremonial" elements of worship will become more clear in the historical argument in Chapter II, especially in the section on the Puritans.

14. John Owen, *The Works of John Owen,* (Johnstone & Hunter, 1854-1855; Reprint, Edinburgh: The Banner of Truth Trust, 1979), Vol. 22, 173.

its administrations."[15] I will merely state the verses and use the best commentators as support of this conclusion, making very few comments of my own.

Hebrews 7:12 "For when the priesthood is changed, of necessity there takes place a change of law also."

This verse asserts the connection between the Levitical priesthood and the ceremonial laws of the Temple worship. When the priesthood is abolished, so also are all the laws of worship connected with them; both stand or fall together. This must include the use of musical instruments. David commanded the use of musical instruments as an inherent part of the Levitical priesthood. When the priesthood is taken away, so must be all of its functions, including its use of musical instruments (1 Chron. 16:4–6, 23:1–5).

John Owen comments that the law here refers to "the whole law of commandments contained in ordinances, or the whole law of Moses, so far as it was the rule of worship and obedience unto the church; for that law it is that followeth the fates of the priesthood."[16] The Lord "should take away, abolish and leave as dead and useless, that whole system of solemn worship which he had appointed in so glorious a manner, and accepted for so many generations."[17] "The law may be considered as it prescribes a way of worship, in its ordinances and institutions, which God did accept. This the people were indispensably obliged unto whilst the law stood in force. But in the gospel our Lord Jesus Christ had now appointed a new, spiritual worship, suited unto the principles and grace thereof. And these were so inconsistent as that no man could at once serve two masters."[18]

Albert Barnes comments,

> The meaning is that since a large number of laws constituting a code of considerable extent and importance was given

15. Ibid., 177.
16. Ibid., Vol. 21, 428.
17. Ibid., 430.
18. Ibid., 429.

for the regulation of the priesthood, and in reference to the rites of religion, which they were to observe or superintend, it followed that when their office was superseded by one of a wholly different order, the law which had regulated them vanished also, or ceased to be binding. This was a very important point in the introduction of Christianity, and hence it is so often insisted upon in the writings of Paul.[19]

Hebrews 8:13 "When He said, 'A new covenant,' He has made the first obsolete. But whatever is becoming obsolete and growing old is ready to disappear."

Owen explains the meaning of the apostle's words:

The general design of the apostle in these discourses is to manifest and prove that the old covenant made with the church at Sinai, with all the ordinances of worship and privileges thereunto belonging, was taken away, or ceased to be of any force in the church. Hereon did a total alteration of the whole present church-state of the Hebrews depend. . . .[20]

To the glorious outward appearance of the administrations of it. This was that which greatly captivated the minds and affections of those Hebrews. They were carnal themselves, and these things, the fabric of the Temple, the ornaments of the priests, the order of their worship, had a glory in them which they could behold with their carnal eyes, and cleave unto with their carnal affections. The ministration of the letter was glorious. "All this glory," saith the apostle, "shall shortly disappear, shall vanish out of your sight."[21]

19. Albert Barnes, *Barnes Notes*, (London: Blackie & Son, 1884-1885; Reprint, Grand Rapids: Baker Book House), Vol. 13, 158–159.
20. Owen, Vol. 22, 177.
21. Ibid.

Hebrews 9:8–10 (NKJV) "the Holy Spirit indicating this, that the way into the Holiest of All was not yet made manifest while the first tabernacle was still standing. It was symbolic for the present time in which both gifts and sacrifices are offered which cannot make him who performed the service perfect in regard to the conscience—concerned only with foods and drinks, various washings, and fleshly ordinances imposed until the time of reformation."

John Owen explains that the "food, drinks, various washings, and fleshly ordinances" mentioned are only representative and the apostle means to include the whole of the Old Covenant worship.[22] This would include the musical instruments of the Temple worship, which were to exist only until "the time of reformation" that came with the death of Christ.

Owen argues that the carnal nature of the Temple ordinances could never bring the people of God to that spiritual worship God desired and had promised:

> All the laws concerning these things were carnal, "carnal ordinances;" such as, for the matter, manner of performance, and end of them, were carnal. This being their nature, it evidently follows that they were instituted only for a time, and were so far from being able themselves to perfect the state of the church, as that they were not consistent with that perfect state of spiritual things which God would introduce, and had promised so to do.[23]

Owen writes regarding the abolition of Old Covenant worship,

> Then did he [Christ] pronounce concerning it and all things belonging unto it, "It is finished."[24]

> It continued until the day of Pentecost; for then, in the coming of the Holy Ghost, was the foundation of the

22. Ibid., 252.
23. Ibid.
24. Ibid., 242.

> gospel church-state, order, and worship, solemnly laid, whereon, a new way of worship being established, the abrogation of the old was declared.[25]

Owen goes on to state regarding the whole of the Temple worship and all of its "fleshly ordinances" that "they were never designed to continue forever."[26] The apostle has "undeniably demonstrated that they were not to be of perpetual use in the church," and "he now declares that there was a certain determinate season fixed in the purpose and counsel of God for their cessation and removal."[27] In referring to the Old Covenant worship, he states that the word "reformation" in Heb. 9:10 means "its utter removal and taking away out of the service of God in the church" and "the introduction of a new animating form and life, with new means and ways of their expression and exercise in new ordinances of worship."[28]

John 4:21–23 "Jesus said to her, 'Woman, believe Me, an hour is coming when neither in this mountain, nor in Jerusalem, shall you worship the Father. You worship that which you do not know; we worship that which we know, for salvation is from the Jews. But an hour is coming, and now is, when the true worshipers shall worship the Father in spirit and truth; for such people the Father seeks to be His worshipers.'"

Jesus states that the hour has come for two great changes in the worship of God. First, the place of worship will now become a matter of indifference. Second, the nature of worship will change as well. The outward and ceremonial worship of the Temple in Jerusalem will be replaced by a more inward and spiritual worship under the gospel. The two stand in contrast to each other and cannot be mixed. The Temple worship must be done away with, "an hour is coming when neither in this mountain, nor in Jerusalem, shall you

25. Ibid.
26. Ibid., 256.
27. Ibid., 257.
28. Ibid.

worship the Father." A new spiritual worship will be established, "an hour is coming, and now is, when the true worshipers shall worship the Father in spirit and truth."

The Puritan George Hutcheson observes,

> The correction and reformation of the worship of God was reserved for the days of the gospel, and to be brought about by Christ. . . .[29]

> The Jewish way (of worship), because temporary, should be abolished, and that partition wall be broken down.[30]

> The true worship of God under the gospel doth not consist in external pomp of ceremonies and observances, but is spiritual, simple, and substantial; for they shall worship the Father in spirit and in truth.[31]

Matthew Henry shares this perspective,

> The way of worship which Christ has instituted is rational and intellectual, and refined from those external rites and ceremonies with which the Old Testament worship was both clouded and clogged. This is called true worship, in opposition to that which was typical. . . The gospel erects a spiritual way of worship.[32]

John Calvin comments, "the meaning is that the repeal of the law is already at hand, so far as relates to the Temple, and priesthood, and other outward ceremonies."[33] On John 4:23 he writes,

---

29. George Hutcheson, *The Gospel of John,* (Edinburgh: The Banner of Truth Trust, reprinted 1985), 64.

30. Ibid., 63.

31. Ibid., 65.

32. Henry, Vol. 5, 906.

33. John Calvin, *Calvin's Commentary,* 22 Vol., (Grand Rapids: Baker Book House Company, Reprinted 1984), Vol. 17, 158.

Now follows the latter clause, about repealing the worship, or ceremonies, prescribed by the law. When He says that "the hour cometh," or "will come," He shows that the order laid down by Moses will not be perpetual. When He says that "the hour is now come," He puts an end to ceremonies, and declares that the time of reformation, of which the apostle speaks, (Heb. 9:10), has thus been fulfilled.[34]

John Owen states that our Lord Jesus was referring to a new spiritual worship in contrast to the outward and carnal worship of the Temple:

For "God is Spirit," and will be "worshipped in spirit;" which our Savior asserts to belong unto the gospel-state, in opposition unto all the most glorious carnal ordinances and institutions of the law, John 4:21–24.[35]

2 Corinthians 3:10–11 "For indeed what had glory, in this case has no glory on account of the glory that surpasses it. For if that which fades away was with glory, much more that which remains is in glory."

Paul makes a comparison between the Old and New Covenants that includes the worship of both. Two points are made: First, the Old Covenant worship is fading away and will be replaced by the gospel worship, which is permanent. Second, the glory of gospel worship far surpasses the glory of Old Covenant worship.

Albert Barnes emphasizes the abolition of the Old Covenant worship:

The splendor that attended the giving of the law; the bright shining of the face of Moses; and the ritual institutions of his religion. It was to be done away with. It was never designed to be permanent. Everything in it had a transient existence, and was so designed. . . .The law he

34. Ibid., 161.
35. Owen, Vol. 21, 419.

calls the thing which was to be made to cease; to be put an end to; to be done away with; to be abolished. It had no permanency; and it was designed to have none. . . .It is implied here, that it was originally designed that the Mosaic institutions should not be permanent; that they should be mere shadows and types of better things; and that when the things which they adumbrated should appear, the shadows would vanish of course. This idea is one which prevails everywhere in the New Testament, and which the sacred writers are often at great pains to demonstrate.[36]

Ephesians 2:14–15 "For He Himself is our peace, who made both groups into one and broke down the barrier of the dividing wall, by abolishing in His flesh the enmity, which is the Law of commandments contained in ordinances."

Matthew Henry observes how Christ has abrogated the Old Covenant worship by His death upon the cross:

By His sufferings in the flesh, He took away the binding power of the ceremonial law, which is here called "the law of commandments contained in ordinances," because it enjoined a multitude of external rites and ceremonies, and consisted of many institutions and appointments about the outward parts of divine worship. The legal ceremonies were abrogated by Christ, having their fulfillment in him. . . . He framed both these parties (Jew and Gentile) into one new society. . . . they being renewed by the Holy Ghost, and now concurring in a new way of gospel worship.[37]

John Owen has the same understanding and writes that Christ has

. . . taken away "the law of commandments contained in ordinances," that is, by abolishing that way of worship

36. Barnes, Vol. 11, 58.
37. Henry, Vol. 6, 694.

which was the Jews' privilege and burden. . . . By bearing
the curse of the law, he reconciled both unto God; by taking
away and abolishing the worship of the law, he took away
all grounds of difference amongst them.[38]

The above passages from the New Testament make it clear
that not just the sacrificial system, which typified the coming of
Christ, but the entire worship of the Old Covenant Temple, in
all of its outward ceremonies and rituals, has been abolished. This
would necessarily include all the musical instruments that were
always considered as part of Temple worship under the Levitical
priesthood. The Old Covenant worship, in all of its ceremonies
and rituals, must be considered as one package. It was instituted
by Moses and David only temporarily until "the time of reformation" should come. That time has come with Jesus Christ, and
Old Covenant worship has now been removed. We can no longer
look to Moses or David for authority in New Covenant worship.
We have no right to bring any aspect of the Temple worship into
the church. The apostles forbid us to do so. This includes any of
the musical instruments instituted under David. In other words,
the fact that David used musical instruments is no longer a valid
authority for us under the New Covenant.[39]

38. John Owen, *The Works of John Owen*, (Johnstone & Hunter, 1850-1853; Reprint,
Edinburgh: The Banner of Truth Trust, 1979), Vol. 9, 53-54.
39. The fact that musical instruments were used in the Old Testament Temple is often
used as justification for their use in the Christian church. For example, after making
an excellent and vigorous defense of the regulative principle of worship, Derek W. H.
Thomas states, "The case needs, then, to be established and maintained that the regulative
principle is an argument based on what is warranted by God in Scripture as a whole, and
not merely in the New Testament church. In this instance, as regards the use of musical
instruments and choral accompaniment, Temple practice provides all the warrant that is
needed." This perspective fails to take into account the distinctions between the Old and
New Testament worship and the abolition of Temple worship that we have seen in these
passages. A full application of this reasoning would revive many other aspects of Temple
worship and throw the worship of the church into confusion. This perspective finds no
support from the commands of the apostles or the examples of any New Testament church.
See Derek W. H. Thomas, "The Regulative Principle Responding to Recent Criticism,"
in *Give Praise to God,* 92.

We should note that the plea of Temple worship was the justification used by the Roman Catholic Church for many of its additions to worship throughout the Medieval Ages. Calvin complained that the Catholics had revived the Temple worship, "A new Judaism, as a substitute for that which God had distinctly abrogated, has again been reared by means of numerous puerile extravagances . . . . The first evil here is, that an immense number of ceremonies, which God had by his authority abrogated, once for all, have been again revived."[40]

We are faced with two questions: Are musical instruments to be used in the New Testament church? If so, what specific instruments are to be used? In answering these questions, we must look to Christ and His apostles in the New Testament alone. Here we find a complete silence in regard to musical instruments in worship. The New Testament gives no command for musical instrumentation in the worship of the church. Neither do we find even a single example of instruments ever being used in any of the churches. There is not a word mentioned concerning musical instruments' being used in any of the New Testament churches.

The regulative principle of worship remains, and what God has not commanded in the New Testament we have no authority to use. He has not commanded the use of any musical instruments as He did in the days of Moses and David. Therefore, we have no authority to bring them into the worship of His church. The complete silence of the New Testament on musical instruments is a most compelling argument that they are not to exist in the church. Only singing is commanded (1 Cor. 14:15, Eph. 5:19, Col. 3:16).

Some will say that the New Testament command to sing implies the use of musical instruments. But we must understand that singing and the playing of musical instruments are two entirely different acts. Each can be performed independent of the other. Singing can

40. John Calvin, *The Necessity of Reforming the Church,* (Edinburgh: Calvin Translation Society, 1844; Reprint, Dallas: Protestant Heritage Press, 1995), 21–22.

be done without the use of any musical instruments and it is in no way dependent upon them. In the Temple worship, it was very clear that both were commanded. In the New Testament, it is very clear that only singing is commanded. Obedience in worship consists in doing God's will, nothing more, and nothing less. "Whatever I command you, you shall be careful to do; you shall not add to nor take away from it" (Deut. 12:32). In the New Testament, God has commanded singing with the voice only, and any addition to God's will is disobedience. The use of musical instruments in Christian worship is such an addition and, therefore, becomes an act of disobedience. This relation between singing and the playing of musical instruments will be considered more fully in the section of "Circumstances of Worship" in Chapter IV.

Some will say that we can assume that the musical instruments of the Temple, or some other instruments, were carried over into the church. But how can we assume that the musical instruments were carried over into the church in the light of the above verses? The apostles make it clear that the Temple worship has been "abolished" and has "become obsolete." It was to exist only until "the time of reformation." Can we assume that the churches to which Paul writes had musical instruments and yet there was never a word mentioned concerning them from his pen? Can we assume that no direction was ever needed concerning their use or that there was never a misuse of them that had to be addressed in any of his letters? Let us consider Paul's pastoral epistles in which he instructs Timothy and Titus how to order the church. Surely if musical instruments were to be present in gospel worship, these young pastors needed instruction concerning their use. Yet not a word is mentioned with regard to musical instruments. Why would the apostle have left these young pastors without any instruction about this critical aspect of church worship? The only explanation of this New Testament silence concerning musical instruments is that they did not exist in the worship of the church.

We may add to this silence the fact that of all the various spiritual gifts listed in the New Testament, there is no gift concerning musical instrumentation (Rom. 12:6–8; 1 Cor. 12:4–11; 1 Pet. 4:10–11). The Holy Spirit has always supplied those gifts needed for God's worship throughout history (Exod. 31:1–11, 35:25, 30–35; 1 Kings 7:13–45; 1 Chron. 28:11–21). We may be certain that the Spirit continues to give every spiritual gift needed for Christian worship, especially since the fullness of His blessings have been poured out upon the church. Yet we find no spiritual gift mentioned at all in regard to musical instrumentation in the New Testament. This absence of any spiritual gift in the use of musical instruments is another compelling argument that they are to have no place in the worship of the church.

Some may say that all of this is only an argument from silence. But silence is the regulative principle of worship. Where God is silent, we do not add to His worship. His silence means He has given no command and we have no authority to act. His silence on musical instruments in the New Testament means we have no authority to bring them into the worship of the church.

Some may say that the musical instruments of the Old Covenant were not part of the sacrificial system that was abolished under the New Covenant. The sacrifices of the Old Covenant worship have been abolished, but the musical instruments may continue. This argument must be rejected for the following two reasons: First, David, under divine direction, instituted the use of musical instruments as part of the Levitical priesthood. It was the Levites alone whom he authorized to use the musical instruments. The Levitical priesthood and the use of the musical instruments cannot be separated from one another. But now in the New Covenant, the Levitical priesthood in its entirety has been abolished (Heb. 7:11–12), and this must include their musical instruments. We have no authority to assume that any aspect of the Levitical priesthood of the Temple continues under the New Covenant. Second, the musical instruments of David were never separated from the sacrificial system in the Temple worship of the Old Testament. On every occasion when the Temple worship was restored, both the sacrifices and the musical instruments were viewed as one divine worship (See 1 Chron. 23:25–32; 2 Chron. 23:16–18, 29:20–30, 35:1–19; Ezra 3:1–11; Neh. 12:31–46). Both stand or fall together. When the sacrifices are abolished, the musical instruments must go with them. Andrew Fuller comments concerning the use of musical instruments, "These appendages to the Temple could not survive the Temple, . . . it was as much abolished when sacrifices ceased as the others were when the Temple was no more."[41] Professor Girardeau writes,

> The Lord Jesus knew the divine decree by which the temporary services of the Temple were destined to be abolished. He himself predicted the utter destruction of the Temple. He knew perfectly that instrumental music was an attachment to the peculiar and distinctive services of the Temple, and therefore he knew that it must share the wreck to which the Temple with all those services was doomed. Did he authorize his church to save the instrumental music from the ruins, and employ it in her worship? He did not. Is she then warranted to do it? Assuredly not.[42]

An important argument must now be considered. The advocates of musical instruments in the church often disagree with the principle of the complete abrogation of the Temple worship. They argue that while the ceremonial and sacrificial system of the Temple was typical of Christ and has therefore now passed away with His accomplished salvation, the musical instruments do not fall into this category. The instruments were not typical and so they may continue. But if this view is correct, we would expect it to be confirmed by the commands and the examples of the apostles. The

41. Fuller, 859.
42. Girardeau, 112.

fact is that we never find the apostles carrying any aspect of the Temple worship over into the New Testament churches, including its musical instruments. If the musical instruments of the Temple are to continue, why do we not find the apostles instituting their use? The advocates of musical instruments are unable to answer this question.

The only view of the Temple worship consistent with the commands and the example of the apostles is its complete abrogation. Never once did the apostles look back to any of the ceremonies and rituals of the Temple, including its musical instruments, and attempt to bring them into the worship of the church. They understood that the Temple worship in its entirety was abolished and they were instituting a new worship that was "in spirit and truth" under the authority of Jesus Christ. The conclusion that the musical instruments of Temple worship are abolished is confirmed by the commands and the example of the apostles. Girardeau calls attention to this point in his comments on John 4:23:

> Jesus has thus declared that the positive enactment which required ceremonial worship at the Jewish Temple is abrogated; and the New testament is utterly silent in regard to any transfer to the Christian church of the services peculiar to that edifice. . . . To retain a part of its services is to suppose the continued existence of the Temple, for God never authorized the employment of those services except in immediate connection with that particular structure, after the tabernacle had given way to it by his inspired direction.[43]

Under the Old Covenant, the Levites were distinguished by God from the rest of the people and set apart with special privileges of drawing near to Him in worship (Num. 8:14–16, 16:8–9; Deut. 8:10). It was based upon this distinction that they were later used

---

43. Girardeau, 87.

for singing and the playing of musical instruments in the Temple (1 Chron. 16:4; 23:1–5; 2 Chron. 29:25–26, 35:3–10; Ezra 3:10; Neh. 12:27, 44–47). Under the New Covenant, no such distinction exists any longer. There is no designated group set apart from the rest of the people to sing and use musical instruments in worship. Yet this is precisely what happens whenever musical instruments are used in the worship of the church. In the New Testament, we have all become priests unto God with equal access into His presence, and, therefore, we are all commanded to sing His praises (1 Pet. 2:9; Rev. 1:6; Heb. 10:19; Col. 3:16). We have no authority to set apart any group for the playing of musical instruments in the church.

We should notice two very striking differences between the Old and New Testaments regarding musical instruments. First, throughout the history of the Old Covenant, the Holy Spirit abundantly recorded the various musical instruments used in worship. On many occasions, throughout the Old Testament, the Spirit spoke profusely concerning the various instruments being used. Musical instruments were never an aspect of worship upon which the Spirit was silent. (See 1 Chron. 13:8, 16:5–6, 15:16, 23:4, 25:1, 6; 2 Chron. 5:12–13, 23:13, 18, 29:27, 34:12; 2 Sam. 6:5; Ezra 3:10; Neh. 12:36. Many passages in the Psalms may be added to this list as well.) This willingness of the Holy Spirit to speak so profusely of musical instruments in the Old Testament leads us to believe that He would do the same in the New Testament if instruments were present. But what do we find in the New Testament? Nothing but complete silence. The abundant record of musical instruments throughout the Old Testament makes the silence of the New Testament all the more convincingly indicate that they were not present in the worship of the early church. Are we to assume that there were musical instruments in the churches just as in the Temple but the Holy Spirit has forgotten to tell us about them? The question must be asked, why is the Holy Spirit so silent on this issue in the New Testament? The only logical conclusion is that musical instruments do not exist in the worship of the New Testament.

A second difference between the Old and New Testaments in regard to musical instruments should also be noted. On every occasion throughout the history of the Temple, whenever its worship was restored, the men of God always looked back to *"the command of David the man of God."* As we have seen, Solomon, Jehoiada, Hezekiah, Josiah, Jeshua, and Nehemiah all established the Temple worship and brought in the musical instruments under the authority of *"the command of David the man of God."* This was the only authority under which musical instruments were ever brought into the Temple worship. But when we come to the New Testament, we never again hear of *"the command of David."* It completely disappears. The apostles never look back to *"the command of David"* as did the men of the Old Testament. They recognized it no longer had authority in the worship of the church. They looked only to the command of Christ as the Head of His church in the establishment of the new gospel worship. The only authority by which musical instruments were brought into the worship of the Temple, namely, *"the command of David,"* completely disappears in the New Testament. The question must be asked, if *"the command of David"* no longer exists, under what authority can men now bring musical instruments into worship? The answer is that men have no authority to do so under the gospel worship.

John Girardeau applies the distinction between the Old and New Testaments:

> The bearing of all this upon the Christian church is as striking as it is obvious. If, under a dispensation dominantly characterized by external appointments, instrumental music could not be introduced into the worship of God's sanctuary, except in consequence of a warrant furnished by him, how can a church, existing under the far simpler and

more spiritual dispensation of the gospel, venture, without such a warrant to incorporate it into its public services?[44]

Girardeau makes extensive arguments that just as the sacrifices of the Old Covenant were typical of the death of Christ, so the emotional joy associated with the use of musical instruments was typical of the spiritual joy of the coming Holy Spirit.[45] I mention this view, not as part of my own argument, but because it has been held by many and we will see it again when we consider the Reformers and Puritans later in Chapter II. Girardeau states in this regard,

> It pleased God to typify the spiritual joy to spring from a richer possession of the Holy Spirit through the sensuous rapture engendered by the passionate melody of stringed instruments and the clash of cymbals, by the blare of trumpets and the ringing of harps. It was the instruction of his children in a lower school, preparing them for a higher.[46]

> The Spirit having been poured out, and that abundant joy of believers having been experienced, the shadow gave way to the substance, the type to the antitype.[47]

> As instrumental music in the Temple worship was one of those types, its employment in the public service of the Christian church is at once unwarrantable and dishonoring to the ever-blessed Spirit.[48]

In his book, *Singing of Psalmes a Gospel Ordinance*, Cotton Mather argues in a similar way, "Instrumental music found in the

44. Ibid., 31–32.
45. For arguments in support of musical instruments as being typical, see Girardeau, 27–79.
46. Ibid., 61–62.
47. Ibid., 63.
48. Ibid., 74–75.

ancient Jewish Temple is merely a type or shadow of the edifying and untheatrical singing with the heart and voice approved and practiced in the New Testament."[49]

In summary, we have seen that God has not left His worship open to the inventions, desires, or preferences of men. Just as with every other aspect of worship, He has regulated the use of musical instruments. In the Old Testament, He placed musical instruments in worship under His authority, and even the specific instruments to be used were only by divine command.

When we come to the New Testament, the following three truths become clear: 1) The Old Testament Temple worship in all of its outward ceremonies and rituals has been abolished; 2) We must look to Christ and His apostles alone for the worship of the church; and 3) With no command, or example, or any indication whatsoever from the Lord Jesus that He desires musical instruments to be used in His church, we have no authority for their use. As will be seen in Chapter II, these three truths will be found over and over again throughout the history of the church. These three simple truths are the thread found in the Scripture and runs throughout the history of the church.

The regulative principle demands that those who would bring any addition into God's worship must prove that they have scriptural warrant for doing so. In this case, the advocates of musical instrumentation must demonstrate from the New Testament that Christ demands their use in His worship. The burden of proof rests upon them, and, apart from such proof, they cannot and should not be used. And if we bring unwarranted additions into Christ's worship, we transgress His authority and prove ourselves violators of His prerogatives.

---

49. Cotton Mather, *Singing of Psalmes a Gospel Ordinance,* quoted in Horton Davies, *The Worship of the American Puritans,* (New York: Peter Lang Publishing, Inc., 1990; Reprint, New York: Soli Deo Gloria Publications, 1999), 128. See also Mather, Vol. 2, 266.

The Origins of the Old Testament Musical Instruments

In this section, we will consider the origins of the musical instruments that God commanded in Old Covenant worship. The Scripture will show that these musical instruments were invented and specifically designed for the worship of God. The significance of this is that it adds further weight to that which has already been established, namely, God's authority over musical instruments in His worship. Not only did God command the specific musical instruments to be used, but both Moses and David were divinely guided by the Holy Spirit to invent those instruments. They did not simply take musical instruments from the surrounding pagan nations (contemporary culture) and bring them into God's worship. They made new instruments under divine guidance to be used in God's worship. Just as all the details of the furnishings and utensils of the Tabernacle and Temple service were specifically designed by God and sanctified for His worship, so also were the musical instruments.

The first musical instrument that God commanded in His worship was the trumpet in the days of Moses. Not only did the Lord command the use of a trumpet, but He also gave Moses its design. Num. 10:1 states, "The Lord spoke further to Moses, saying, 'Make yourself two trumpets of silver, of hammered work you shall make them.'" God's design here specifies both the material to be used, "silver," and the manner in which it is to be formed, "of hammered work you shall make them."

The trumpet as a musical instrument existed prior to the time of Moses and probably first appeared in ancient Egypt.[50] The Egyptian trumpets of that time were curved like a ram's horn, and, being educated among the Egyptians, Moses would surely have known of them. But Moses was not commanded to take his trumpet from the Egyptians. For God's worship he was to make a new trumpet that

---

50. *The Treasury of Scripture Knowledge,* (McLean, VA: MacDonald Publishing Company, Inc., 1982), 100.

was straight and not curved.[51] Josephus informs us that in making his trumpet according to the divine command, Moses refashioned the existing trumpets and became the inventor of the trumpet used by the Israelites. Josephus writes, "Moses was the inventor of the form of their trumpet, which was made of silver. Its description is this: In length it was little less than a cubit. It was composed of a narrow tube, somewhat thicker than a flute."[52]

The Holy Spirit guided Moses in all the details of the construction of the Tabernacle. He was commanded to make the Tabernacle and all its furnishings "after the pattern for them, which was shown to you on the mountain" (Exod. 25:40). This guidance of the Spirit would have included the trumpet as the first musical instrument used in public worship. Matthew Henry makes this same point when commenting on God's command to Moses to design the trumpet in Num. 10:1:

> In a thing of this nature, one would think Moses needed not to have been taught of God: his own reason might teach him the conveniency of trumpets; but the constitution of Israel was to be in everything divine, and therefore even in this matter, small as it seems.[53]

No additional musical instruments were commanded by God for use in worship until the days of King David. David introduced various new instruments that became known as "the instruments of David." Just as the Holy Spirit guided Moses, He guided David in all the details of the construction of the Temple with its furnishings and utensils. "David gave his son Solomon . . . the plans for all that he had by the Spirit" (1 Chron. 28:11–12, NKJV). "All *this,*" said *David,* "the LORD made me understand in writing by His hand upon me, all the details of this pattern" (1 Chron. 28:19). As we

51. Ibid.
52. Josephus, *Josephus Complete Works,* (Grand Rapids: Kregel Publications, 1981), 82.
53. Henry, Vol. 1, 601.

will see, this divine guidance of the Holy Spirit would have included the musical instruments of David as well.

We will now consider two passages which show that David actually "invented" his musical instruments. The prophet Amos, who lived approximately 200 years after David, tells us clearly that David "invented" his musical instruments. Amos 6:5 (NKJV), "Who sing idly to the sound of stringed instruments, And *invent* for yourselves musical instruments like David." In the context, the prophet condemns those who have a sinful and luxuriant life. They are those "who are at ease in Zion" (6:1), "who recline on beds of ivory" (6:4), and "who drink wine from sacrificial bowls" (6:6). They also invented musical instruments like David had done. But rather than using them for God's purposes, they used them as sensual aids in their drinking parties. The invention or use of musical instruments in itself is not condemned, but their employment for sinful purposes is.

The verb "invent" (*hashab*) used by Amos means to employ the mind in conceiving and devising new artistic productions. It speaks of an ingenious creative activity that results in new or original artistic devices.[54] "Reference is not so much to 'understanding,' but to the creating of new ideas."[55] When Amos tells us that David "invented" his musical instruments, he means that David employed his ingenious creative gifts in constructing new or original instruments that did not exist before.

The same verb is found during the construction of the Tabernacle in the wilderness. Bezalel was chosen by God and given special creative gifts by the Spirit of God for the design and fabrication of all the furnishings of the Tabernacle. In Exod. 31:3–5, the Lord says,

---

54. Francis Brown, *The New Brown–Driver–Briggs–Gesenius Hebrew and English Lexicon*, (Peabody: Hendrickson Publishers, 1979), 362–363.

55. R. Laird Harris, Ed., *Theological Wordbook of the Old Testament*, (Chicago: Moody Press, 1992), Vol. 1, 330.

And I have filled him [Bezalel] with the Spirit of God in wisdom, in understanding, in knowledge, and in all kinds of craftsmanship, *to make* artistic designs for work in gold, in silver, and in bronze, and in the cutting of stones for settings, and in the carving of wood, that he may work in all kinds of craftsmanship.

We find the same verb used as well in Exod. 35:35 (KJV):

Them hath he filled with wisdom of heart, to work all manner of work, of the engraver, and of the cunning workman, and of the embroiderer, in blue, and in purple, in scarlet, and in fine linen, and of the weaver, even of them that do any work, and of those that *devise* cunning work.

(See also Exod. 35:32; 36:8, 35; 38:23.) This same verb is used to refer to the creative workmen who invented instruments of war under King Uzziah. 2 Chron. 26:15 reads, "And in Jerusalem he made engines of war *invented* by skillful men to be on the towers and on the corners, for the purpose of shooting arrows and great stones."

The Spirit of God provided men with the inventive and creative gifts to construct every detail of the Tabernacle that He commanded. From the use of *hashab* in the Scripture, we may conclude that the Spirit gave the same inventive and creative gifts to David in designing the musical instruments commanded for worship. As the prophet Amos tells us, David "invented" his musical instruments.

Keil and Delitzsch emphasize David's creative activity in commenting on Amos 6:5, "As David invented stringed instruments in honor of his God in heaven, so do these princes invent playing and singing for their god, their belly. The meaning to invent or devise. . . . is established beyond all doubt by Exod. 31:4."[56]

John Gill agrees,

56. Keil & Delitzsch, Vol. 10, 300.

As David made songs and invented several instruments
of music to sing them upon and to, in religious worship,
and for the praise and glory of God; so these men invented
new ones to indulge their carnal mirth and jollity, in which
they thought themselves to be justified by the example of
David.[57]

A second passage that adds support to the Holy Spirit's giving
creative gifts to David to invent his musical instruments is found
in 1 Chron. 23:4–5 (NKJV) when David appoints the Levites for
their various functions in the Temple: "Of these. . . four thousand
praised the LORD with musical instruments, *"which I made," said
David, "for giving praise."* David was divinely blessed with unusual
musical gifts. In this passage, he states that he used his musical gifts
to make the instruments he brought into worship.

The same word, "made" (*asa*), which David uses here, is often
used in Genesis concerning God's creative activity. It speaks of
God's fashioning the formless mass into order. "Thus God *made*
the firmament" (Gen. 1:7), "And God saw all that He had *made*,
and behold, it was very good" (Gen. 1:31). This same verb is often
used to speak of men fashioning or forming an object.[58] I will give
two examples: "So it came to pass, at the end of forty days, that
Noah opened the window of the ark which he had *made*" (Gen.
8:6). "And they shall *construct* an ark of acacia wood; two and a half
cubits shall be its length, a cubit and a half its width, and a cubit
and a half its height" (Exod. 25:10). In each of the above cases,
the objects formed were made under very specific divine direction.
God gave precise plans to Noah for the design of the ark and to the
Israelites for the construction of the ark of worship.

Once again, this verb (*asa*) indicates that David actually invented and designed his musical instruments specifically for God's

57. Gill, Vol. 4, 678.
58. R. Laird Harris, ed., *Theological Wordbook of the Old Testament*, (Chicago: Moody
Press, 1980), Vol. 2, 701.

worship. The Spirit of God inspired David's mind with the plan for them, and David fashioned them according to God's plan. In the same way that Noah *"made"* the ark and the people of Israel *"made"* the ark of acacia wood, David *"made"* these instruments.

John Owen explains David's words in 1 Chron. 23:5 (NKJV), "which I made," to mean that, "he did it by the direction of the Spirit of God; otherwise he ought not to have done it. . . . It was all revealed to him by the Holy Spirit, without which he could have introduced nothing at all into the worship of God."[59] Alfred Edersheim draws the same conclusion, "The music of the Temple owed its origin to David, who was not only a poet and a musical composer, but who also invented musical instruments (Amos 6:5; 1 Chron. 23:5), especially the ten-stringed Nevel or lute (Ps. 33:2; 144:9)."[60]

As we have seen, from David's time forward, the various instruments he brought into worship become known as "the musical instruments of David" (2 Chron. 29:26; Neh. 12:36). John Gill comments on 2 Chron. 29:26 that "the instruments of David. . . . were invented, directed, and ordered to be used by him."[61] On Neh. 12:36, Gill states, "the musical instruments of David the man of God which were invented by him, and ordered by him to be used in religious service, under divine direction."[62]

We see the same word, "made" (*asa*), used again when Solomon dedicated the Temple in Jerusalem in 2 Chron. 7:6 (NKJV), "And the priests attended to their services, the Levites also with instruments of the music of the LORD, which King David had *made* to praise the LORD. . . ."

It is true that some of David's instruments are mentioned in the Bible before his invention of them (i.e., the lyre in Gen. 4:21 and the harp in 1 Sam. 10:5). Though the same name is used for

59. Owen, Vol. 9, 463.
60. Alfred Edersheim, *The Temple*, (Peabody: Hendrickson Publishers, 1994), 51.
61. Gill, Vol. 2, 520.
62. Ibid., 575.

these instruments prior to David's time, this does not necessarily mean that they were identical instruments. David may have taken existing instruments and refashioned or remodeled them to such an extent that they became, in a sense, new instruments. However it came to pass, it is clear that the instruments of David were specifically designed under the guidance of the Holy Spirit and sanctified for use in God's worship. When David was done, the Scripture can say that he "made" and "invented" his instruments for divine worship.

The view that Moses and David "invented" their musical instruments is consistent with God's commandment not to look to the nations for their worship:

> You shall not do what is done in the land of Egypt where you lived, nor are you to do what is done in the land of Canaan where I am bringing you; you shall not walk in their statutes (Lev. 18:3).

> Beware that you are not ensnared to follow them, after they are destroyed before you, and that you do not inquire after their gods, saying, "How do these nations serve their gods, that I also may do likewise?" (Deut. 12:30).

We can be sure that both Moses and David did not violate God's command by taking their musical instruments from the surrounding nations. Rather, Moses "invented" the silver trumpet and David "invented" his musical instruments for the worship of God according to specific divine directions.

We conclude that the Holy Spirit guided both Moses and David in all the details of the construction and the worship of the Tabernacle and Temple, respectively. Nothing was left to human preference or expediency. Everything was to be done under divine direction and thus sanctified and set apart as holy to Him. This included the trumpet of Moses and the musical instruments of David, which were "invented" and "made" for use in God's worship. The invention of the specific instruments to be used in the Old Covenant further confirms what we have already seen, that the regulative principle of worship extends to musical instruments. Matthew Henry comments on the divine origin of the Temple,

> The Temple must be a sacred thing . . . therefore it must not be left to man's art or invention to contrive it, but must be framed by divine institution. Christ the true Temple, the church the gospel Temple, and heaven the everlasting Temple, are all framed according to the divine councils, and the plan laid in the divine wisdom, ordained before the world for God's glory and ours."[63]

---

63. Henry, Vol. 2, 908.

CHAPTER II

The History of Musical Instruments in the Christian Church

S
OME may wonder if perhaps we have too rigorously applied the regulative principle of worship to the use of musical instruments in the previous chapter. In this chapter, which is an overview of the use of musical instruments throughout the history of the Christian church, we will discover that this is not at all the case. We will hear the testimony of the greatest theologians Christ has given to His church and discover that this application of the regulative principle is consistent with historic and Reformed Christianity.

The question is often asked, how do we interpret the silence of the New Testament Scripture on musical instruments? Does this silence mean that musical instruments in Christian worship were simply assumed by the apostles and therefore nothing was written about them? Or does this silence mean that musical instruments did not exist in the apostolic church? There are two historical facts that provide powerful evidence in answering this question. The first is found in the origins of Christian worship in the Jewish synagogue.

The Origins of Christian Worship in the Jewish Synagogue

The origin and divine warrant of the Jewish synagogue can be traced to the entrance of the Jewish nation into the land of Canaan.[1] Psalm 74:8, which was most likely written during the invasion of Nebuchadnezzar's army, seems to refer to existing synagogues, "They have burned all the meeting places of God in the land." It is important to realize that the local synagogues, not the Temple in Jerusalem, were the center of the religious life of the Jewish people every Sabbath. The Jewish males were commanded to travel to the Temple in Jerusalem only three times each year during the national feasts (Deut. 16:16). But on every weekly Sabbath throughout the year, the Jewish people gathered in their local synagogues scattered throughout the land. That the synagogue was central in the religious life of the Jewish people is seen by our Lord's custom of worshipping there on the Sabbath.[2] By the time of Christ, synagogues were located in every community of Jews throughout Palestine and the Greco–Roman world.[3] The apostle James states in Acts 15:21, "For Moses from ancient generations has in every city those who preach him, since he is read in the synagogues every Sabbath."

The sacrificial and ceremonial elements of the Temple in Jerusalem never found their way into the synagogues. The synagogue worship was focused on the more spiritual elements of the reading and exposition of the Scripture, with prayer and praise through the singing of Psalms.[4] One of the distinctions of the synagogue singing as compared to that of the Temple was that it was unaccompanied by musical instruments. Musical instruments had been commanded by God in the Temple in Jerusalem, but they were

---

1. A discussion of the divine warrant for synagogue worship can be found in Girardeau, *Instrumental Music in the Public Worship of God*, 41–47.

2. Luke 4:16.

3. William D. Maxwell, *An Outline of Christian Worship*, (London: Oxford University Press, 1955), 2–3.

4. Douglas D. Bannerman, *The Scripture Doctrine of the Church*, (Grand Rapids: Baker Book House, 1976), 333.

never introduced into the worship of the synagogues. It was the unaccompanied singing of Psalms that became an important feature of synagogue worship.[5] Professor Girardeau writes, "In regard to the synagogue . . . its worship was destitute of instrumental music . . . no instrumental music entered into the services of the Jewish synagogue."[6] Robert Douglas writes on the synagogue in his book *Church Music Through the Ages*, "Instrumental music is not known to have been used in connection with this worship."[7]

It was the worship of the synagogue that became the direct inheritance of the early Christian church.[8] Philip Schaff writes, "As the Christian Church rests historically on the Jewish Church, so Christian worship and the congregational organization rest on that of the synagogue, and cannot be well understood without it."[9] The elements of Christian worship, while under the authority of Christ and His apostles, were patterned after the worship of the Jewish synagogue.[10] This included the unaccompanied singing of the Psalms. Professor James McKinnon, perhaps the leading scholar of the 20th century on music in the early church, writes,

> Early Christianity inherited its musical practices and attitude from Judaism, especially from the Synagogue. Unlike the Temple, the Synagogue employed no instruments in its services. . . . instruments had no function in the unique service of the Synagogue. . . . The Synagogue's rites were

5. Best & Hutter, 315.

6. Girardeau, 39–40.

7. Robert Douglass, *Church Music Through the Ages*, (Nashville: Convention Press, 1967), 8. Cotton Mather states, "Tho' instrumental musick was admitted and appointed in the worship of God under the Old Testament, yet we do not find it practised in the synagogue of the Jews, but only in the Temple." Mather, Vol. 2, 266.

8. Maxwell, 2. Hughes Oliphant Old, *Worship That Is Reformed According to Scripture*, (Atlanta: John Knox Press, 1984), 43.

9. Philip Schaff, *History of the Christian Church*, (New York: Charles Scribner's Sons, 1910: reprint ed., Vol. 1, Grand Rapids: Eerdmans, 1985), 456, 461–65.

10. Douglas Bannerman writes, "The worship of the apostolic Church at home was just in substance the worship of the Hebrew synagogue or proseucha." Bannerman, *The Scripture Doctrine of the Church*, 361.

absorbed into the early Christian Mass, and the vocal music of the Synagogue, especially psalmody, was fostered by Christians with considerable enthusiasm.[11]

Girardeau states,

> The elements of public worship actually enumerated in the New Testament are precisely those which existed in the synagogue. As then, the use of musical instruments was unknown in the worship of the synagogue it was not introduced into the Christian church.[12]

In addition to the ceremonial worship of the Temple being fulfilled by Christ, there are three historical reasons why the worship of the synagogues became the basis of early Christian worship.

First, by the time of Christ, the simple and spiritual worship of the synagogues had become far more prominent than the ceremonial and sacrificial worship, even in the Temple in Jerusalem. Bannerman writes regarding the worship of the Temple, "When we pass to the worship of our Lord's time, we find that a silent revolution has taken place. . . . a significant change is apparent as regards the Temple worship itself. In it, too, those elements are now conspicuous which specially belonged to the synagogue, prayer, confession of sins, exposition of the Scriptures, and oral popular address. . . . The old sacrificial system indeed still goes on. . . . but there is a manifest change with respect to the place and importance assigned to the material and ceremonial, as compared with the spiritual elements in worship."[13] In other words, the outwardly ornate and ceremonial worship of David's day had already faded by the time of the apostles and had been replaced by a worship that was more according to the synagogues.

---

11. James McKinnon, *The Church Fathers and Musical Instruments,* (Ann Arbor: University Microfilms, Inc., 1965), Abstract, 1.

12. Girardeau, 102.

13. Bannerman, *Scripture Doctrine of the Church*, 333.

Second, by the time of Christ, the vast majority of Jews of the Dispersion, scattered throughout the Greco-Roman world, had never even seen the Temple worship in Jerusalem. Even within Palestine, the religious home of the Jewish people was the synagogue. Bannerman writes, "all that was best and highest in the religious life of Israel had, since the exile, come to centre in the synagogue rather than in the Temple."[14] It was the simple worship of the synagogue to which the Jews and Gentile proselytes were accustomed every Sabbath Day, and when they were converted to Christ, it was the worship of the synagogue which they brought into the Christian church. The Temple worship, of course, meant little or nothing to those Gentiles who were converted from paganism.

Third, after the Temple was destroyed in A.D. 70, it was never rebuilt, and instrumental music among the Jews appears to have completely disappeared.[15] It was the singing of the synagogues, unaccompanied by musical instruments, which continued both among the Jews and the early Christian church.

For these reasons, we may conclude that the worship of the apostolic church grew out of the simple and spiritual elements of the synagogue, including the singing of psalms, unaccompanied by any musical instruments. The hymns of the early church were primarily sung by the whole congregation with their voices united.[16] There are a few examples of solo hymns and antiphonies, or responsive songs, which were probably begun by Ignatius of Antioch.[17]

The Rejection of Musical Instruments by the Church Fathers

The second historical fact we must consider is the worship of the church immediately following the days of the apostles. The early

---

14. Ibid.
15. Maxwell, 2.
16. William C. Rice, *A Concise History of Church Music,* (New York: Abingdon Press, 1964), 13.
17. Joseph Bingham, *The Antiquities of the Christian Church,* 2nd ed. (London: Simpkin, Marshall, and Co., 1870), Vol. 1, 711.

Church Fathers were unanimous and vehement in condemning musical instruments in the worship of the church. They opposed instrumental music on three grounds: 1) They believed that musical instruments and other ceremonies of the Old Testament Temple were characteristic of the church in its infancy, but now, with the coming of Christ, the church had come to its maturity and they were no longer to be used; 2) They believed that the many references to musical instruments in the Old Testament should be interpreted figuratively; and 3) They considered musical instruments to be associated with pagan cults and immoral practices.[18] This last objection seems to have been the most common among the Church Fathers and to have caused many of them to reject the use of musical instruments, not only in public worship, but also in private.[19]

The second century and the centuries following provide a uniform testimony to vocal singing without the use of any musical instruments. The unaccompanied human voice became the norm for Christian worship following the death of the apostles. James McKinnon states, "The antagonism which the Fathers of the early Church displayed toward instruments has two outstanding characteristics: vehemence and uniformity."[20] Girardeau writes, "Instrumental music had no place in the early Christian churches."[21] Edmund S. Lorenz writes in *Church Music* that in regard to the singing of the early church, "there was no instrumental accompaniment."[22]

18. David W. Music, *Instruments in Church*, (London: The Scarecrow Press, Inc., 1998), 27.

19. William Rice states on instrumental music in the early church, "The leaders (of the church)....were worried by its secular associations. Instrumental music retained that stigma for centuries and has never been accepted by certain denominations." *A Concise History of Church Music*, 12. David Music writes, "The early Christian writers opposed musical instruments in any area of life; to be a player of a musical instrument was equated with being an immoral person, regardless of where the instrument was played or what music was performed." *Instruments in Church*, 27–28.

20. McKinnon, *The Temple, the Church Fathers and Early Western Chant*, 69.

21. Girardeau, 102–103.

22. Edmund Lorenz, *Church Music*, (New York: Fleming H. Revell Company, 1923), 217.

We return now to our question concerning how we are to interpret the silence of the New Testament on musical instruments. Does this silence mean that musical instruments were simply assumed by the apostles and nothing was written about them? Or does this silence mean that musical instruments did not exist in the apostolic church? The historical evidence of unaccompanied singing in both the Jewish synagogue before the apostles and the church of the second century after the apostles provides the most powerful evidence in interpreting the silence of the New Testament. If the worship of the synagogue, from which the worship of the church was derived, and the worship of the second century immediately following the apostles were both without musical instruments, then surely the apostolic churches had no musical instruments either. How can it possibly be assumed that musical instruments existed in the apostolic church when they were absent from the periods immediately prior and following? It is placed beyond any doubt, by these historical facts, that the silence of the New Testament must be interpreted to mean that musical instruments did not exist in the apostolic churches. Those who hold to the regulative principle of worship believe that the church today should follow the apostolic model. The question must be asked, if musical instruments did not exist in the times of the apostles, then under whose authority do we bring them into the church today? John Girardeau answers the question:

> Our Lord, as a man, was perfectly familiar with the worship of the synagogue. It is said that there were in his day at least four hundred and fifty synagogues in the great city of Jerusalem itself, churches in which the population worshipped from Sabbath to Sabbath, just as a Christian people now worship in theirs. His custom was to attend the synagogue wherever in his blessed itinerary he chanced to be. He full well knew the absence of instrumental music from its services, and he knew that his church,

when established as such, would follow the precedents
of stated Sabbath worship, which reached immemorially
back through the history of his ancient people. Did he
leave a command to his church to depart from that order,
and introduce instrumental music into its stated Sabbath
worship? He did not; and the defect of such a command
is sufficient to settle the question.[23]

We will now survey some quotations from the Church Fathers
that confirm their vehement rejection of musical instruments in
the church. As we read their words, we should remember those
three principles of worship we found back in Chapter 1: 1) The
Old Testament Temple worship in all of its outward ceremonies
and rituals has been abolished, 2) We must look to Christ and
His apostles alone for the worship of the church, and 3) With no
command, example, or any indication whatsoever from the Lord
Jesus that He desires musical instruments to be used in His church,
we have no authority for their use. While we may not find these
principles stated in these same words, it will become clear that they
lie in the background and often form the theological basis of the
rejection of musical instruments by the Church Fathers.

Ignatius of Antioch (ca. 35–107) was one of the first to use an
allegorical interpretation of the Old Testament musical instruments.
While we would not agree with this method of interpretation, it
does show one of the ways in which the Church Fathers denied
the validity of musical instruments in the worship of the church.
Ignatius compared the unity of the bishop and presbyters to the
well-tuned strings of a harp, "Wherefore it is fitting that ye should
run together in accordance with the will of your bishop, which thing
also ye do. For your justly renowned presbytery, worthy of God, is
fitted as exactly to the bishop as the strings are to the harp. Therefore
in your concord and harmonious love, Jesus Christ is sung. And do
ye, man by man, become a choir, that being harmonious in love,

23. Girardeau, 112.

and taking up the song of God in unison, yet may with one voice sing to the Father through Jesus Christ . . ."[24] In his Letter to the Philadelphians, Ignatius compared the obedience of the bishop to God's commandments to the strings of a harp, "For he is in harmony with the commandments (of God), even as the harp is with its strings."[25]

Justin Martyr (ca. 100–165) was the leading apologist of the early church in the face of intense Roman persecution. His defense of Christianity ultimately lead to his martyrdom. Concerning the distinction between Old and New Covenant worship, Martyr wrote about A.D. 140, "The use of singing with instrumental music was not received in the Christian churches as it was among the Jews in their infant state, but only the use of plain song."[26] Plain song refers to singing with the voice unaccompanied by musical instruments. Martyr also writes, "Musical organs pertain to the Jewish ceremonies and agree no more to us than circumcision."[27]

Clement of Alexandria (150-ca. 215), an apologist of the early church, based his objection to musical instruments upon their association with idolatry and immorality. "Leave the pipe to the shepherd, the flute to the men who are in fear of gods and are intent on their idol-worshipping. Such musical instruments must be excluded from our wineless feasts . . . ."[28] Clement believed that the instruments of the Old Testament were now replaced by the instruments of the human body, "'Praise Him with harp,' for the tongue is a harp of the Lord; 'and with the lute, praise Him,' understanding the mouth as a lute moved by the Spirit . . . ."[29] "But

24. Alexander Roberts and James Donaldson, eds., *The Ante-Nicene Fathers,* (Buffalo: The Christian Literature Publishing Company, 1885), Vol. 1, 50–51.

25. Ibid., 79.

26. Quoted in Charles H. Spurgeon, *The Treasury of David,* (McLean, VA: MacDonald Publishing Company), Vol. 1, Part 2, 111. Quoted in Bingham, Vol. 1, 316.

27. Quoted in William Ames, *A Fresh Suit Against Human Ceremonies in God's Worship,* (Gregg International Publishers Limited, reprinted, 1971), 405.

28. Clement of Alexandria, *Christ the Educator,* translated by Simon P. Wood, (New York: Fathers of the Church, Inc., 1954), 130.

29. Ibid., 131.

as for us, we make use of one instrument alone: only the Word of peace, by whom we pay homage to God, no longer with ancient harp or trumpet or drum or flute. . . ."[30]

Origen (ca. 185-ca. 254), a pupil of Clement and perhaps the greatest scholar of the early Church Fathers, comments on Ps 33:2, "The kithara (lyre) is the active soul being moved by the commandments of God, the psalterion (harp) is the pure mind being moved by spiritual knowledge. The musical instruments of the Old Covenant understood spiritually are applicable to us. The kithara, speaking figuratively, is the body, the psalterion the spirit. These are in tune for the wise man who employs the members of the body and powers of the soul as strings. He who makes melody with the mind makes melody well, speaking spiritual songs and singing in his heart to God."[31]

Arnobius of Sicca (d. ca. 330) ridiculed the pagan cults for their use of musical instruments to appease their gods. "To what purpose is the rattling of castanets: that the deities might hear them, have respect to the performance, and forget their burning anger?. . . . Are the almighty deities soothed by the shrill sound of pipes, and do

---

30. Ibid. Clement did write favorably of the use of musical instruments as being an imitation of King David, "And even if you wish to sing and play to the harp or lyre, there is no blame. Thou shalt imitate the righteous Hebrew king in his thanksgiving to God. 'Rejoice in the Lord, ye righteous; praise is comely to the upright,' says the prophecy. 'Confess to the Lord on the harp; play to Him on a psaltery of ten-strings. Sing to Him a new song.' And does not the ten-stringed psaltery indicate the Word Jesus, who is manifested by the element of the decade." This quotation has been used as evidence of the use of musical instruments in the early church. However, James McKinnon states that the larger context of this quotation shows that Clement was expressing approval of the use of these instruments at a Christian banquet and not a worship service. It should also be noted that Clement writes allegorically of instruments in this passage. The quotations given above clearly demonstrate Clement's antagonism to instruments in Christian worship, which is consistent with the unanimous opinion of the Church Fathers. Further quotations of Clement condemning musical instruments will be given in Chapter III. McKinnon also notes that many musicologists, in an effort to produce evidence that instruments were employed in the early church, have either mistranslated or misinterpreted passages (often allegorical) from the Church Fathers. See McKinnon, *The Church Fathers and Musical Instruments,* 151–155, 261–262.

31. Quoted in Everett Ferguson, *A Cappella Music in the Public Worship of the Church,* (Abilene, TX: Biblical Research Press, 1972), 57.

they relax at the rhythm of cymbals, their indignation mollified?"[32] The use of instruments by the cults was one reason why Arnobius banished them from Christian worship.

Eusebius, Bishop of Caesarea (ca. 260-ca. 339), was the leading historian of the early church. If musical instruments had existed in the worship of the church, he surely would have recorded their use. But Eusebius states that it was the universal practice of the churches to sing unaccompanied psalms. In his commentary on Ps. 91:4, he contrasts the worship of the church in its infancy under the Old Covenant with its maturity under the New Covenant, "When formerly the people of the circumcision worshipped through symbols and types, it was not unreasonable that they raised hymns to God on psalteries and cithara. . . . we however. . . . upon a living psaltery and an animate cithara and in spiritual songs that we render the hymn. And so more sweetly pleasing to God than any musical instrument would be the symphony of the people of God, by which, in every church of God, with kindred spirit and single disposition, with one mind and unanimity of faith and piety, we raise melody in unison in our psalmody."[33]

Athanasius (ca. 293–373) of Alexandria, who led the struggle against Arianism, was opposed to the use of musical instruments in Christian worship. His views will be considered later in Chapter III.

Hilary of Poitiers (d. 367), who made significant contributions in the trinitarian debates of the fourth century, shared the same perspective as the rest of the Church Fathers.[34]

---

32. Arnobius of Sicca, "Disputationum adversus gentes," VII, 32, J.P. Migne, ed., *Patrologiae Cursus Completus Series Latina,* 221 Vols., (Garnier Fratres, 1878–1890), hereafter listed as *PL,* V, 1262, quoted in Music, 38.

33. Eusebius of Caesarea, "In psalmum," XCI, 4, J.P. Migne, ed. *Patrologiae Cursus Completus Series Graeca,* 161 Vols., (Paris: 1857–1887), hereafter listed as *PG,* XXIII, 1172–1173, translated by James McKinnon, *Music in Early Christian Literature,* (Cambridge: Cambridge University Press, 1987), 97–98.

34. McKinnon, *The Church Fathers and Musical Instruments,* 3.

Chrysostom (ca. 345–404) was Bishop of Constantinople and one of the greatest preachers of the early church. He comments on Ps. 33:2 and contrasts the use of musical instruments under the Old and New Covenants, "It was only permitted to the Jews, as sacrifice was, for the heaviness and grossness of their souls. God condescended to their weakness, because they were lately drawn off from idols: but now instead of organs, we may use our own bodies to praise him withal."[35] This word "organs" used here was a Latin word referring to musical instruments of any kind and not to the instrument we now call an organ.[36]

Evagrius Ponticus (346–399) spiritually interpreted musical instruments as the soul and parts of the human body. "Praise the Lord on the cithara, sing to him on the psaltery of ten strings, etc. The cithara is the practical soul set in motion by the commandments of God; the psaltery is the pure mind set in motion by spiritual knowledge. The musical instruments of the Old Testament are not unsuitable for us if understood spiritually; figuratively the body can be called a cithara and the soul a psaltery, which are likened musically to the wise man who fittingly employs the limbs of the body and the powers of the soul as strings. Sweetly sings he who sings in the mind, uttering spiritual songs, singing in his heart to God."[37]

Ambrose (ca. 340–397), Bishop of Milan, opposed the use of musical instruments in worship, criticizing those who would rather play the lyre and psaltery than sing psalms and hymns.[38]

Jerome (ca. 340–420) was unsurpassed as a scholar in the early church. His greatest achievement was his translation of most of the Bible into Latin from the original languages (later known as the Vulgate). Jerome rejected the use of musical instruments on the basis of their immoral associations and stated that, "A Christian

---

35. Quoted in Spurgeon, Vol. 1, Part 2, 111.
36. Music, xvii.
37. Evagrius of Pontus, "Selecta in psalmos," XXXII, 2–3, *PG*, XII, 1304, translated by McKinnon, 38.
38. Lorenz, 220.

maiden ought not even to know what a lyre or flute is, or what it is used for."[39]

Augustine of Hippo (354–430) was the most influential theologian of his time. In his comments on Ps. 33:2, Augustine declares singing to continue in the church, but not the use of instruments, "'Praise the Lord with harp; sing unto Him with the psaltery of ten strings,' For this even now we sang, this expressing with one mouth, we instructed your hearts. Hath not the institution of these Vigils in the name of Christ brought it to pass that harps should be banished out of this place? And, lo, the same are bid to sound, 'Praise the Lord,' saith he, 'with harp; sing unto Him with the psaltery of ten strings.' Let none turn his heart to instruments of the theatre."[40] In his comments on Ps. 57:8, Augustine allegorically interpreted the psaltery and the harp as the divine miracles and the human sufferings of Christ, respectively. "But what is the psaltery? What is the harp? Through his own flesh the Lord worked two kinds of actions, miracles and sufferings: the miracles were from above, the sufferings from below. Indeed, those miracles that were done were divine, but they were done through the body and the flesh. Thus, the flesh working the divine is the psaltery; the unyielding flesh of humanity is the cithara."[41]

Isidore of Pelusium (d. ca. 440) compares the use of musical instruments with the other ceremonies of the Old Testament, all of which were done away with in the church. "If God bore with bloody sacrifices, because of men's childishness at that time, why should you wonder he bore with the music of a harp and a psaltery?"[42]

Theodoret of Cyrrhus (ca. 393-ca. 458), as late as the 5th century, writes concerning the sacrifices and musical instruments of the Old Covenant, "What he ordained in the Law, then, concerning

---

39. Quoted in Lorenz, 220.

40. Augustine, *Expositions of the Book of Psalms*, (Oxford: James Parker and Co. and Rivingtons, 1877), 311–312.

41. Augustine, "Enarrationes in Psalnum," Ps. 57, 16, *PL*, XXXVI, 671, quoted in Music, 32.

42. Quoted in Girardeau, 158.

these things, was because of their weakness, not their need or their intention . . . . And again he cries, 'Take away from me the sound of your songs; to the voice of your instruments I will not listen' (Amos 5:23)."[43] Theodoret goes on to state concerning the musical instruments of the Temple, "Wherefore the use of such instruments and other things appropriate to those who are childish is dispensed with in the churches and singing alone has been left over."[44]

Niceta, Bishop of Remesiana from 370 until his death about 414, spoke of the discontinuation of the ceremonial laws of the Temple, including its use of musical instruments. He writes, "For what is fleshly is rejected, including circumcision, the sabbath, sacrifices, discrimination in foods, trumpets, harps, cymbals, drums: which now are all understood to resonate better in the members of the human being. Daily baptisms, observance of new moons, and painstaking inspection for leprosy have entirely ceased and been abrogated, even if these were necessary for a time because of their childishness. On the other hand, spiritual things—among which are faith, piety, prayer, fasting, patience, chastity, and praise—have been increased, not lessened."[45]

Not only did the Church Fathers as individuals condemn the use of musical instruments in worship, but the early church councils did so as well. The Council of Laodicea (367) forbid the use of musical instruments in worship, and this has remained the policy of the Eastern Orthodox Church to the present day.[46] In 416, the

43. Theodoret, "Graecarum affectionum curatio de sacrificiis," 34–35, *PG*, LXXXIII, 1001–2, quoted in McKinnon, 107.

44. Theodoret of Cyrrhus, "Quaestiones et responsiones ad orthodoxos," CVII, *PG*, VI, 1353, translated by McKinnon, 107.

45. Niceta of Remesiana, "De psalmodiae bono," in *Journal of Theological Studies*, April 1923, Vol. 24, 237–238, quoted in Music, 33–34.

46. Douglass, 15. McClintock and Strong state, "Never has either the organ or any other instrument been employed in public worship in Eastern churches; nor is mention of instrumental music found in all their liturgies, ancient, or modern." John McClintock and James Strong, *Cyclopedia of Biblical, Theological and Ecclesiastical Literature*, (New York: Harper & Brothers, Publishers, 1879), 739.

Council of Carthage addressed this issue and declared, "On the Lord's day let all instruments of music be silenced."[47]

We have heard the unanimous rejection of musical instruments by the Church Fathers throughout the early centuries of the church. Several things should be stated concerning the above quotations: 1) It should be noted that the Church Fathers are not debating with other Christians over the use of musical instruments in worship. Neither are they trying to correct an abuse that had crept into the church. They did not need to do so, because there was no debate, but rather unanimity, on this issue. There were no musical instruments in the worship of the early Christian churches for many centuries, 2) Some have suggested that persecution was the reason the Church Fathers rejected instruments, since they would draw attention to their worship. But as we can see from their own words, it was always other factors, and not persecution, upon which the Church Fathers based their objections.

The significance of this rejection of musical instruments in worship by the Church Fathers cannot be underestimated. It provides the most convincing historical evidence that musical instrumentation in worship was not commanded by the apostles or practiced in the churches of their time. If the apostles had commanded and used musical instruments in the early church, then surely this practice would have been carried on by the Church Fathers. But here we have seen that musical instruments had no place in Christian worship for centuries after the apostles. How can we account for this historical fact? Can we assume that the Church Fathers completely revolted against an apostolic command and practice? And this they did, not by one or two, but by all of them in mass? This cannot be. Is it possible that musical instruments were used in all the churches of the New Testament, and yet immediately after the death of the apostles, the Church Fathers were able to completely eradicate them from worship, and that, as we shall see, for over a thousand

47. Quoted in Girardeau, 67.

years? The thought is absurd. All the historical evidence leads to only one conclusion, that there were no musical instruments in the apostolic churches.

With the reign of Constantine (311–337), Christianity was established as the national religion of the Roman Empire in A.D. 313 and great changes began to take place in its outward worship. Magnificent buildings were constructed and worship became marked by increasingly elaborate ceremonies, including more complex tunes in singing. This complexity of tunes eventually made congregational singing impossible and gave rise to the use of skillful choirs. But despite the increase of external pomp beginning in the 4th century, musical instruments did not enter into the worship of the church until many centuries later.

In the late 6th century, Gregory the Great (ca. 540–604) developed his monodic melodies, which became known as the Gregorian chant. These became the standard throughout the western church into the 7th century, and it is a well-known fact that they continued to be sung without musical accompaniment.[48] McClintock and Strong state, "Even Gregory the Great, who towards the end of the 6th century added greatly to the existing church music, absolutely prohibited the use of instruments."[49]

David Music summarizes the history of the post-apostolic church, "The vehement and unanimous objections of the Church Fathers to musical instruments apparently succeeded in suppressing their use in Christian worship for many centuries."[50] Andrew Fuller writes, "The history of the church during the first three centuries affords many instances of the primitive Christians engaging in singing; but no mention, that I recollect, is made of instruments. Even in the times of Constantine, when every thing grand and

---

48. Rice, 14–15.
49. McClintock and Strong, Vol. 6, 759.
50. Music, 43.

magnificent was introduced into Christian worship, I find no mention made of instrumental music."[51]

It cannot be argued that the reason musical instruments were not used in the early church was that they were not present or popular in the world at that time. Musical instruments were commonly used for secular purposes in the contemporary society of the early church. They played a central role in the worship of the mystery cults and were used in the celebrations of various feast days of the Roman Empire. The fact that musical instruments were prominent in the surrounding culture makes it all the more remarkable that they were successfully resisted by the Church Fathers and did not find an entrance into Christian worship for many centuries. Edward Dickinson, Professor of the History of Music at Oberlin College, writes, "while the pagan melodies were always sung to an instrumental accompaniment, the church chant was exclusively vocal."[52]

The Rise of Musical Instruments During the Dark Ages

Church historians agree that the first recorded example of a musical instrument in Christian worship was an organ introduced in about 670 in a Roman Catholic Church in Rome by Pope Vitalianus.[53] In France, in 757, nearly one hundred years after the first organ appeared in Rome, Emperor Constantine V sent an organ as a gift to King Pepin.[54] This organ was to be used in the king's court and not in a church. The organ was still so uncommon in Europe at that time that when this gift arrived it was regarded as a

---

51. Fuller, 861.

52. Edward Dickinson, *Music in the History of the Western Church,* (New York: Charles Scribner's Sons, 1902), 54.

53. Schaff, Vol. 4, 439; Lyman Coleman, *The Antiquities of the Christian Church,* (Andover: Gould, Newman & Saxton, 1841), 192; *The New International Encyclopedia,* Vol. 13, 446; M.C. Kurfees, *Instrumental Music in the Worship,* (Nashville: Gospel Advocate Co., 1950), 152.

54. Thomas Hirst, *The Music of the Church,* (London: Whittaker, & Co.; Simpkin, Marshall, & Co., 1841), 75.

great novelty.[55] The second occasion of an instrument's being used in church worship occurred in 812, when Pepin's son, Charlemagne, had a copy of this organ made for the Roman Catholic Cathedral at Aix-la-Chapelle.[56] By the 9th century, only two organs had been used in Christian worship. In the churches of England, the organ probably made its first appearance in the 9th century,[57] and through the influence of St. Dunstan, archbishop of Canterbury, it became more common by the end of the 10th century.[58] The organ, however, continued to face strong opposition and remained only isolated in its use for hundreds of years. There was no general acceptance of it in the churches until at least the late 1200s.

It was not long after the organ was introduced into the church that men began to speak out against its abuse. Wulstan of Winchester (d. 990) tells of the massive organ installed in the cathedral at Winchester, England. The organ was so large that to work its bellows required "seventy strong men, labouring with their arms covered with perspiration, each inciting his companions to drive the wind up with all his strength . . . ."[59] "The noise is so loud, reverberating everywhere, that everyone stops his open ears with his hand, not being able to bear the powerful roaring made by the clashing of the various sounds."[60]

Although the organ was the most common musical instrument in worship and the only one sanctioned by the Roman Catholic Church, other instruments such as the harp, violin and cither eventually came into use as well.[61] Ethelred, the Abbot of Rievaulx Abbey, Yorkshire (1109–1166), complained of the adverse effect of the organ and other instruments upon the singing of the human voice, "Let me speake now of those who, under the show of religion,

55. Music, 43.
56. Lorenz, 406.
57. Ibid., 407.
58. Music, 46.
59. Quoted in Lorenz, 407.
60. Wulstan of Winchester, "Letter to Elfege," *PL*, I, 110–111, quoted in Music, 47.
61. Nick Needham, "Worship Through the Ages," in *Give Praise to God*, 392.

doe obpalliate[62] the business of pleasure. . . . Whence hath the church so many organs and musical instruments? To what purpose, I pray you, is that terrible blowing of belloes, expressing rather the crakes of thunder, than the sweetness of a voyce?"[63]

While there appear to be isolated examples of the organ's being used as early as the 9th century, most historians agree that there was considerable resistance to it by the church, and its acceptance was only gradual over the next five hundred years. Professor Girardeau writes, "When the organ was introduced into its worship it encountered strong opposition, and made its way but slowly to general acceptance."[64] It was not until at least the late 13th century that the organ began to be more common.[65] Thomas Aquinas (1225–1274) was one of the most prominent Roman Catholic theologians of the Middle Ages and one who surely knew how worship was conducted in his time. As late as 1260, he wrote, "The Church does not use musical instruments such as the harp or lyre when praising God, in case she should seem to fall back into Judaism. . . . For musical instruments usually move the soul more to pleasure than create inner moral goodness. But in the Old Testament, they used instruments of this kind, both because the people were more coarse and carnal, so that they needed to be aroused by such instruments and with worldly promises, and also because these bodily instruments were symbolic of something."[66] Cajetan, a Roman Catholic Cardinal of the 16th century said, "It is to be observed the church did not use organs in Thomas's time; whence, even to this day, the Church of Rome does not use them in the Pope's presence."[67]

Joseph Bingham, the famous church historian, in his *Antiquities of the Christian Church,* writes concerning the use of musical

---

62. An old English word meaning "to extenuate an offense."
63. Quoted in Percy A. Scholes, *The Puritans and Music,* (London: Oxford University Press, 1934), 215.
64. Girardeau, 161.
65. Rice, 19.
66. Quoted in Needham, 393.
67. Quoted in Girardeau, 161–162.

instruments in worship, "that there were no such things in use in the ancient churches for many ages. Music in churches is as ancient as the apostles, but instrumental music not so: for it is now generally agreed among learned men that the use of organs came into the church since the time of Thomas Aquinas, Anno 1250."[68] Professor Girardeau writes,

> There is no evidence, but the contrary, to show that instrumental music was commonly introduced into the church until the thirteenth century.[69] The church, although lapsing more and more into defection from the truth and into a corruption of apostolic practice, had no instrumental worship for 1200 years.[70]

It was during the dark ages of the 14th and 15th centuries that the organ gained prominence in the worship of the Roman Catholic Church.[71] Girardeau writes, "In spite of opposition, the organ, during the fourteenth and fifteenth centuries, steadily made its way toward universal triumph in the Romish church."[72] By the early 1500s, an organ was found in almost every important church of Europe, and its use became one of the distinguishing traits of the Roman Catholic liturgy. Once music became a major emphasis in the worship of the church, it continued in various forms until the Reformation.[73] The use of other musical instruments increased dramatically in the Roman church, especially during the 16th century.[74]

Cotton Mather, writing in about 1700, states that

> Instrumental musick in the worship of God is but a very late invention and corruption in the church of the New

68. Bingham, Vol. 1, 315.
69. Girardeau, 156.
70. Ibid., 179.
71. Music, 55, 71.
72. Girardeau, 162.
73. Maxwell, 86.
74. McKinnon, *The Temple, the Church Fathers and Early Western Chant*, 239–240.

Testament. The writings that go under the name of Justin Martyr deny it and decry it. Chrysostom speaks meanly of it. Even Aquinas himself, about 400 years ago, determines against it, as Jewish and carnal. Bellarmine himself confesses that it was but late received in the church.[75]

Andrew Fuller writes that musical instruments in worship "originated in the dark ages of popery, when almost every other superstition was introduced under the plea of its according with the worship of the Old Testament. At present it is most in use where these kinds of superstitions are most prevalent, and where the least regard is paid to primitive simplicity."[76]

Robert L. Dabney, a professor of theology and church history for over forty years at Union Theological Seminary in Richmond, Virginia, writes in regard to the exclusion of musical instruments from Christian worship, "Such has been the creed of all churches, and in all ages, except of the Popish communion after it had reached the nadir of its corruption at the end of the thirteenth century, and its prelatic imitators."[77]

McClintock and Strong state,

> Students of ecclesiastical archaeology are generally agreed that instrumental music was not used in churches till a much later date; for Thomas Aquinas, A.D. 1250, has these remarkable words: "Our Church does not use musical instruments, as harps and psalteries, to praise God withal, that she may not seem to Judaize." From this passage

---

75. Mather, Vol. 2, 266–267. Benjamin Keach, a leading Baptist theologian in the late 17th century states, "We find no mention in the least of any other singing, but that of united voices, in Eusebius, nor Tertullian, &c.," Benjamin Keach, *The Breach Repaired in God's Worship,* (London: John Marshall, 1700), 68. *Early English Books,* 1641–1700, (Ann Arbor, MI: University Microfilm International), hereafter listed as *EEB,* 1641–1700, Reel 1951:4.

76. Fuller, 861.

77. Robert L. Dabney, *The Presbyterian Quarterly,* July 1889, http://www.naphtali. com/dabney's_review_of_girardeau.htm (accessed March 24, 2004).

we are surely warranted in concluding that there was no ecclesiastical use of organs in the time of Aquinas.[78]

We should not miss the significance of what we have just read. A number of the most esteemed Christian historians and leaders testify with one voice that musical instruments were not an accepted part of the worship of the church for over 1300 years. They were "a very late invention" and did not have any prominence in worship until the dark ages of Roman Catholicism in the 14th and 15th centuries.

The Protestant Reformation

Throughout the Medieval Age, the worship of the Roman Catholic Church had grown increasingly sensuous and idolatrous. The worship of God had become, to a large extent, an effort to gratify the physical senses. For the eyes, there were idols, candles, various man-made ceremonies, magnificent church architecture, and the host transformed into the body of Christ; for the touch, there were images and relics; for the smell, there was incense; and for the ears, there was the use of musical instruments, especially the organ. The reformers saw this sensuous worship as idolatrous. They believed that God must be worshipped according to His commands and not by human inventions. The sensuous worship of the Medieval church was directly opposed to the spiritual worship of the New Testament. "God is spirit," and He must be worshipped "in spirit and truth." Any man-made attempt to worship Him through the material world was a contradiction of His Being and a violation of His will in the gospel.[79]

To the reformers, reformation was necessary not only in regard to false doctrine, but also in regard to false and idolatrous worship. The recovery of biblical doctrine must have its legitimate expression

78. McClintock and Strong, Vol. 8, 739.
79. Charles Garside, *Zwingli and the Arts,* (New Haven: Yale University Press, 1966), 36.

in the recovery of biblical worship. True doctrine can exist and be maintained only in the context of true worship. The Protestant Reformation therefore became to a large extent a movement to return the church to the simplicity and purity of apostolic worship. No small part of the sensuous worship of the medieval church that had to be reformed was its use of musical instruments. As we shall see, from the earliest stages of Reformation, the reformers fervently cried out against this corruption of worship.

John Wycliffe (1320–1384), "the morning star of the Reformation," censured the English churches of his day for their extreme sensuousness in worship. He considered the many ceremonies and images of the church, along with its use of the organ, "a relapse into Judaism, which seeks after signs, and a departure from the spiritual nature of Christianity."[80] Wycliffe protested that the churches were filled with nominal believers who "feed their senses to excess in religion . . . their eyes with the sumptuous spectacle of the Church's ornaments, their ears with bells and organs and the new art of striking the hour of the day by the wonderful chimes, not to mention many other sensuous preparations by which their other senses are moved, apart altogether from religious feeling."[81] Wycliffe strongly encouraged the unaccompanied singing of psalms by the entire congregation.[82]

In the early 1400s, John Hus (1369–1415) faced similar corruptions in the churches of Bohemia. Hus complained that when the people come to church they "gape at the pictures, the vestments, chalices and other marvelous furnishings of the churches. Their ears are filled with the sound of bells, organs, and small bells, by frivolous singing which incites to dance rather than to piety."[83] Hus and his followers reformed worship by forbidding the use of musical

80. Professor Lechler, *John Wycliffe and His English Precursors,* (London: The Religious Tract Society, 1904), 324.
81. Quoted in Lechler, 326.
82. McClintock and Strong, 739.
83. Quoted in Matthew Spinka, *John Hus' Concept of the Church,* (Princeton: Princeton University Press, 1966), 306.

instruments and returning to primitive simplicity with unison congregational singing.[84] Hus himself wrote many hymns in the vernacular and became the founder of Bohemian hymnody.[85]

In the medieval church, singing was not performed by the congregation but by well-trained or professional choirs. The singing was usually in Latin and was so complex and elaborate that it could not be understood by the people. Music had become a major emphasis in the worship of the church. Erasmus (ca. 1466–1536) complained of how contrary this emphasis on music was to apostolic worship, "Modern church music is so constructed that the congregation cannot hear one distinct word. The choristers themselves do not understand what they are singing, yet according to priests and monks it constitutes the whole of religion. Why will they not listen to Paul? In college or monastery it is still the same: music, nothing but music. There was no music in St. Paul's time."[86] Erasmus also complained against the detrimental effects musical instruments had upon singing:

> We have introduced into churches a type of laborious and theatrical music, a confused chattering of diverse voices such as I do not think was ever heard in the theatres of the Greeks or the Romans. They perform everything with slide-trumpets, trombones, cornetts, and little flutes, and with these the voices of men contend.[87] Men run to church as to a theatre, to have their ears tickled.[88]

On October 31, 1517, Martin Luther (1483–1546) sparked the Protestant Reformation by nailing his ninety-five theses on the door of the Wittenberg church. Prior to his discovery of the

84. Gustave Reese, *Music in the Renaissance*, (New York: W. W. Norton & Company, Inc., 1959), 732–733. Douglass, 37.

85. Dickinson, 233.

86. Quoted in J. A. Froude, *Life and Letters of Erasmus*, (New York: Charles Scribner's Sons, 1894), 122–123.

87. Quoted in Garside, 32.

88. Quoted in Girardeau, 162.

doctrine of justification by faith alone, Luther's own experience was one of intense spiritual struggle. Perhaps because of his own personal anguish, Luther's main concern throughout the rest of his life was the centrality of preaching justification as the gospel way of salvation. Luther did not hold to a biblical view of the regulative principle of worship. He believed that unless a practice was expressly forbidden by the Word of God it could be allowed.

As a result, Luther never considered the reformation of worship a matter of priority as did the other leading reformers.[89] He never fully understood the sinfulness of idolatry or of man-made ceremonies and inventions in the worship of God.[90] So long as the preaching of the Word of God was central, Luther was willing to retain many of the existing forms of medieval worship, including images, the altar, the wearing of vestments, and the sign of the cross.[91] Luther himself declared images in worship to be a matter of indifference, "I must admit that images are neither here nor there, neither evil nor good, we may have them or not, as we please."[92] If Luther did not object to the use of images in worship, we should not be surprised that he did not object to the use of musical instruments either. The fruit of Luther's view of worship can be seen in the many man-made corruptions that remain in the Lutheran and Anglican churches today. Despite his acceptance of musical instruments, Luther did however often lead the church in unaccompanied congregational singing.[93]

Andreas Bodenstein of Carlstadt (1480–1541), more commonly known as Carlstadt, was Dean of the Faculty of Theology at the University of Wittenberg. It was Carlstadt who conferred the

89. Garside, 35–36.
90. William Cunningham, *The Reformers and the Theology of the Reformation,* (Edinburgh: The Banner of Truth Trust, Reprinted, 2000), 104.
91. Williston Walker, *A History of the Christian Church,* (New York: Charles Scribner's Sons, 1985), 435.
92. Martin Luther, *Luther's Works,* (Philadelphia, Muhlenberg Press, 1959), Vol. 51, 86.
93. Douglass, 39.

doctorate degree on Martin Luther in 1512, and he later became an ardent supporter of the Reformation. When the papal bull of excommunication was issued in October 1520, Carlstadt's name appeared along with Luther's as a condemned heretic. In the late summer of 1521, he became the first reformer to write a critique of music in worship entitled, *Disputation on Gregorian Chant*.[94] He opposed the Gregorian chant because it had become an unintelligible mumbling of words, and was therefore without edification to the congregation. In his *Disputation,* Carlstadt rejected the use of musical instruments in Christian worship. His overarching thesis was an historical argument in which he connected the fall of the church in the Middle Ages with the increased use of music. Carlstadt maintained that the increase of ecclesiastical music from the time of Pope Gregory, including the use of instruments, was one of the marks of the apostasy of the church.[95] He also argued that the concentration required to play a musical instrument rendered the worship of the instrumentalist psychologically impossible. Church music had become too theatrical and performance oriented. It was an exhibition of the technical skills of both the musicians and the composer. For these reasons, all musical instruments should be removed from Christian worship. Carlstadt wrote, "On the grounds that it is everywhere a hindrance to devotion, we completely reject the measured chant from the church. Therefore, together with it and the organ, we relegate trumpets and flutes to the theatre of entertainments and the halls of princes."[96] Carlstadt believed that church music should be comprised of the unaccompanied singing of the psalms by the entire congregation.[97]

An event that came to be known as "the Wittenberg Movement" illustrates Luther's indifference to reforms in worship. In 1521, while Luther was hidden away in the Wartburg castle, Carlstadt

94. Garside, 28.
95. Ibid., 30–31.
96. Quoted in Garside, 46.
97. Ibid., 31.

and Melancthon became the leaders of the Reformation back in Wittenberg. During Luther's absence, many of the monks and students, along with a number of the citizens in Wittenberg, became increasingly impatient with the lack of reform in the worship of the church. Rioting broke out and some of the idols and images were torn down and removed from the churches. Melancthon himself became anxious for further reforms in worship and urged Carlstadt to make changes.[98] On Christmas day, 1521, Carlstadt celebrated the first evangelical Eucharistic service of the Reformation.[99] He began to preach against the use of vestments, pictures, organs, and other inventions of Romish worship. There is no evidence that the use of the organ was discontinued,[100] but it certainly would have been if Carlstadt had been able to carry out all his reforms. Many in Wittenberg desired the city council to enact Carlstadt's reforms more quickly, and when they seemed to drag their feet, the public disorders in the city only increased.

In March of 1522, Luther returned to Wittenberg and quelled the disturbance by declaring the reforms of worship to involve only externals of secondary importance. In eight powerful sermons, Luther maintained that so long as the gospel was preached, the forms of worship were matters of indifference. Nearly all of Carlstadt's reforms were reversed. Even the images were brought back into the church and virtually all of the medieval practices were reinstated.[101] Carlstadt's efforts to reform worship according to the commands of Scripture were suppressed, and Luther continued to maintain

98. James S. Preus, *Carlstadt's Ordinaciones and Luther's Liberty,* (Cambridge: Harvard University Press, 1974), 19. See also David C. Steinmetz, *Reformers in the Wings,* 2nd Ed., (Oxford: Oxford University Press, 2001), 127.

99. Carlstadt conducted the service without the normal priestly garments and pronounced the words of consecration in German without making reference to the mass as a sacrifice. He refused to elevate the host and served both elements to the entire congregation. Carlstadt also declared that the confessional was not necessary before partaking of the Eucharist.

100. Garside, 31.

101. Walker, 434–435.

that so long as the Word of God was central there could be great liberty in matters of worship.

The other leading reformers strongly disagreed with Luther's view of worship. For them, the Reformation had to extend beyond doctrine and affect the worship of the church. They believed that the truth of the gospel could be maintained only in the context of a biblically ordered worship. God alone has the prerogative to order His worship, and man has no right to intrude his own inventions and devices into it. Whereas for Martin Luther the central issue of the Reformation was justification by faith, for the other leading reformers, the central issue was the restoration of pure and spiritual worship according to the New Testament.[102]

Huldriech Zwingli (1484–1531), pastor of the Great Minster Church in Zurich, became the leader of the Swiss Reformation in the early 1520s. Zwingli was influenced by Carlstadt's writings and agreed with his objection to the use of musical instruments in worship.[103] But unlike Carlstadt, who based his arguments on historical and psychological grounds, Zwingli derived his arguments from scriptural principles. He was the first reformer to clearly articulate what we know today as the regulative principle of worship: only what Christ has explicitly commanded in His Word should be part of the worship of the church.[104] Zwingli applied this principle to the use of musical instruments. Since Christ had not commanded them in the New Testament, they should not be used in His church. Zwingli summarized his view of worship in 1523, when he wrote, "Everything which is added to the true institutions of Christ is an abuse."[105]

Zwingli was well aware of the turmoil that Carlstadt's reforms had caused in Wittenberg. He exercised great care that the same

---

102. Carlos M. N. Eire, *War Against Idols,* (Cambridge: Cambridge University Press, 1986), 2, 195–233.
103. Garside, 28.
104. Ibid., 38–39.
105. Quoted in Garside, 54.

disorders did not result in Zurich. Zwingli made sure that the people were fully instructed, and he waited for the approval of the city council before any reforms were implemented. The outcome of Zwingli's patience was that all of his reforms were accomplished without disturbance and the organ in the Great Minster Church ceased to be used after June 1524.[106]

Zwingli went so far as to remove not only musical instruments but all vocal singing from the churches in Zurich. He was aware of the apostle's commands concerning singing in Eph. 5:19 and Col. 3:16 but interpreted these to refer to inward worship with the mind rather than outward singing with the voice. Zwingli wrote, "For we are not unaware that the words of Paul in Ephesians 5:19 and Colossians 3:16 concerning psaltery and singing in the heart give no help to those who protect their swan songs by them. For in the heart, he says, not with the voice. Therefore, the psalms and praises of God ought to be treated as if our minds sing to God."[107] Although Zwingli removed vocal singing in Zurich, the norm of the Reformed churches throughout Switzerland was unaccompanied congregational singing.[108] In 1598 vocal singing was once again permitted in the Zurich churches.[109]

We should be careful to note that Zwingli's reforms were not the result of a personal aversion to music. The very opposite was true. Zwingli was a great lover of music and had studied it for over ten years in the schools and universities of Bern, Vienna and Basel.[110] He was an accomplished musician and composer who "possessed an astonishing skill in playing almost a dozen musical instruments."[111] Throughout his entire life, he enjoyed singing

106. Ibid., 61.
107. *Huldrych Zwinglis Samtliche Werke*, (Berlin-Zurich, 1905—), Vol. 2, 621, translated in Garside, 53.
108. Music, 57–58.
109. Garside, 60.
110. Ibid., 8–15.
111. Walter Kohler, in his biography of Zwingli, quoted in Garside, *Zwingli and the Arts*, 22. See also Timothy George, *Theology of the Reformers*, (Nashville: Broadman Press, 1988), 131.

and the use of musical instruments in his own home. To Zwingli, instruments were a means of personal relaxation and recreation. But he would not bring them into the church because Christ had not commanded their use in worship. Charles Garside summarizes Zwingli's views,

> Music, choral or instrumental, no matter how religiously inspired, artistically beautiful, or superlatively performed, must be prohibited from worship because Scripture has made its existence there impossible. Zwingli the servant of the Word, rather than Zwingli the musician, is prohibiting music from liturgy.[112]

Heinrich Bullinger (1504–1575) succeeded Zwingli as the Chief Pastor at Zurich and the leader of the Reformation in Switzerland. He played a prominent role in drawing up the first and second Helvetic Confessions (1536 and 1566). Bullinger continued the commitment to the simplicity of New Testament worship and excluded all musical instruments from the church.

In the medieval church, musical instruments were often played by themselves, without singing. Because of this, the Reformers would at times object to them on the grounds that they were like the unknown tongues of 1 Cor. 14. Neither musical instruments nor unknown tongues could edify the people of God, and, therefore, they should not be present in Christian worship. Bullinger refers to this when he recorded the demolition of the organs in Zurich, "Since they also are not in accord with the apostle's teaching in 1 Corinthians 14, the organs in the great cathedral of Zurich were demolished on the 9th of December in this year of 1527. Then the people no longer desired either songs or organs in the churches . . ."[113]

---

112. Garside, 47.
113. Heinrich Bullinger, *Heinrich Bullinger's Reformationsgeschichte,* (Frauenfeld: Ch. Beyel, 1838), Vol. 1, 418, quoted in Music, 58.

The central concern of the great reformer John Calvin (1509–1564) was the restoration of the church to the simplicity and purity of apostolic worship. To Calvin, the way in which we worship God was so vital that he placed it first among the concerns of true Christianity and the Reformation. Calvin summarized "the whole substance of Christianity" as "first, of the mode in which God is duly worshipped; and, secondly, of the source from which salvation is to be obtained."[114]

Calvin further enlarged upon the regulative principle that worship must be according to God's commands in the Scripture. He wrote, "we may not adopt any device which seems fit to ourselves, but look to the injunctions of him who alone is entitled to prescribe. Therefore, if we would have him to approve our worship, this rule, which he everywhere enforces with the utmost strictness, must be carefully observed . . . the Lord, in condemning and prohibiting all ficticious worship, requires us to give obedience only to his own voice."[115]

In addition to the regulative principle, Calvin also clearly understood the distinction between Old and New Testament worship. He writes, "For, if we would not throw everything into confusion, we must never lose sight of the distinction between the old and new dispensations, and of the fact that ceremonies, the observance of which was useful under the law, are now not only superfluous, but vicious and absurd."[116]

Based upon the regulative principle and the distinction between Old and New Covenant worship, Calvin was committed to the authority of the New Testament in the worship of the church. He vehemently objected to the use of musical instruments in Christian worship, believing that they were part of the Temple ceremonies that had been abolished by Christ. While the New Testament was his final authority in worship, Calvin was also a scholar of the early

114. John Calvin, *The Necessity of Reforming the Church,* 15.
115. Ibid., 17.
116. Ibid., 48.

Church Fathers and often looked to them for confirmation of his views.[117] Calvin's contribution in this area of church life has been felt down through the centuries in the Reformed churches of the European continent, England, Scotland, Ireland, and America. David Music writes,

> Calvin's enormous personal influence led to the exclusion of musical instruments in the church that followed his model of church life, including Reformed congregations in Geneva and the Low Countries, English and American Puritans and Separatists, and Scottish Presbyterians.[118]

Because of Calvin's great influence throughout the Reformed churches, we will review some of his thoughts concerning musical instruments in Christian worship. As we have seen with the Church Fathers, we will find the same three truths underlying Calvin's words (and those of other reformers later): 1) The Old Testament Temple worship in all of its outward ceremonies and rituals has been abolished, 2) We must look to Christ and His apostles alone for the worship of the church, and 3) With no command, or example, for the use of musical instruments in the New Testament, we have no authority to bring them into the church.

Calvin notes the distinction between the public praise of God under the Old and New Covenants in his comments on Ps. 33:2, "Sing praises to Him with a harp of ten strings." He writes,

> There is a distinction, however, to be observed here, that we may not indiscriminately consider as applicable to ourselves, every thing which was formerly enjoined upon the Jews. I have no doubt that playing upon cymbals, touching the harp and the viol, and all that kind of music, which is so frequently mentioned in the Psalms, was a part

---

117. Horton Davies, *Christian Worship, Its History and Meaning,* (New York: Abingdon Press, 1957), 55. See also Hughes Oliphant Old, *The Patristic Roots of Reformed Worship,* (Zurich: Theologischer Verlag, 1975).

118. Music, 59.

of the education; that is to say, the puerile instruction of the law: I speak of the stated service of the Temple. For even now, if believers chose to cheer themselves with musical instruments, they should, I think, make it their object not to dissever their cheerfulness from the praises of God. But when they frequent their sacred assemblies, musical instruments in celebrating the praises of God would be no more suitable than the burning of incense, the lighting up of lamps, and the restoration of the other shadows of the law. The Papists, therefore, have foolishly borrowed this, as well as many other things from the Jews. Men who are fond of outward pomp may delight in that noise; but the simplicity which God recommends to us by the apostle is far more pleasing to him.[119]

On Ps. 71:22, "I will also praise Thee with a psaltery . . . I will sing praises with the harp," Calvin comments,

In speaking of employing the psaltery and the harp in this exercise, he alludes to the generally prevailing custom of that time. To sing the praise of God upon the harp and psaltery unquestionably formed a part of the training of the law, and of the service of God under that dispensation of shadows and figures; but they are not now to be used in public thanksgiving. We are not, indeed, forbidden to use, in private, musical instruments, but they are banished out of the churches by the plain command of the Holy Spirit, when Paul, in 1 Cor. 14:13, lays it down as an invariable rule, that we must praise God, and pray to him only in a known tongue.[120]

On Ps. 81:2–3, "Raise a song, strike the tabret, The sweet sounding harp with the psaltery. Blow the trumpet at the new

119. John Calvin, Vol. 4, 539.
120. Calvin, Vol. 5, 98.

moon," Calvin writes, "with respect to the tabret, harp, and psaltery, we have formerly observed, and will find it necessary afterwards to repeat the same remark, that the Levites, under the law, were justified in making use of instrumental music in the worship of God; it having been his will to train his people, while they were as yet tender and like children, by such rudiments, until the coming of Christ. But now when the clear light of the gospel has dissipated the shadows of the law, and taught us that God is to be served in a simpler form, it would be to act a foolish and mistaken part to imitate that which the prophet enjoined only upon those of his own time. From this, it is apparent that the Papists have shown themselves to be very apes in transferring this to themselves."[121]

Calvin argues that to bring in such "childish elements" as musical instruments is "to bury the light of the Gospel" and to "introduce the shadows of a departed dispensation." In his comments on Ps. 92:4, Calvin writes,

> In the fourth verse, he more immediately addresses the Levites, who were appointed to the office of singers, and calls upon them to employ their instruments of music — not as if this were in itself necessary, only it was useful as an elementary aid to the people of God in these ancient times. We are not to conceive that God enjoined the harp as feeling a delight like ourselves in mere melody of sounds; but the Jews, who were yet under age, were astricted to the use of such childish elements. The intention of them was to stimulate the worshippers, and stir them up more actively to the celebration of the praise of God with the heart. We are to remember that the worship of God was never understood to consist in such outward services, which were only necessary to help forward a people, as yet weak and rude in knowledge, in the spiritual worship of God. A difference is to be observed in this respect between his

121. Ibid., 312.

people under the Old and under the New Testament; for now that Christ has appeared, and the Church has reached full age, it were only to bury the light of the Gospel, should we introduce the shadows of a departed dispensation. From this, it appears that Papists, as I shall have occasion to show elsewhere, in employing instrumental music, cannot be said so much to imitate the practice of God's ancient people, as to ape it in a senseless and absurd manner, exhibiting a silly delight in that worship of the Old Testament which was figurative, and terminated with the Gospel.[122]

In his homily on 1 Sam. 18:1–9, Calvin tells us of how musical instruments were a detriment to the edification of the people,

In Popery there was a ridiculous and unsuitable imitation (of the Jews). While they adorned their Temples and valued themselves as having made the worship of God more splendid and inviting, they employed organs, and many other such ludicrous things, by which the Word and worship of God are exceedingly profaned, the people being much more attached to those rites than to the understanding of the divine Word.[123]

He goes on to state concerning singing that the "pure and simple modulation is sufficient for the praise of God, if it is sung with the heart and with the mouth. Instrumental music, we therefore maintain, was only tolerated on account of the times and the people, because they were boys . . . but in gospel times we must not have recourse to those unless we wish to destroy the evangelical perfection, and to obscure the meridian light we enjoy in Christ our Lord."[124]

122. Ibid., 494–495.
123. Quoted in Girardeau, 165.
124. Ibid.

We have heard from his own words how John Calvin, the greatest leader of the Protestant Reformation, was vehemently opposed to the use of any musical instruments in Christian worship. In 1571, the French Protestant Church, formed under the influence of Calvin, numbered more than two-thousand one hundred congregations, many of which had over ten-thousand members. These churches held to the views of their founder in the unaccompanied singing of psalms.[125]

Since such a practice is so rare in our day, one might wonder about the aesthetic beauty of the *a cappella* singing. A refugee to Strasbourg in 1545 after Calvin's reform gives us this account:

> On Sundays . . . we sing a psalm of David or some other prayer taken from the New Testament. The psalm or prayer is sung by everyone together, men as well as women, with a beautiful unanimity, which is something beautiful to behold. For you must understand that each one has a music book in his hand; that is why they cannot lose touch with one another. Never did I think that it could be as pleasing and delightful as it is. For five or six days at first, as I looked upon this little company, exiled from countries everywhere for having upheld the honor of God and His gospel, I would begin to weep, not at all from sadness, but from joy at hearing them sing so heartily, and, as they sang, giving thanks to the Lord that He had led them to a place where His name is honored and glorified. No one could believe the joy which one experiences when one is singing the praises and wonders of the Lord in the mother tongue as one sings them here.[126]

As we have seen above, Calvin (as well as other reformers) was not opposed to the use of musical instruments outside the worship

125. Ibid., 167–168.
126. Howard L. Rice and James C. Huffstutler, *Reformed Worship,* (Louisville, KY: Geneva Press, 2001), 104.

of the church. They believed that music had great power to move men's hearts for either good or evil, depending on how it was used. Their rejection of musical instruments from worship was not based upon any personal aversions or cultural considerations, but solely on scriptural principles. Calvin himself took great delight in music and wrote, "Now among the other things which are appropriate for recreating man and giving him pleasure, music is either the first or one of the principal, and we must value it as a gift of God deputed to that use."[127] In Calvin's mind there was a distinction between music in private and music in the church. The purpose of the first is the entertainment of men, and so long as it is "neither light nor frivolous" and does not lead to sensuality and licentiousness, musical instrumentation should be allowed. But the purpose of the second is the worship of God, which must be regulated by His Word alone. Calvin writes, "There is a great difference between the music which one makes to entertain men at table and in their homes, and the psalms which are sung in the Church in the presence of God and His angels."[128]

Theodore Beza (1519–1565) became Calvin's successor in Geneva and the one of the most prominent leaders of the Reformation. Beza also excluded the use of musical instruments in worship and wrote,

> If the apostle justly prohibits the use of unknown tongues in the church, much less would he have tolerated these artificial musical performances which are addressed to the ear alone, and seldom strike the understanding even of the performers themselves.[129]

127. W. Baum, E. Cunitz, and E. Reuss, eds., *Ioannis Calvini Opera Quae Supersunt Omnia,* (Brunswick, C.A.: Schwetschke and Sons, 1863–1900), Vol. VI, 165–172, quoted in Charles Garside, Jr., *The Origin's of Calvin's Theology of Music: 1536–1543,* (Philadelphia: The American Philosophical Society, 1979), 33.

128. Ibid., 32.

129. Quoted in Girardeau, 166.

Menno Simons (1496–1561), the wise and peace-loving leader of the Anabaptists, believed that what is not expressly commanded in the New Testament should not be permitted in Christian worship.[130] Menno applied this principle to musical instruments and wrote,

> There is not a word to be found in Scripture concerning their anointing, crosses, caps, togas, unclean purifications, cloisters, chapels, organs, choral music, masses, offerings, ancient usages, etc.; but under these things the lurking wolf, the earthly sensual mind, the anti-Christian seductions and bloody abominations are readily perceived.[131]

Martin Mohler (1547–1606), German reformer and Professor of Theology at Munich, comments on Ps. 150,

> It is no wonder, therefore, that such a number of musical instruments should be so heaped together; but although they were a part of Paedagogia Legalis (the instruction of the law), yet they were not for that reason to be brought into Christian assemblies. For God willeth that, after the coming of Christ, his people should cultivate the hope of eternal life and the practice of true piety by very different and more simple means than these.[132]

Wilhelm Zepperus (1550–1607), another leading scholar during the Protestant Reformation, writes, "Instrumental music in the religious worship of the Jews, belonged to the ceremonial law, which is now abolished."[133] David Pareus (1548–1622), a Reformed scholar and Professor of Theology at Heidelberg University, comments on 1 Cor. 14:7,

---

130. George, 273–274.
131. Menno Simons, *The Complete Writings of Menno Simons,* (Scottdale: PA, Herald Press, 1956), 172.
132. Quoted in Girardeau, 171.
133. Ibid., 170.

In the Christian church the mind must be incited to spiritual joy, not by pipes and trumpets and timbrels, with which God formerly indulged his ancient people on account of the hardness of their hearts, but by psalms and hymns and spiritual songs.[134]

It was not long before the views of the continental reformers regarding musical instruments took hold among the English reformers as well. Robert Holgate (ca. 1481–1555) became the bishop of Llandaff in 1537 and archbishop of York in 1545. In 1552, he banned the playing of the organ in the church, declaring,

> We will and command that there be no more playing of the organs, either at the Morning Prayer, the Communion, or the Evening Prayer within this Church of York, but that the said playing do utterly cease . . . forsomuch as playing of the organs ought and must be ceased and no more used within the Church of York . . . .[135]

Robert Horne (1514–1579) was made bishop of Winchester, and in 1571 he issued a similar injunction forbidding the use of the organ in that city.[136]

John Marbeck (1510-ca. 1585) served as the organist at St. George's Chapel, Windsor. By 1550, he was convinced of Calvin's arguments against musical instruments in the church. In his most famous musical publication, *The Boke of Common Praier Noted* (1550), Marbeck writes,

> But when they haunt their holy assemblies, I think that musicall instruments are no more meet for ye setting forth of Gods praises, then if a man shall call againe sensing

---

134. Ibid.
135. Robert Holgate, "Injunctions given by Robert Archbishop of York," *Visitation Articles and Injunctions of the Period of Reformation,* Vol. 15 of Alciun Club Collections (London: Longmans, Green, 1910), II, 320, quoted in Music, 63.
136. Music, 64.

and lames, & such other shadowes of the lawe. Foolishly therfore haue ye Papists borowed this & many other things of the Jewes. Men yt are giuen to outward pomps, delight in such noise, but God lyketh better the simplicitie which he commendeth to vs by his Apostle . . .[137]

In 1562, a proposal was brought before the English Convocation for the removal of all organs from the Church of England. When the votes were initially counted, the proposal passed by a considerable margin. But when all the proxy votes were counted later, it was denied by only a single vote.[138] Within the following year, however, the second prayer book of the Church of England (1563) declared organs as "belonging to superstitious and idolatrous manners" and are now "utterly abolished."[139]

In Scotland, by the early 1500s, the worship of the Roman Catholic Church was dominated by the singing of choirs, with the organ as prominent, and other instruments probably used as well.[140] Under the leadership of John Knox (1513–1572), the principles of the Protestant Reformation began to take hold by the 1550s. When persecution arose under the reign of bloody Mary, Knox went into exile in Geneva, where he spent nearly six years with John Calvin. Knox found himself to be one mind with the great Reformer. Charles W. Baird writes of the unity that existed between Knox and Calvin on matters of worship, "As on all important points of faith and discipline these great Reformers perfectly agreed, so, too, in respect to forms of public worship their practice was harmonious."[141] This certainly would have included Calvin's strong views

137. John Marbeck, *A Booke of Notes and Common Places, with Their Expositions, Collected and Gathered out of the Works of Diuers Singular Writers, and Brought Alphabetically into Order,* (London: Thomas East, 1581), 754–755, quoted in Music, 65.

138. Girardeau, 173–4.

139. Quoted in Scholes, 221.

140. Isobel Woods Preece, *Music in the Scottish Church up to 1603,* (Glasgow: The Universities of Glasgow and Aberdeen, 2000), 91, 98, 274.

141. Charles W. Baird, *The Presbyterian Liturgies,* (Grand Rapids: Baker Book House, 1957), 97.

on the exclusion of musical instruments. Knox was so impressed with Calvin's reforms of worship that he wrote to a friend back in England that the Geneva church "is the most perfect school of Christ that ever was in the earth since the days of the apostles. In other places, I confess Christ to be truly preached; but manners and religion to be so sincerely reformed, I have not yet seen in any other place beside."[142]

The restoration of the simplicity and purity of apostolic worship became the central concern of John Knox upon his return to Scotland in 1562. Knox followed Calvin's example and introduced unaccompanied congregational singing of psalms and paraphrases of other biblical passages in the Reformed churches. Knox viewed the New Testament alone as regulative for the worship of the church. W. Stanford Reid writes,

> That this had long been Knox's position all the evidence proves. The service of God's worship, including the administration of the sacraments, was to be determined completely by New Testament precept and example. Biblical simplicity without humanly devised rituals was his objective.[143]

The legacy of John Knox, in the exclusive vocal singing of the Scottish Reformed churches, has continued for hundreds of years even down to the present day. Percy Scholes tells us that from the days of John Knox the Reformed churches of Scotland have had "furious opposition to instrumental music in the Kirk."[144]

It was not just the individual Reformers who opposed the use of musical instruments in worship, but various synods growing out of the Reformation did so as well. In August 1560, the first Reformation Parliament of Scotland met in Edinburgh and ordered

142. Quoted in Baird, 97.
143. W. Stanford Reid, *Trumpeter of God,* (Grand Rapids: Baker Book House, 1982), 136.
144. Scholes, 220.

the removal of the organ and all other musical instruments from the worship of the churches.[145] Soon after the Reformation, the Synods of the Dutch Reformed Church decided very strongly against the use of musical instruments. In 1581, the National Synod of Middleburg rejected instruments, and in 1594, the Synod of Holland and Zeland declared, "That they would endeavor to obtain of the magistrate the laying aside of organs, and the singing with them in the churches, even out of the time of worship, either before or after the sermons."[146] Girardeau writes, "The Provincial Synod of Dort also inveighed severely against their use."[147]

The Synod of the Reformed Churches of the Netherlands held in Zeland wrote a letter to the commissioners of the General Assembly of the Church of Scotland. The letter exhorts the Scottish Reformed churches to assist their English brethren in the process of reformation, and to maintain the purity and simplicity of the gospel ordinances against all corruptions of Roman Catholicism, no matter how small they may appear. The Synod of Zeland recognized that perhaps the first inroad of Romish false worship was the use of the organ as an accompaniment to psalm singing. The Synod wrote concerning the Roman Catholics,

> They perceive that the reformed kirks do extremely abhor their idolatry: therefore they despair to introduce the same wholly and together: but they essay to creep in by degrees. They labor to persuade, that there is no danger, if with the singing of psalms, organs be joined as a part of divine worship.

After mentioning several other man-made additions to true worship, the letter states, "And in end, what shall be the end, if this

---

145. Preece, 274.
146. Quoted in Girardeau, 170.
147. Ibid.

door shall once be opened? Therefore we must not pass from the primitive worship?"[148]

The Irish Presbyterian Church maintained the simple singing of praise without musical instruments from the time of the Reformation to at least the end of the 19th century.[149]

McClintock and Strong note that previous attempts to return the church to apostolic simplicity had finally reached their goal in the Reformation.

> The Reformers, observing the excessive attention to musical services, endeavored to return to the plainness of apostolic times. There had previously been repeated efforts at such a transformation. "The Albigenses, during the hottest seasons of persecution, are stated to have solaced themselves, in the very prospect of death, with singing the psalms and hymns of their Church. Psalmody was cherished by the disciples of Wycliffe. The Bohemian Brethren published a hymnbook with musical notes, from which it appears that the melodies they used originated in the chants to which the ancient Latin hymns of the Western Church were sung" . . . That psalmody was cultivated by the persecuted ancient Vaudois (Waldenses) is evident from the fact that a large manuscript collection of their psalms and hymns is preserved in the library of Geneva . . . But it was the Reformation in the 16th century which restored to the people their right to participate in this primitive and edifying part of public worship.[150]

The Protestant Reformation showed unrelenting zeal to remove the idolatrous practices introduced by the Roman Catholic

---

148. Synod of Zeland, *A Letter from the Synod of Zeland to the Commissioners of the General Assembly of the Kirk of Scotland,* (Edinburgh: Evan Tyler, 1643), 16–17. *Thomason Tracts,* (Ann Arbor, MI: University Microflim International, 1977–1981), hereafter listed as *TT,* Reel 11.

149. Girardeau, 177–178.

150. McClintock and Strong, Vol. 8, 739.

Church, including its use of musical instruments. The reformers had witnessed the sensuality of Romish worship, of which musical instruments played an important role. They would take no rest until instruments were removed. So passionate were they against their use, that one reformer said of the organ, "There's a demon in every pipe." By the late 1500s, this corruption of church worship, which had crept in during the dark ages, had been effectively banished from the Reformed churches. The greatest spiritual revival since the days of the apostles had returned the church to the apostolic simplicity of unaccompanied congregational singing.

The Puritan Era

In the 1600s, the Puritans held to the same views of musical instruments in worship as the Reformers. Both the English and American Puritans rejected their use in church worship. As with the Church Fathers and the Reformers, the Puritans were convinced of those same three principles we have seen before: 1) The Old Testament Temple worship in all of its outward ceremonies and rituals has been abolished, 2) The church must look to Christ and His apostles alone for the ordinances of worship, 3) In the New Testament, we find neither command nor example of any musical instrument in worship, and, therefore, we have no warrant for their use.

While the Puritans believed in the final authority of Scripture in all matters of faith and practice, they also looked back to the Church Fathers and the Reformers in confirmation of their exclusion of musical instruments. Henry Wilder Foote writes,

> The Puritans were not, of course, peculiar in their disapproval of instrumental music in church. They could quote Tertullian, Clement of Alexandria, St. Chrysostom,

St. Ambrose, St. Augustine, St. Jerome, and others of the early Church Fathers in support of their opinion.[151]

The Puritans clearly had ample precedent as well as good sense to support their objection to elaborate church music. They proposed to "sing Psalms like rational beings," set to simple but noble and beautiful music, and sung in unison without accompaniment.[152]

David Music writes, "The Puritans adhered to the Calvinist belief that musical instruments and other "popish" ornaments had no place in Christian worship . . ."[153]

Horton Davies, in *The Worship of the American Puritans*, comments that "the Puritans objected to elaborate church music because it distracted the attention of the worshippers . . .; the Puritans welcomed instrumental music in their homes while refusing its assistance in their meetinghouses. This restriction is based, in part, on the demand for simplicity and sincerity in worship, but also on their interpretation of Scripture and the finality of the authority of the New Testament for them."[154] Davies goes on to write,

> The Puritans insisted in their worship on the divine mandate, and that therefore every ordinance had to be plainly instituted or approved in the New Testament as the final Word of God. It was not enough that the Book of Psalms was ancient Israel's anthology of praise unless it was also used and approved by Christ or His apostles, and therefore ratified as the continuing will of God. If there was no evidence of the use of instrumental music in the gatherings

---

151. Henry Wilder Foote, *Three Centuries of American Hymnody,* (Cambridge, MA: Harvard University Press, 1940), 86.
152. Ibid., 90.
153. Music, 85.
154. Davies, *The Worship of the American Puritans,* 126.

of the early Christians, then it must be rejected by the seventeenth-century Christians too.[155]

We will now survey the testimony of some of the most prominent Puritans concerning their rejection of musical instruments in Christian worship. William Perkins (1558–1602), one of the leading theologians among the early Puritans, writes, "The worship of God for outward ceremonies is most simple and plain."[156] In commenting on things forbidden in the second commandment, Perkins includes, "Will-worship, when God is worshipped with a naked and bare good intention not warranted by the Word of God . . . to these may be added consort in music in divine service, feeding the ears, not edifying the mind."[157] Perkins looks back to the example of the early Church Father, Justin Martyr, in support of his own rejection of musical instruments and writes, "Justin Martyr in his book of *Christian Quest. and Ans.* 107, 'It is not the custom of the churches to sing their meters with any such kind of instruments, but their manner is only to use plain-song.'"[158]

Henry Ainsworth (1571–1622), is best known for his metrical Psalm book, which was widely used in his day, and for his *Annotations on the Pentateuch and the Psalms.* In his book, *The Old Orthodox Foundation of Religion: Left for a Pattern to a New Reformation*, Ainsworth states that the musical instruments of the Temple worship have ceased under the gospel,

> The manner of singing, is to be holy, reverent, grave, orderly, with understanding, feeling, and comfort, to the edification of the church. . . Instruments of musicke were so annexed to the songs in the Temple, as incense to the

155. Ibid.
156. Quoted in Ian Breward, *The Works of William Perkins,* (Berkshire: The Sutton Courtenay Press, 1970), 306.
157. William Perkins, *A Golden Chain,* (London: John Legatt, 1621), 152. Early English Books, 1475–1640, (Ann Arbor, MI: University Microfilm International), hereafter listed as *EEB, 1475–1600,* Reel 1823:7.
158. Ibid., 153.

prayers, 2 Chron. 29. Such shadows are ceased, but the substance remaineth.[159]

In another book, *An Arrow Against Idolatrie*, Ainsworth complains of "Romish idolatry" including that "they learned to make . . . reading and singing their prayers upon a book with organs and melodie."[160]

William Ames (1576–1633), a leading theologian among the early English Puritans, is most known for his book *The Marrow of Theology*. In 1633, just prior to his death, Ames wrote *A Fresh Suit Against Human Ceremonies in God's Worship*. Among the human ceremonies to which Ames protested was the use of the organ and other musical instruments. In condemning their use in Christian worship, he quotes from Erasmus,

> I make no question but all that kind of music was a part of the legal pedadodie. In the solemn worship of God, I do not judge it more suitable, than if we should recall the incense, tapers, and other shadows of the law, into use. I say again, to go beyond what we are taught is most wicked perversity.[161]

159. Henry Ainsworth, *The Old Orthodox Foundation of Religion: Left for a Pattern to a New Reformation,* (London: E. Cotes, 1653), 71–72. *EEB, 1641–1700,* Reel 830:17. After stating that musical instruments are not to be used, Ainsworth recognizes that there are circumstances of worship which must be determined by the church for the sake of decency and order. He writes, "The times of psalms were not prescribed, but left to the discretion of the singers, each country therefore is to use the most decent order and manner of singing, according to the form given, 1 Cor. 14:40; Ps. 93:5," Ibid., 72. Thus, while recognizing that circumstances of worship exist, Ainsworth does not recognize that the use of musical instruments is among them. This issue of circumstances of worship will be discussed in more detail in Chapter IV.

160. Henry Ainsworth, *An Arrow Against Idolatrie,* (Printed 1640), 94–95. *EEB,* 1475 1640, Reel 1761:9.

161. William Ames, *A Fresh Suit Against Human Ceremonies in God's Worship,* (Gregg International Publishers Limited, reprinted, 1971), 405–406. Ames states that it would be too burdensome to mention all the English Reformers before him who agreed with his rejection of musical instruments in worship, "It would be too tedious, if I should reckon up all that have assented to these. I will add only the two and thirty grave learned men, which were chosen in King Edwards days, to reform ecclesiastical laws, and observances: they judge this law fitting. 'It likes us well to have this tedious kind of music taken away,'"

Robert Browne (1550–1633), an early Puritan separatist, was so influential in the beginning of the Congregationalists in England that they were often called "Brownists." In his treatise, *True and Short Declaration* (1583), Browne wrote concerning the use of organs in the churches, "Thus thei have a shewe of religion, but in deed thei turne it to gaming, and plaie mockholidaie with the worship of God."[162]

David Calderwood (1575–1650) was a minister and leading historian of the Scottish Reformed churches. In the early 1640s, Calderwood co-authored the *Directory of Public Worship*. In his treatise *The Pastor and the Prelate*, Calderwood contrasts the Puritan pastor with the clergymen of the Church of England and writes,

> The pastor loveth no music in the House of God but such as edifieth, and stoppeth his ear at instrumental music as serving the pedagogy of the outward Jews under the law, and being figurative of that spiritual joy whereunto our hearts should be opened under the Gospel. The Prelate loveth carnal and curious singing to the ear, more than the spiritual melody of the gospel, and therefore would have antiphony and organs in the Cathedral churches, upon no greater reason than other shadows of the law of Moses, or lesser instruments as lutes, citherus or pipes might be used in other churches.[163]

David Dickson (1583–1662), a Scottish pastor and professor of Divinity in Glasgow and Edinburgh, comments on Ps. 33:2,

> There is no exercise whereunto we have more need to be stirred up, than to praise; such is our dullness, and such is the excellency and necessity of the work, as the ceremonial use of musical instruments in the pedagogy of Moses did

Ibid., 406.
162. Quoted in Scholes, 217.
163. David Calderwood, *The Pastor and the Prelate*, (Edinburgh: Alexander Henderson, 1692), 9.

signify and import; the religious use whereof, albeit it be taken away with the rest of the ceremonial law . . . yet the thing signified, which is the bending all the powers of our soul and body to praise God, is not taken away.[164]

John Owen (1616–1683), perhaps the greatest English speaking theologian, writes on David's use of instruments in the Temple:

> He was the first that brought in a great number of musical instruments into the worship of God. And he speaks expressly, in 1 Chron 23:5, of praising God with instruments of music, "which," says he, "I made." He did it by the direction of the Spirit of God; otherwise he ought not to have done it: for so it is said, 1 Chron. 28:12, when he had established all the ordinances of the Temple . . . . It was all revealed to him by the Holy Spirit, without which he could have introduced nothing at all into the worship of God.[165]

Of this entire Temple worship, which would have included its use of musical instruments, John Owen writes, in many other places, to this effect, "that the Lord Christ, in and by this gospel has altered and abolished all that solemn worship, all those ordinances and institutions, which God Himself had set up under the Old Testament, to continue unto the time of reformation; and hereby He rendered it absolutely unlawful for any one to serve God according to those institutions."[166]

John Bunyan (1628–1688) is best known as the author of *Pilgrim's Progress*. In his book *Solomon's Temple Spiritualized*, Bunyan states that the Old Testament Temple worship is now completely abolished, "We are not now to worship God in these methods, or

---

164. David Dickson, *A Commentary on the Psalms*, (Edinburgh: The Banner of Truth Trust, reprinted 1985), 171.
165. Owen, Vol. 9, 463.
166. Ibid., Vol. 7, 218.

by such ordinances, as once the old church did."[167] Bunyan believed that many of the Temple rituals were typical of gospel worship. In regard to the Temple singing and its use of musical instruments, Bunyan writes, "These songs were sung with harps, psalteries, cymbals, and trumpets; a type of our singing with spiritual joy, from grace in our hearts. 1 Chron. 25:6; 2 Chron. 29:26–28; Col. 3:16."[168]

Even those within the Church of England complained of the use of musical instruments in worship. Jeremy Taylor (1613–1667) wrote that they may "add some little advantage to singing, but they are more apt to change religion into aires and fancies and take off some of its simplicity." Instrumental music "does not . . . make a man wiser or instruct him in anything." Instruments may "guide the voice . . . but they are but a friend's friend to religion."[169]

When the Westminster Assembly of Divines met in 1643–1644 to write *The Directory for Worship*, they were in agreement that musical instruments were not a part of Christian worship.[170] Iain Murray comments that the Westminster Assembly recognized the dangers of music in the medieval churches and made a complete reversal of it: "The worship from which the reformed churches began to emerge at the time of the Reformation was worship which placed much emphasis upon the physical and the external. The requirements of the church were satisfied if men went to consecrated buildings to

167. John Bunyan, *The Works of John Bunyan,* (Edinburgh: The Banner of Truth Trust, reprinted 1991), Vol. 3, 462.

168. Ibid., 496.

169. Quoted in Scholes, 218. In his *Histriomastix* (1633), the Puritan William Prynne bemoaned the over emphasis of music and the costly employment of professional musicians in the churches of his time, "But now-a-dayes musicke is growne to such and so great licentiousnesse, that even at the ministration of the holy sacrament all kinde of wanton and lewde trifling songs, with piping of organs, have their place and course. As for the divine service and common prayer, it is so chaunted and minsed and mangled of our costly hired, curious, and nice musitiens (not to instruct the audience withall, nor to stirre up mens mindes unto devotion, but with a whorish harmony to tickle the eares)." Prynne says that the end result was that "the authority and power of judgment is taken away both from the minde and from the eares utterly," Ibid., 217–218.

170. Girardeau, 132–135

behold ceremonies, to hear music and to partake of sacraments. The more beautiful the vestments, the churches, and the music, the more wonderful worship was held to be. The worship envisaged in the *Directory* is not merely a modification of that view; it is a total reversal of it. Dress, music, buildings, all disappear. They are not so much as mentioned. The glory of true worship, it is affirmed, consists in the enjoyment of the presence of God. Medieval worship had gone back to the material, the visual, and the symbolic, because it had lost the truth that believers now have 'boldness to enter into the holiest by the blood of Jesus' (Heb. 10:19)."[171]

The reason why the use of musical instruments is "not so much as mentioned" is that it was no longer an issue at the time of the Assembly. In 1644, the Solemn League and Covenant of the Scots declared organs to be among the "superstitious monuments" that had been "utterly abolished" from the churches. Girardeau explains, "Before the Westminster Assembly of Divines undertook the office of preparing a *Directory for Worship*, the Parliament had authoritatively adopted measures looking to the removal of organs, along with other remains of Popery, from the churches of England."[172] This refers to the fact that in 1644 the Long Parliament in England passed "An Ordinance for the further demolishing of Monuments of Idolatry, and Superstition." In this ordinance they ordered "the speedy demolishing of all organs, images, and all matters of superstitious monuments in all Cathedralls, and Collegiate or Parish-Churches and Chapels, throughout the Kingdom of England and Dominion of Wales; the better to accomplish the blessed reformation so happily begun, and to remove all offenses and things illegal in the worship of God . . ."[173]

171. Iain Murray, "The Public Directory for Worship," in *To Glorify And Enjoy God*, John L. Carson and David W. Hall, eds., (Edinburgh: The Banner of Truth Trust, 1994), 182–183.

172. Girardeau, 132.

173. Quoted in Andrew Wilson-Dickson, *The Story of Christian Music*, (Minneapolis: Fortress Press, 1996), 101–102. Diarmaid MacCulloch states that "in English parish churches . . . nationwide from about 1570 organs were nearly all removed or terminally

On May 20, 1644, the Scottish commissioners to the West-minster Assembly, who were especially zealous for the removal of musical instruments, wrote a letter to their own church stating their approval of how quickly the reformation was proceeding. Among the reforms accomplished were "the great organs at Pauls and of Peters in Westminster taken down, images and many other monuments of idolatry defaced and abolished."[174]

When the Westminster Assembly later prepared their *Directory for Worship*, the situation in England was such that the singing of psalms unaccompanied by musical instruments prevailed almost universally.[175] Thus, when they prescribed that Christian worship should include the "singing of psalms with grace in the heart," they meant the simple singing of praise without musical accompaniment. As we will see in the quotations below, this was clearly the practice of the men who wrote the confession. The Scottish commissioners especially would have vehemently and uncompromisingly opposed any measure supporting the use of musical instruments. Such was the agreement among them that when the issue was considered it was settled quickly with no debate. The only point of discussion was concerning the reading of psalms by line. "Lightfoot, who was a member of the Assembly, in his '*Journal of its Proceedings*' tells us: 'This morning we fell upon the *Directory* for singing of psalms; and, in short time, we finished it.'"[176]

We shall now hear from the leaders of the Westminster Assembly of their rejection of musical instruments in Christian worship. George Gillespie (1613–1648), the leader of the Scottish delegation to the Westminster Assembly, writes in his *Assertion of the Government of the Church of Scotland,*

neglected, as they were in Zurich or Scotland." Diarmaid MacCulloch, *The Reformation*, (New York, NY: Viking, 2003), 570.

174. "The Letter from the Commissioners at London to the General Assembly," in *The Acts of the General Assemblies of the Church of Scotland,* 1638–1649, (Edinburgh: George Mosman, 1691), 228, *EEB*, 1641–1700, Reel 1353:1.

175. Girardeau, 133.

176. Ibid., 133.

The Jewish Church, not as it was a church but as it was Jewish, had an High Priest, typifying our great High Priest, Jesus Christ. As it was Jewish, it had musicians to play upon harps, psalteries, cymbals and other musical instruments in the Temple.[177]

Samuel Rutherford (1600–1661), another prominent member of the Scottish delegation to the Westminster Assembly, was also "a zealous opponent of the use of musical instruments in the church."[178] Rutherford declares that "altars, organs, Jewish ephods, or surplice, masse-cloaths, and Romish crossing, bowing to altars, images, are badges of Jewish and Popish religion."[179]

Thomas Goodwin (1600–1680), the leader of the Independents in the Assembly, comments on the harps of Rev. 5:8 that they are an "allusion to the Levitical service in the Temple, where they had musical instruments . . . not that musical instruments are to be in the worship of God now."[180] Goodwin states that the harps are symbolic of the spiritual melody of our hearts, "so those harps were of that 'spiritual melody,' as the Apostle calls it, which we make in our hearts to God, even of 'spiritual songs,' Eph 5:19."[181]

Although he was not a member of the Westminster Assembly, Thomas Manton (1620–1677) was chosen to write the preface to the *Westminster Confession of Faith*.[182] In a sermon on Eph. 5:19, Manton makes it clear that the only instrument to be used in Christian worship is the human voice, "the very external act is

177. George Gillespie, "Assertion of the Government of the Church of Scotland," in *The Presbyterian's Armoury,* (Edinburgh: Robert Ogle and Oliver and Boyd, 1844–46), Vol. 1, 13, quoted in Girardeau, 67.
178. William MacMillan, *The Worship of the Scottish Reformed Church,* 1550–1638, (London: The Lassodie Press, Ltd., 1930), 99.
179. Quoted in David Hay Fleming, *The Reformation in Scotland,* (London: Hodder and Stoughton, 1910), 310.
180. Thomas Goodwin, *The Works of Thomas Goodwin,* (Edinburgh: James Nichol, 1861), Vol. 3, 13.
181. Ibid.
182. Old, *Worship That Is Reformed According to Scripture,* 83.

by singing, the usual vent of our joy."[183] He contrasts the use of instruments by the world with the use of the voice alone in God's worship when he writes, "as it is the custom of nations to proclaim what they would have noted and observed, by sound of drum and trumpet, so by singing we manifestly own God's worship and service."[184]

The expressed convictions of these men, as the leaders of the Westminster Assembly, confirms that this body of divines stood in opposition to the use of musical instruments in Christian worship. This continued to be the understanding of later Puritan commentators as they looked back on the work of the Westminster Assembly. Thomas Ridgeley (1667–1734) was a leading Puritan who lived shortly after the Assembly. In his highly esteemed lectures on the Assembly's Larger Catechism, Ridgeley reflects their views in regard to the Temple worship:

> We very often read of their praising God with the sound of the trumpet, psaltery, harp, organ, and other musical instruments. This is the principal argument brought for the use of musical instruments by those who defend it and conclude it an help to devotion . . . But what may sufficiently determine this matter, is that we have no precept nor precedent for it in the New Testament, either from the practice of Christ, or his apostles.[185]

Matthew Henry (1662–1714), the well-known Bible commentator, followed in the footsteps of the Westminster divines, believing that the musical instruments of the Old Covenant are no longer to be used in gospel worship. Commenting on David's bringing the ark up to Jerusalem in 1 Chron. 15, he writes,

---

183. Thomas Manton, *The Complete Works of Thomas Manton,* (Worthington, PA: Maranatha Publications), Vol. 19, 415.

184. Manton, Vol. 16, 157.

185. Thomas Ridgeley, *A Body of Divinity,* (Edinburgh: A. Fullarton and Co., 1844), 435, 437.

This way of praising God by musical instruments had not hitherto been in use. But David, being a prophet, instituted it by divine direction, and added it to the other carnal ordinances of that dispensation, as the apostle calls them, Hebrews 9:10. The New Testament keeps up singing of psalms, but has not appointed church-music.[186]

On Ps. 149:3, Matthew Henry writes,

Let God be "praised in the dance with timbrel and harp," according to the usage of the Old Testament church very early (Exod. 15:20), where we find God praised with timbrels and dancing. Those who from this urge the use of music in religious worship must by the same rule introduce dancing, for they were together, as David's dancing before the ark, and Judg. 21:21. But, whereas many scriptures in the New Testament keep up singing as a gospel ordinance, none provide for the keeping up of music and dancing; the gospel canon for psalmody is to "sing with the spirit and with the understanding."[187]

During the late 1600s, many Particular Baptists in England believed that singing in public worship was an ordinance of the Jewish ceremonial law that was not to be continued under the gospel. Benjamin Keach (1640–1704), the leading Baptist theologian of his time, labored to convince his brethren that singing was a New Testament ordinance. In 1691, he published *The Breach Repaired in God's Worship,* in which he shows from the Scripture that singing, just like prayer and preaching, is a moral, or natural duty incumbent upon all men in all times. Men have always been

---

186. Henry, Vol. 2, 875.

187. Henry, Vol. 3, 786, On Ps. 81:2, Henry writes, "It was then to be done by musical instruments, the timbrel, harp, psaltery; and by blowing the trumpet... It was then and is now to be done by singing psalms, singing aloud, and making a joyful noise. The pleasantness of the harp and the awfulness of the trumpet intimate to us that God is to be worshipped with cheerfulness and holy joy, with reverence and godly fear.," Ibid., 548.

obligated to perform such moral or natural duties even before they were made part of the divine institutions. Singing the praises of God existed as moral worship before the ceremonial law (Job 38:7; Gen. 4:26; Exod. 15:1–2), under the ceremonial law (Ps. 84:1–2, 95:1–2, 100:1–2; 1 Chron. 16:9), and under the gospel (Eph. 5:19; Col. 3:16; James 5:13), and it will continue to exist in heaven (Rev. 5:9; 15:3). But when it comes to the use of musical instruments, Keach regards them as part of the ceremonial law, which ceases under the gospel. The moral duty of singing continues, but the ceremonies of Temple worship are abolished, musical instruments being among them.

Benjamin Keach writes, "There is no doubt but the singing of David's psalms with instruments of music, was suited to the order of the Levites and to the Temple worship."[188] "There is now no other instrument to be used in singing but that of the tongue, well tuned with grace, from a holy and spiritual heart. . . singing is given forth afresh in the New Testament, and no instruments of music mentioned."[189] To use musical instruments is to "corrupt" the ordinance of singing and "to add poison to it."[190] Keach saw the use of musical instruments in the Temple as typical of the joy of the saints under the gospel, "Doubtless their singing of old, with musical instruments, was a figure of that sweet spiritual melody the saints should make from a well-tuned heart, and with united and melodious tongues together in the gospel days . . ."[191]

The Presbyterian and Independent Puritans believed that their singing should be limited to the inspired writings of the book of Psalms. It was Benjamin Keach, and not Isaac Watts as is commonly thought, who was the first Puritan to write hymns of human composition. The first hymns of Watts were published in 1694, while

188. Keach, 129–130.
189. Ibid., 54.
190. Ibid., 68.
191. Ibid., 131.

those of Keach had appeared thirty years earlier.[192] Commenting on the phrase "a new song" found in the Psalms and in Rev. 14:3, Keach writes, "'A new song,' signifies a song which praises God for new benefits received from him. . . . This shows other spiritual songs may be sung besides David's psalms in gospel days."[193]

The Reformers and Puritans believed that true rational and spiritual worship could be offered only through the praise of the human soul and not by the use of a mechanical device such as a musical instrument. True rational and spiritual worship could be offered only through the mind and heart fixed on the glory of God and expressed by the human tongue. It was this kind of worship God had always desired and had instituted under the gospel. It was this kind of worship that would continue in heaven. To the Puritans, it was inconceivable that once God had abolished the mechanical devices used under the ceremonial law and established true spiritual worship under the gospel He would revert to them again in heaven through the use of harps. Thus, they interpreted the harps in the book of Revelation figuratively as being the human heart filled with the Holy Spirit.

Hanserd Knollys (1599–1691), another leader among the English Particular Baptists, also excluded the use of musical instruments in the church. Commenting on Rev 5:8, Knollys states, "'Having every one of them harps;' that is, hearts filled with the Holy Spirit, Eph. 5:18–19, and 1 Cor. 14:14,15, prepared to pray and praise the Lord." On the "new song" in Rev. 5:9, he writes, "This is called a new song, because, first, it contains new matter of thanksgiving unto God, as Ps. 98:1, &c. and second because the hearts (harps) of these singers were put into a new frame by the fresh anointing of the Holy Spirit."[194]

---

192. Horton Davies, *The Worship of the English Puritans*, 179.
193. Keach, 129.
194. Hanserd Knollys, *An Exposition of the Whole Book of the Revelation*, (London: Newgate Street, 1688), 75–76. *EEB*, 1641–1700, Reel 1387:26.

The exclusion of musical instruments from Christian worship by Benjamin Keach and Hanserd Knollys is of great significance to Reformed Baptists today. These men were two of the most prominent leaders of the Particular Baptists of the late 17th century. They were both among the original signers of the *Second London Baptist Confession of Faith*. Their convictions regarding musical instruments were representative of the churches who signed our Confession of Faith. As Reformed Christians, we should have a high regard for the convictions of our forefathers who have gone before us. We should not overturn their convictions without the clearest evidence from Scripture that we must do so.

Isaac Watts (1674–1748), perhaps the greatest hymn writer in the history of the church, agrees that musical instruments are to have no place in Christian worship. Commenting on the song of Moses in Rev. 15:3, Watts writes,

> The church now under the salvation and instructions of the Lamb, sings with the voice to the glory of the vengeance and the grace of God, as Israel under the conduct of Moses sung with harps . . . it would be as unreasonable to prove from this text, that we must sing the very words of the 15th of Exodus in a Christian church, as to prove from this book of the Revelation that we must use harps and altars, censers, fire and incense.[195]

Referring to the apostolic churches, he writes, "we can never suppose the primitive church in those days had instruments of music."[196]

John Gill (1697–1771), a leading Baptist theologian of the 18th century, stated that instruments in public worship were abolished under the gospel.[197] Commenting on Ps. 81:2, Gill writes that

195. Isaac Watts, *The Works of Isaac Watts*, (London: John Barfield, Wardour Street, 1810), Vol. 4, 373.
196. Ibid., 372.
197. J. Spencer Curwen, *Studies in Worship Music*, (London: J. Curwen & Sons, 1890), 104.

Asaph exhorts men to "make use of all these musical instruments in singing, and so make an agreeable melody: these were used in the times of the Old Testament, and were typical of the spiritual joy and melody in the heart, expressed by vocal singing, under the New Testament."[198] On the various instruments of Ps. 150, Gill writes,

> Now these several instruments of music are named, not as to be used in Gospel times; but, being expressive of the highest praise and joy shown in former times, are mentioned to set forth the highest strains and notes of praise in New Testament saints; as well as to denote their heartiness, agreement, and unanimity in this service, Rom. 15:6.[199]

The American Puritans followed with the same view of musical instruments as their English brethren. John Cotton (1585–1652), a leading Puritan minister in Boston, Massachusetts, writes, "Singing with instruments was typical, and so a ceremonial worship, and therefore ceased. But singing with heart and voice, is a moral worship, such as is written in the hearts of all men by nature."[200] "Singing of Psalms with lively voice, is not a ceremonial but a moral duty, and so continues now in the days of the New Testament."[201]

Samuel Mather writes, "Take this inference, namely, the unwarrantableness of musical instruments in the worship of God under the gospel. You see of old there was an institution for them, there

198. Gill, Vol. 3, 201.
199. Ibid., 425.
200. John Cotton, *Singing of Psalmes: A Gospel Ordinance,* (London: Sunne and Fountaine in Pauls-Churchyard, 1650), 5–6, *TT,* Reel 61. For those who object to instrument's being viewed as typical, Cotton writes, "Or suppose singing with instruments were not typical, but only an external solemnity of worship, fitted to the solace of the outward senses of children under age, (such as the Israelites were in the Old Testament, Gal. 4:1,2); yet now, in the grown age of the heirs of the New Testament, such external pompous solemnities are ceased, and no external worship reserved, but such as holdeth forth simplicity and gravity; nor is any voice now to be heard in the church of Christ, but such as is significant and edifying by signification (1 Cor. 14:10, 11, 26), which the voice of instruments is not," Ibid., 6.
201. Ibid., 23.

is not so now. They are a very late invention of the Church of Rome."[202] Mather speaks to our own time in denouncing "ministers of music," which are so common in our modern churches, "This cathedral music introduces into the Church of God a rabble of church-officers which the Lord never appointed, and which never came into his heart, the choristers and singing-men, and that is a very great evil. It is not in the power of men, but it is the great prerogative of Jesus Christ to appoint officers in his church who has appointed none but pastors and teachers, elders and deacons."[203]

Cotton Mather (1663–1729) states,

> Now there is not one word of institution in the New Testament for instrumental music in the worship of God. And because the holy God rejects all that He does not command in His worship, He now therefore in effect says unto us, "I will not hear the melody of thy organs."[204] If we admit instrumental musick in the worship of God, how can we resist the imposition of all the instruments used among the ancient Jews?—yea, dancing as well as playing, and several other Judaic actions? or, how can we decline a whole rabble of church-officers, necessary to be introduced for instrumental musick, whereof our Lord Jesus Christ hath left us no manner of direction?[205]

Benjamin Keach summarizes the unanimous practice of unaccompanied singing from the early Reformation and notes, "the Waldenses practice in singing, &c. and all other godly Christians since the beginning of the Reformation; how zealous were the godly Puritans (as they were called) for this blessed ordinance . . . also our brethren of the Independent and Presbyterian persuasion are

---

202. Samuel Mather, *The Figures or Types of the Old Testament,* (New York, Johnson Reprint Corporation, reprinted 1969), 439.
203. Ibid., 440.
204. Cotton Mather, Vol. 2, 266.
205. Ibid., 267.

as well established in this sweet ordinance . . . I thought it could not be amiss to take notice of the unanimous agreement, and joint consent and practice of the churches and godly Christians in the succeeding ages next after the apostles, and to this very day."[206] Among other Puritans who opposed the use of musical instruments in Christian worship are such names as William Whittingham (Knox's successor in Geneva), Oliver Cromwell, Thomas Shepard, and Increase Mather.[207]

It is acknowledged that Richard Baxter differed from his Puritan brethren on the use of musical instruments in worship, as he did on other issues as well. Baxter considered their use lawful, and the reader is invited to consider his thoughts under Question 127 in his *Christian Directory*. One leaves disappointed at the weakness and unscriptural nature of his arguments. Baxter actually takes the view of Luther and the Anglicans in regard to the regulative principle and states, "No Scripture forbiddeth it, therefore it is not unlawful."[208] His arguments on this matter are proof that even a great mind such as Baxter's cannot give any solid justification to the use of musical instruments in worship.

I should state that in all that we have seen, I have not been selective in the material I have presented. Martin Luther and Richard Baxter are the only two men among the Reformers and Puritans whom I have found who considered the use of musical instruments lawful. Both of these men held to unbiblical views of the regulative principle of worship. All the other Reformers and Puritans who have said anything upon this issue have been decidedly against the use of musical instruments in Christian worship. If there are others who have held a proper view of the regulative principle of worship and have developed a sound theology for the use of instruments, I have not been able to find them.

---

206. Keach, 69.
207. Davies, *American Puritans,* 124–145.
208. Richard Baxter, *The Practical Works of Richard Baxter,* (Ligonier, PA: Soli Deo Gloria Publications, reprinted 1990), Vol. 1, 705.

Charles Spurgeon summarizes the almost unanimous views of the Reformers and the Puritans on musical instruments when he writes,

> There was a typical signification in them; and upon this account they are not only rejected and condemned by the whole army of Protestant divines, as for instance, by Zuinglius, Calvin, Peter Martyr, Zepperus, Paroeus, Willet, Ainsworth, Ames, Calderwood, and Cotton; who do with one mouth, testify against them, most of them expressly affirming that they are a part of the abrogated legal pedagogy; so that we might as well recall the incense, tapers, sacrifices, new moons, circumcision, and all the other shadows of the law into use again.[209]

We should note that the three theological principles of worship established in Chapter I and seen among the Church Fathers have now also been found among the Reformers and Puritans. These principles are: 1) The Old Testament Temple worship in all of its outward ceremonies and rituals has been abolished, 2) The church must look to Christ and His apostles alone for the ordinances of gospel worship, 3) In the New Testament, we find neither command nor example of any musical instrument in worship, and therefore, we have no warrant for their use. These simple principles, proven from the Scripture, have now been traced throughout the history of the church down to the age of the Puritans. They will continue to be the theological principles for those who hold to a biblical and Reformed view of worship.[210]

209. Spurgeon, Vol. 2, Part 1, 223.
210. We have also seen that many of the Reformers and Puritans believed that the musical instruments of the Temple worship were typical of the joy of the Holy Spirit to come under the gospel. This was not part of the theological argument presented earlier in Chapter I. For those who are interested in a thorough discussion of this matter, it can be found in Girardeau, *Instrumental Music in the Public Worship of the Church*, 47–79. This view of musical instruments as typical is not necessary to establish these three principles of worship we have listed above. The abolition of Temple worship, which would include its use of musical instruments, is clearly established from the New Testament and is confirmed by

It should be noted that the Puritans did not have an aversion for music in general. They often enjoyed musical instruments in the privacy of their own homes, and many of them were accomplished musicians.[211] But they refused to bring their own personal desires, including their musical instruments, into God's worship without specific divine command. They were committed to the purity of worship according to the New Testament. Henry Wilder Foote writes,

> The essential point to be noted in the Puritan attitude towards all instrumental music, including the use of organs, is the clear distinction which they drew between the use of instrumental music in church, of which they disapproved, and music for social enjoyment, which they approved within reasonable limits.[212]

Horton Davies summarizes the view of the early American Puritans, "It was not that they disliked music, but that they loved the religion of Christ's ordinances more."[213]

The reader is cautioned that sometimes the Reformers and Puritans are misquoted as if they approved the use of musical instruments in Christian worship. It should be understood that when the Reformers and Puritans speak favorably of "music" in worship, they are referring to *a cappella* singing and not to the use of musical instruments. When they speak favorably of musical instruments, they are approving their use in private or social settings and not in the worship of the church. When such quotations are misused, they can be very misleading and give the false impression that the speakers are approving of instruments in worship.[214]

the commands and the example of the apostles. From all that we have seen, the Reformers and Puritans are in full agreement with these basic principles.

211. Davies, *American Puritans,* 143.

212. Henry Wilder Foote, 79.

213. Davies, *American Puritans,* 145.

214. I will note two examples of this in two recently published books. First, in *How God Wants Us to Worship Him,* by Joe Morecraft (San Antonio: The Vision Forum, Inc.,

The 18th and 19th Centuries

The question now before us is how did the Protestant churches, which once held to the principles of the Reformers and Puritans, lose their convictions? How did musical instruments come to have such a dominant presence in much of the worship of the modern evangelical church? We shall now trace the gradual erosion of the Reformation and Puritan principle of the exclusion of musical instruments from worship that took place in the 18th and 19th centuries.

In general, those churches in England and America that were guided by the Reformation continued firm in their opposition to all musical instruments in worship until the early to mid 1700s. The first inroads of musical instruments began with the relatively unobtrusive orchestral-type instruments (bass viol, cello, clarinet, etc.) in the first half of the 18th century. Some small country churches, which could not afford an organ (like the Lutheran

2001), 158. In a section in which Morecraft supports the use of musical instruments in Christian worship, he quotes John Calvin as if the reformer shared his views. Morecraft's book reads as follows, "John Calvin, who believed that music was a gift of God, wrote that music 'has the power to enter the heart like wine poured into a vessel, with good or evil effect.' In worship, in particular, it 'has great force and vigor to move and inflame the hearts of men to invoke and praise God with a more vehement and ardent zeal.'" Morecraft uses this quotation as if Calvin were supporting the use of musical instruments in worship. He gives the source of this quotation as James Hastings Nichols, *Corporate Worship in the Reformed Tradition,* (Philadelphia: The Westminster Press), 35. But when Nichol's book is read in context, it becomes clear that Calvin's approval of music in worship is referring to *a cappella* singing and not to the use of musical instruments. The original quotation is from Calvin's Psalter of 1542. Second, in an article by Timothy Keller, "Reformed Worship in the Global City," in *Worship by the Book,* D. A. Carson, ed., (Grand Rapids, Zondervan, 2002), 212. Keller claims that Calvin took a middle course between the Lutherans, who used complex musical instrumentation, and the Anabaptists, who rejected the use of all instruments in worship. He writes, "Therefore, while Anabaptist theology of art would preclude accompaniment and choirs per se from worship, Calvin's theology does not. His 'middle way' between the Anabaptists and the Lutherans points the way for Reformed worship today to include the judicious use of accompaniment, ensembles, and solos – provided Calvin's over-arching purposes of simplicity, transcendence, and edification are honored." Keller gives no quotation from Calvin to support this perspective. To claim that Calvin's theology allows "the judicious use of accompaniment" is to clearly misrepresent the reformer. We know from Calvin's practice and we have heard from his own words how strongly he opposed the use of musical instruments in Christian worship.

and Anglican churches), began to form what were called "gallery orchestras" because they would gather in the west gallery or the balcony of the church. These "gallery orchestras" were used to accompany the psalm singing or the choir if one existed.

In the early years of the American colonies, there were relatively few musical instruments of any kind. The hardships associated with settling the new land and the expense of importing instruments from England and Europe prohibited their presence to any significant degree. By the early 1700s, with growing prosperity and improved means of shipment, small orchestra-type instruments became more common. The use of these instruments was first felt in singing schools, which usually met in schoolhouses. For a time, there was no effect upon the churches. But Henry Wilder Foote notes how these instruments gradually passed from the schoolhouses into the churches:

> The awakening of interest in instrumental music had no immediate effect upon the churches. . . . but when the singing school met in the schoolhouse there was no objection to the use of a pitch pipe to set the pitch or of a bass viol to support the singing. But the young people, once accustomed to such instrumental support, naturally desired it when they sat in the singers' gallery in church. So the pitch pipe was introduced, almost by stealth perhaps, and then, usually, the bass viol—"the Lord's fiddle," because it became so much associated with psalm singing, whereas the violin had secular associations with dancing.[215]

It was the entrance of these relatively small orchestra-type instruments, as noted above, that seems to have gradually broken down the opposition of many churches to the use of the larger and more conspicuous organ.[216] By the end of 18th century, the principles of the Reformation, which had guided such churches

215. Foote, 112.
216. Music, 119.

for centuries, had largely disappeared. Some of the arguments in support of the organ included its rising popularity among the churches, its appeal to the younger members of the church, and its supposed usefulness in evangelism.[217] We see that many of the arguments in favor of instruments are the same today.

Opposition to such changes was voiced early in the 1700s. In New England, a pamphlet approved by a church council meeting on January 30, 1722, was written by three Independent ministers, Peter Thacher, John Danforth, and Samuel Danforth. These pastors expressed their desires to continue in the use of unaccompanied singing of the Psalms.[218]

In 1763, an anonymous pamphlet was published in Phila-delphia entitled *The Lawfulness, Excellency, and Advantages of Instrumental Musick in the Publick Worship of God.* This pamphlet, which seems to have gained wide distribution, was written to encourage Presbyterians and Baptists to reconsider their opposition to the use of instruments in worship. The only scriptural argument was the assumption that because musical instruments were used in the Old Testament Temple, they should be used in the church. Other arguments were that instruments created a "divine Melody" and a "heavenly Enthusiasm which spread itself through the whole Assembly." This supposedly increased the devotion of the people and was declared to be "not only a strong Proof of the Propriety and Expediency of the Institution, but gives a pleasing Idea, that the Cause of Christianity in such Churches is not so desperate . . ."[219] To this was added an argument from the increasing popularity of musical instruments among the churches. The author writes, "What a glorious Appearance would an Organ make in some of their Churches, especially in this and the neighboring Cities! Nor would one look out of Character in the meanest Building in the Country." Those who held to the old ways of no musical instruments

---

217. Ibid., 127.
218. Davies, *American Puritans*, 130.
219. Quoted in Music, 130–131.

were mocked as being "ridiculous" and "weak but well-meaning Professors," "who, if properly informed, might know better." The pamphlet confidently declares that the use of musical instruments will "not bring us one Jot nearer to Popery or Episcopacy than we were before."[220]

These are the kinds of shallow, man-centered, and unscriptural arguments that usually lie behind the addition of unappointed elements in worship. John Owen states,

> Three things are usually pleaded in the justification of the observance of such rites and ceremonies in the worship of God: First, that they tend unto the furtherance of the devotion of the worshippers; secondly, That they render the worship itself comely and beautiful; thirdly, that they are the preservers of order in the celebration thereof. And therefore on these accounts they may be instituted or appointed by some, and observed by all.[221]

The first Puritan church to have an organ was the First Congregational Church in Providence, Rhode Island, in 1770.[222] The organ was installed only after much debate. Henry Wilder Foote records the general opposition to instrumental music in the churches at that time:

> Sometimes members of a congregation would leave the meetinghouse in indignation when the instrument was introduced. By the latter part of the century such instrumental accompaniment of singing became general, and in some instances the church or the town bought and kept in the meetinghouse a bass viol for use at the Sunday services, until eventually it bought an organ.[223]

220. Ibid., 131–132.
221. Owen, Vol. 15, 467.
222. Charles H. Lippy and Peter W. Williams, ed., *Encyclopedia of the American Religious Experience,* (New York: Charles Scribner's Sons, 1988), Vol. 3, 1292.
223. Foote, 113.

By 1795, one minister wrote, "The fondness for instrumental music in churches so increases, that the inclination is not to be resisted."[224]

Even among the Anglicans, who often had an organ, there were some who stood against its use into the late 1700s. Dr. Tho. Bradbury Chandler, a New England Episcopalian minister, had resisted an organ against the increasing pressure of his congregation. After his farewell sermon in 1785, realizing that the end of his life was near, he told his people, "that it would not be long before he was in his grave—he knew that before his head was cold there, they would have an Organ—and they might do as they pleased."[225]

In America, the Baptists were among the last to give way before the rising flood of the use of organs. David Benedict (1779–1874), a New England Baptist pastor and historian, states that the first organ in a Baptist church was about 1820 in Pawtucket, Rhode Island. In his book entitled *Fifty Years Among the Baptists,* he records the sad account of how the people, being desensitized by the previous entrance of smaller instruments, were willing to give way more easily to the larger organ:

> The changes which have been experienced in the feelings of a large portion of our people has often surprised me. Staunch old Baptists in former times would as soon have tolerated the Pope of Rome in their pulpits as an organ in their galleries, and yet the instrument has gradually found its way among them, and their successors in church management, with nothing the jars and difficulties which arose of old concerning the bass viol and smaller instruments of music.[226]

224. William Bentley, *The Diary of William Bentley,* (Gloucester, MA: Peter Smith, 1962), Vol. 1, 418, quoted in Music, 124.

225. Ezra Stiles, *The Literary Diary of Ezra Stiles,* ed. Franklin Bowditch Dexter, (New York: Charles Scribner's Sons, 1901), Vol. 3, 162.

226. David Benedict, *Fifty Years Among the Baptists,* (New York: Sheldon & Company, 1860), 283.

The objections of the New England Puritans to musical instruments gradually decreased over the course of the 18th century. One example of how is in regard to the Brattle Square Congregational Church in Cambridge, Massachusetts. A man by the name of Thomas Brattle, whose brother William was the pastor of the church, was a successful Boston merchant. He owned an organ in his home, and when he died in 1713, he bequeathed it to the church. The church, still holding to its principle of no musical instruments in worship, refused to accept Brattle's gift. Mr. Brattle apparently anticipated the church's decision and made a backup provision in his will that if this happened, the organ was to be given to an Anglican congregation. By 1797, however, the convictions of the same Brattle Square Church had been abandoned, and the church installed its first "fine organ" and boasted that it was "one of its most attractive features."[227]

The Scottish Presbyterian churches, founded by John Knox in the 16th century, maintained their no-instrumental convictions for well over three hundred years, nearly one hundred years longer than their brethren in England and America. It was not until the late 19th century that the organ began to enter into the worship of the Scottish Reformed churches. The famous American revivalist team of Moody and Sankey seems to have been one means of eroding the convictions of these churches. In 1873, Dwight L. Moody and Ira D. Sankey began an evangelistic tour of the British Isles. Sankey sang solo gospel songs while accompanying himself with a portable organ. When they came to Scotland, "on the whole. . . . Sankey and his instrument seem to have been readily accepted and probably went a good way toward breaking down the resistance to the use of organs among the Scotch."[228] From that point forward, organs gained increased popularity in the Scottish churches.[229]

227. Music, 136, 140.
228. Ibid., 155.
229. Ibid., 159.

Despite this slow decline during the 18th and 19th centuries, there remained many prominent examples of those who held their ground against the rising flood of musical instruments. Thomas Chalmers (1780–1847), was minister at Kilmany, Scotland, and later Principal and Professor of Theology in New College. He is recognized as the greatest preacher of the 19th century in Scotland. Chalmers was a strong opponent of the use of instruments in Christian worship.[230]

Andrew Fuller (1754–1815), minister in Kettering and one of the leading Baptist theologians of early 19th century, also rejected the use of musical instruments. Fuller writes,

> Of priests, altars, sacred garments, and instrumental music in Christian worship, the New Testament "saith nothing." Is it improper then to infer that no such things were known in the times of the first Christians?[231] Instrumental music, the more I think of it, appears with increasing evidence to be utterly unsuited to the genius of the gospel dispensation. There was a glare, if I may so express it, which characterized even the divine appointments of Judaism. An august Temple, ornamented with gold and silver, and precious stones, golden candlesticks, golden altars, priests in rich attire, trumpets, cymbals, harps; all of which were adapted to an age and dispensation when the church was in a state of infancy. But when the substance is come, it is time that the shadows flee away. The best exposition of harps in singing is given by Dr. Watts, "Oh may my heart in tune be found, like David's harp of solemn sound."[232]

As late as the 1880s, Charles Spurgeon continued to hold to the principles of the Reformers and Puritans and rejected the use of any musical instruments in worship, including the organ, which

230. Dabney, *Presbyterian Quarterly*, July 1889.
231. Fuller, 861.
232. Ibid., 860.

had become so prevalent in his day.[233] In a sermon entitled "The New Song and the Old Story," Spurgeon states his opposition to musical instrumentation in worship:

> What a noble instrument the human voice is! . . . Is not our tongue the glory of our frame? Had I no conscientious objection to instrumental music in worship, I should still, I think, be compelled to admit that all the instruments that were ever devised by men, however sweetly attuned, are harsh and grating compared with the unparalleled sweetness of the human voice. When it is naturally melodious and skillfully trained. . . . there can be no music under heaven that can equal the combination of voices which belong to men, women, and children whose hearts really love the Savior. . . . If you want the sensual gratification of music's melting, mystic lay, let me commend to you the concert-room, there you will get the enchanting ravishment; but when ye come to the house of God, let it be to "sing unto the Lord."[234]

Spurgeon comments on Ps. 42:4,

> David appears to have had a peculiarly tender remembrance of the singing of the pilgrims, and assuredly it is the most delightful part of worship and that which comes nearest to the adoration of heaven. What a degradation to supplant the intelligent song of the whole congregation by the theatrical prettinesses of a quartette, the refined niceties of a choir, or the blowing off of wind from inanimate bellows and pipes! We might as well pray by machinery as praise by it.[235]

233. Curwen, 427.

234. Charles Spurgeon, *Metropolitan Tabernacle Pulpit,* Sermon No. 2850 (1903; reprint, Pasadena, Texas: Pilgrim Publications, 1977; Rio, WI, Ages Digital Library, Ages Software Inc., 2000), Vol. 49, 601–602.

235. Spurgeon, *The Treasury of David,* Vol. 1, Part 2, 272.

Spurgeon warns his own congregation what would happen if they were to prove unfaithful as a church:

> If the Spirit of God were gone, you would say, "Well, we are still a large and influential congregation; we can afford to pay a talented minister, money will do anything;" and you would get the man of talents, and then you would want an organ and a choir, and many other pretty things which we now count it our joy to do without . . . Alas! for the carnal, spasmodic efforts we have seen made in some churches! Prayer-meetings badly attended, no conversions, but still the people have said, "It is imperative upon us to keep up a respectable appearance; we must collect a congregation by our singing, by our organ, or some other outward attraction;" and angels might have wept as they saw the folly of men who sought almost anything except the Lord who alone can make a house His Temple.[236]

John Spencer Curwen visited the Metropolitan Tabernacle and records the *a cappella* singing in *Studies in Worship Music*:

> The first hymn on Sunday morning last was "God is our refuge and our strength," to the tune "Evan." Mr. Spurgeon read it slowly through, then he announced the tune and read the first verse again. As the people stood up the precentor advanced from the back of the platform and started the melody with a clear voice. Like a giant that needs a moment to arouse himself the congregation allows a note or two to pass before they entered in full strength. Then the heavy tide of sound streamed forth from every part of the building. Many churches have more cultivated congregational singing than Mr. Spurgeon's, but, from the numbers engaged, no other singing touches the heart

---

236. Charles Spurgeon, *The Autobiography of Charles H. Spurgeon,* (New York: Fleming H. Revell Company, 1899), Vol. 3, 256.

with such an indefinable pleasure, and makes the frame glow with such a sense of worshipful sympathy. "There are waterfalls," it has been said, "more beautiful than Niagara, but none so overwhelming." To yield oneself to the power of this great human voice, to let the spirit sink and rise with the swell of this mighty bosom, is to know the force of human sympathy, and feel the joy that companionship in worship inspires.[237]

John L. Dagg (1794–1884) was one of the most respected Baptist theologians in America during the late 19th century. In his *Manual of Theology,* Dagg wrote, "Instrumental music formed a part of the Temple worship; but it is nowhere commanded in the New Testament; and it is less adapted to the more spiritual services of the present dispensation."[238]

Prominent leaders among the Southern Presbyterians such as James Henley Thornwell, Robert L. Dabney , and Dr. R. J. Breckinridge refused to admit musical instruments into the worship of their churches into the late 19th century.[239] In 1889, Dabney wrote,

Christ and his apostles ordained the musical worship of the New Dispensation without any sort of musical instrument, enjoining only the singing with the voice of psalms, hymns, and spiritual songs. Hence such instruments are excluded from Christian worship. Such has been the creed of all churches, and in all ages, except of the Popish communion after it had reached the nadir of its corruption at the end of the thirteenth century, and its prelatic imitators.[240]

---

237. Curwen, 427.
238. John L. Dagg, *Manual of Theology,* (Harrisonburg, VA: Gano Books, 1982), Second Part, 240.
239. Girardeau, 202.
240. Dabney, *Presbyterian Quarterly*, July 1889. Dabney wrote this article as a review of John Girardeau's book on *Instrumental Music in the Public Worship of the Church.*

Girardeau laments the changes that took place so quickly after the deaths of Breckinridge and Thornwell:

> How it is that such men as Breckinridge and Thornwell, in the American Presbyterian church, were hardly cold in their graves before, in the very places where they had thundered forth their contentions for the mighty principle which demands a divine warrant for every element of doctrine, government, and worship, and where they had, in obedience to that principle, utterly refused to admit instrumental music into the church, the organ pealed forth its triumph over their views?[241]

Robert L. Dabney (1820–1898) looks back at the decline in his generation and writes,

> The first organ I ever knew of in a Virginian Presbyterian church was introduced by one of the wisest and most saintly of pastors, a paragon of old school doctrinal rigor. But he avowedly introduced it on an argument, the most unsound and perilous possible for a good man to adopt, that it would be advantageous to prevent his young people from leaving his church to run after the Episcopal organ in the city.[242]

In 1880, John Spencer Curwen wrote of how churches of various denominations that had once opposed musical instruments had yielded to the popular demand for the organ,

> Men still living can remember the time when organs were very seldom found outside the Church of England. The Methodists, Independents, and Baptists rarely had them, and by the Presbyterians they were stoutly opposed. But since these bodies began to introduce organs, the adoption

---

241. Girardeau, 202.
242. Dabney, *Presbyterian Quarterly*, July 1889.

of them has been steady and unchecked. Even the Presbyterians are giving way, and if we read the future by the past, we can hardly doubt that, in a few years, unaccompanied singing will very seldom be heard.[243]

We can see from the scene of the modern church how accurate was Curwen's prediction of the future.

Dr. D. Martyn Lloyd-Jones did not oppose the use of an organ in worship, but he makes a plea for the modern church to reevaluate the musical innovations of the 19th century and to return to the worship of the Reformation and the Puritans:

> Nothing is needed more urgently than an analysis of the innovations in the realm of religious worship in the nineteenth century—to me in this respect a devastating century. The sooner we forget the nineteenth century and go back to the eighteenth, and even further to the seventeenth and sixteenth century, the better. The nineteenth century and its mentality and outlook is responsible for most of our troubles and problems today. It was then that a fatal turn took place in so many respects, as we have been seeing, and very prominent among the changes introduced was the place given to music in various forms. Quite frequently, and especially in non-episcopal churches, they did not even have an organ before that time. Many of the leaders were actively opposed to organs and tried to justify their attitude from Scripture. . . . My point is that. . . . the entirely new emphasis on music which came in about the middle of the last century was a part of that respectability, and pseudo-intellectualism which I have already described.[244]

243. Curwen, 179.
244. D. Martyn Lloyd-Jones, *Preaching & Preachers,* (Grand Rapids: Zondervan Publishing House, 1996), 265–266.

The 20th Century

The piano came into prominence in many American and English churches in the early 20th century. David Music writes,

> In the same way that the organ was introduced into Scottish Presbyterian churches, through its use in the evangelistic meetings of Moody and Sankey, the piano came to play an important role in many American congregations through the influence of later revival musicians, particularly Charles M. Alexander. Other factors certainly eased the way for the piano, including its inexpensiveness, ready availability, and simple playing technique—at least in comparison with the pipe organ.[245]

Alexander popularized the use of the piano when he accompanied evangelists such as R. A. Torrey and J. Wilbur Chapman and led the music in tours of the United States, England, and Australia.

From 1880 to 1920, many churches were adversely affected by the concert ambitions of choirs and quartets who were more interested in performance than worship. William Rice writes,

> Many large congregations listened each Sunday to the operatic effusions of a well-paid quartet whose concern for worship was often negligible. Others listened to equally operatic, but less efficient quartet choirs. Smaller congregations did their best to fall into line, using whatever talents were at hand. Choirs, where they existed, were often used for the display of talent, temperament, and jealousies—often all to the detriment of the church.[246]

After World War II, the expanding radio and recording industries fueled the spread of popular music styles such as jazz, folk, and country and western. In the 1950s and 60s, the western world was

245. Music, 165.
246. Rice, 93, 101.

shocked by the rapid popular success of rock-and-roll music among young people. Many instruments that had rarely, if ever, been used in worship before, such as the guitar, drums, saxophone, etc. began to find acceptance in many churches. With the development of technology, the electronic keyboard and synthesizer, along with amplification, were also added. By the end of the 20th century, the entire ethos of the world had found its way into the church through music. In many worship services today, little difference can be found between a rock-and-roll concert and the music of the church. It was in the atmosphere of these musical instruments that the development of "Contemporary Christian Music" took place. This modern style of church music is dependent upon and cannot be separated from the instruments used in its development. David Music writes, "The advent of Contemporary Christian Music naturally involved the introduction of the instruments used to accompany this music."[247]

With the loss of biblical principles, we now see what confusion has entered into the worship of the modern church. The convictions of the Reformers and Puritans have been entirely lost, and the use of any kind of musical instruments is accepted in almost every branch of Christianity. The choice of what musical instrument to use is now purely a matter of personal preference. The most subjective and foolish arguments are set forth to promote one over the other. In 1993, Chuck Kraft, a writer for *Worship Leader* magazine, argued that the organ gives us a "view of God as distant and unapproachable" while the guitar represents the incarnation of Christ and the nearness of God. His only biblical support for using the guitar over the organ is John 1:14, "the Word became flesh and dwelt among us," a verse which, of course, has nothing to do with musical instruments. Mr. Kraft goes on to ask, "Can you imagine

247. Music, 175.

Jesus playing an organ? How about a guitar? Somehow, worship with guitars seems to bring Him close again."[248]

As we look back over the entire history of the church, the evidence rejecting the use of musical instruments in New Testament worship is overwhelming. For hundreds of years before the coming of Christ, the Jewish synagogues, from which the apostolic church derived its worship, knew nothing of musical instruments. For 1300 years after the apostles, the vast majority of the church continued to deny their use. It was only during the dark ages of Roman Catholicism in the 14th and 15th centuries that we find the rise of musical instruments in the worship of the church. The Church Fathers, the Reformers, the English and American Puritans, the Scottish, Irish, and American Presbyterians, and many of the most prominent theologians since have all declared that musical instruments are to have no part in Christian worship.

Lessons from Church History

There are several lessons that can be learned from this historical data:

1) We should remember the three theological principles of worship established in Chapter I. These principles are: 1. The Old Testament Temple worship in all of its outward ceremonies and rituals has been abolished; 2. The church must look to Christ and His apostles alone for the ordinances of gospel worship; and 3. In the New Testament, we find neither command nor example of any musical instrument in worship, and, therefore, we have no warrant for their use. These simple principles, proven from the Scripture, have now been traced throughout the history of the church. We have found them among the Church Fathers, the Reformers, the Puritans, and many others down through the centuries who have held to a biblical and Reformed view of worship.

---

248. Quoted in Music, 176–177.

2) The exclusion of musical instruments from Christian worship is the historic Reformed tradition. While a diversity in other aspects of historic Reformed liturgies can be recognized and appreciated, the use of musical instruments is not among them. We have heard the strongly held convictions on this subject from all the major Reformers. This tradition, which is based upon the application of the regulative principle of worship, was passed on from the Reformers to the Puritans. We have seen how the Puritans maintained and expanded upon this principle. From the Puritan era, down through the centuries, those Christians who have desired to maintain biblical and Reformed worship have continued to hold to this same position. We have also seen how this issue transcends the distinctions between Baptists and Paedo-Baptists within the Reformed churches. The historical evidence is clear, and there can be no doubt that the exclusion of musical instruments is part of the classic Reformed practice of worship.[249]

Reformed Christians who would bring musical instruments into worship must realize that they are departing from the historic traditions of Reformed and biblical worship. The reformation of worship was central to the Reformers, and the rejection of musical instruments was no small part of that work. Both the Reformers and the Puritans viewed their use in worship as one of the manifestations of Roman Catholic sensuality, which they vehemently opposed. It is clear from the historical facts that if we bring musical instruments into worship, we are reversing one of the great works of the Protestant Reformation and abandoning one of the strongest held convictions of the Reformed churches throughout the centuries.

---

249. Scholars of historic Reformed worship share this same conclusion that the exclusion of musical instruments is the classic Reformed tradition. I cite six such references:
1) Hughes Oliphant Old, *Worship That Is Reformed According to Scripture,* 159–160;
2) James Hastings Nichols, *Corporate Worship in the Reformed Tradition,* 34–41;
3) Howard L. Rice and James C. Huffstutler, *Reformed Worship,* 100–106;
4) Nick Needham, "Worship Through the Ages," in *Give Praise to God,* 401;
5) Elsie Anne McKee, "Reformed Worship in the Sixteenth Century," in *Christian Worship in Reformed Churches Past and Present,* ed. Lukas Vischer, 3–31.
6) John L. Girardeau, *Instrumental Music in the Public Worship of God,* 163–179.

The question must be asked: If a church no longer conscientiously walks in the historic traditions of the Reformed churches, can it honestly still claim to be among them?

3) This study reveals how far the modern evangelical church has drifted from the principles of the Protestant Reformation. In regard to the use of musical instruments, the modern church has come nearly full circle since the days prior to the Reformation. In many churches, the emphasis on music has once again become central in worship. The modern church is in desperate need of another reformation of its worship. The words of Erasmus concerning musical instruments are as applicable today as they were when he first spoke them, "according to priests and monks it constitutes the whole of religion. Why will they not listen to Paul? In college or monastery it is still the same: music, nothing but music. There was no music in St. Paul's time."[250] "The church rings with the noise of trumpets, pipes, dulcimers; and human voices strive to bear their part with them. Men run to church as to a theatre, to have their ears tickled."[251]

4) Christian history indicates a connection between the use of musical instruments and the spiritual decline of the church. It was during the spiritual darkness of Medieval Roman Catholicism that musical instruments had their greatest prominence in worship.[252] We have seen how Carlstadt made this historic connection between the rise of music and the apostasy of the church throughout the Middle Ages. Andrew Fuller states that musical instruments in worship, "originated in the dark ages of popery, when almost every other superstition was introduced under the plea of its according with the worship of the Old Testament."[253]

---

250. Quoted in Scholes, 216.
251. Quoted in Girardeau, 162.
252. Andrew Wilson-Dickson comments on the musical developments of the Middle Ages and writes, "The musical changes were creative, stimulating and positive, but they occurred alongside a depressing and shameful spiritual decline." Wilson-Dickson, 55.
253. Fuller, 861.

The movement of many modern churches to what is called "contemporary worship," which is often dominated by instrumental music, is not really a step of reformation and enlightenment as it is often portrayed. It is rather another departure from the biblical principles of the Protestant Reformation and a bold step backward toward the sensuality that dominated Medieval Roman Catholic worship.

As we look back over the entire history of the church, there are only two periods in which musical instruments have had great prominence in worship. The first was the dark ages of Roman Catholicism in the 14th and 15th centuries, and the second is our own generation. This historic perspective is confirmed by Professor Vincent Lenti, a longtime member of the faculty at the Eastman School of Music in Rochester, New York. Professor Lenti states that because of the wide variety of musical instruments available today and the electronic amplification that is so common, the scene we are witnessing in the modern church is unparalleled in history. In his words, "Never before have men and women been subject to such a cacophony as they are on Sunday mornings today." In this sense, our modern situation is worse than before the Protestant Reformation. We have witnessed, in our own generation, the continuing advance of a man-centered theology and worship in the modern evangelical church. What God desires in His worship is hardly a consideration. What appeals to man and what makes him feel comfortable in church is the theme of countless books on worship. The increasing use of musical instruments and the sensuality of modern worship is a manifestation of this man-centeredness. This is what our Reformed brethren from the past are crying out to us about. The Reformers, the Puritans, and others since have seen the connection between the use of musical instruments and the sensuality of false worship. We have heard their words, and they warn us in the strongest terms that the use of musical instruments is part of the road back to the sensuality of Medieval worship.

In 1889, Robert L. Dabney saw that the increasing use of musical instruments was part of the darkness descending over the evangelical church of his day. Dabney warns,

> Nothing is needed but the lapse of years enough for this drift, of which this music is a part, to send back great masses of our people, a material well prepared for the delusion, into the bosom of Rome and her kindred connections. . . . This is the pernicious mistake which has sealed up millions of self-deceived souls for hell. Rome encourages the delusion continually.[254]

Dabney goes on to write,

> But these organ-grinding Protestant churches are aiding and encouraging tens of thousands of their members to adopt this pagan mistake. Like the besotted Papist, they are deluded into the fancy that their hearts are better because certain sensuous, animal emotions are aroused by a mechanical machine, in a place called a church, and in a proceeding called worship.[255]

We have seen Dabney's words come true in many ways in our own day. And should not we, as Reformed Christians, take heed from the warnings of history and deliver ourselves from such dangers?

5) We should recognize that many of the Reformers, Puritans, and others since have spoken against the use of even a single musical instrument, especially the organ. They saw even in this a violation of a biblical principle, which opens the door to greater abuses. We have seen how the principle of the exclusion of musical instruments recovered during the Reformation was gradually eroded throughout the 18th and 19th centuries. Very often it was the introduction of a single musical instrument that marked the loss of principle and the beginning of a downward trend. The use of a single instrument

---

254. Dabney, *Presbyterian Quarterly*, July 1889.
255. Ibid.

was the beginning of a natural progression to the use of others as well, until we have arrived in our present circumstances. We have also seen that these changes were based, not upon Scripture, but upon human expediency.

John Calvin gives us this warning, "such is our folly, that when we are left at liberty, all we are able to do is go astray. And then when once we have turned aside from the right path, there is no end to our wanderings, until we get buried under a multitude of superstitions."[256] Calvin's words have been fulfilled in the modern church in regard to the use of musical instruments. The church's wandering from biblical principle began with a single instrument and has resulted in the confusion we see all around us today. Those who continue to accept the use of even a single instrument should ask themselves how they will avoid this wandering into the use of multiple instruments so clearly demonstrated in church history?

6) As Reformed Christians, we place great value on our religious heritage and on the light God has given to those who have gone before us in the faith. If we were to study the doctrine of justification, we would not pretend to be the first to open our Bibles on that great subject. We would look back to those who have gone before us. Should we not do the same in regard to musical instruments in worship? There needs to be no sense of novelty as if no one has dealt with it before. When we do look back through the centuries, we find overwhelming testimony declaring that musical instruments are to have no part in the worship of the church. There is hardly an issue on which historical theology speaks more clearly than this one.

Can we ignore this massive evidence from church history? Can we actually believe that from the days of the apostles, for well over a millennium, the Christian church was ignorant of the will of Christ in regard to musical instruments in worship? Do we believe that we are more enlightened than the Reformers and

256. John Calvin, *Necessity of Reforming the Church*, 17.

the Puritans? Can we really think that such vast segments of the Christian church have misunderstood the will of God in worship, and that we have somehow arrived at a better understanding? The fact is that the advocates of musical instruments stand opposed to the greatest theologians of the church. Who is willing to take his stand on this issue against all the Church Fathers: Ignatius, Justin Martyr, Clement, Eusebius, Chrysostom, Theodoret, Athanasius, Augustine, and over a thousand years of church history? We add to this the likes of John Wycliffe, John Hus, John Calvin, John Knox, Zwingli, Bullinger, Beza, Menno Simons and the other Reformers, along with the synods of the Reformation. Then we have the Puritans: John Owen, Henry Ainsworth, William Ames, John Bunyan, William Perkins, David Calderwood, George Gillespie, Samuel Rutherford, Thomas Goodwin and Thomas Manton. Standing with them are Matthew Henry, Cotton Mather, John Cotton, Isaac Watts, John Gill, Benjamin Keach, and Hanserd Knollys along with the Westminster Assembly and the English and American Puritans who followed in their footsteps. We cannot forget those since: Thomas Chalmers, Andrew Fuller, Charles Spurgeon, and John Dagg, along with James Henley Thornwell, Robert L. Dabney, and John Girardeau as representatives of their churches. The historic unanimity on this issue is decisive. What does it say about us if we are willing to oppose the collective testimony of the greatest men throughout the history of the church?

Someone may say that these are only men and we must follow the Scriptures alone. This is true. But where is the New Testament evidence that demands the use of musical instruments? These men were all filled with the Holy Spirit as they studied their Bibles. They are among those pastors whom Christ has given to the church so that "we are no longer to be children, tossed here and there by waves and carried about by every wind of doctrine, by the trickery of men, by craftiness in deceitful scheming" (Eph. 4:14). Before we depart from their ways, we must have clear and convincing evidence from the Scriptures to do so. Until that evidence is presented, we must obey the command to "be subject to one another in the fear of Christ" (Eph. 5:21).

7) What is the source of this pressure on our generation to to have musical instruments? It does not come from the New Testament Scripture, and it certainly does not come from church history. One is left to suspect that the real source of this pressure is from the world and from a modern church that has embraced so much of the world with little regard for God's rights in His worship. Dabney comments on the organ's being used by more and more churches in his day,

> I know, by an intuition which I believe every sensible observer shares, that the innovation is merely the result of an advancing wave of worldliness and ritualism in the evangelical bodies. These Christians are not wiser but simply more flesh-pleasing and fashionable . . .[257]

8) A no-instrument position will surely seem radical to most modern Christians. We have become so accustomed to the use of instruments in church that we simply assume they should be there. We cannot possibly imagine anything else. Many in our generation will dismiss a no-instrument position as "extreme" and "austere" and "rigid." But those who say such things must place these very same labels on the greater part of the Christian church and all those who have been named above. When one looks back over the history of the church, it is not the no-instrument position that is surprising, but the fact that so many of us have willingly accepted the use of instruments in our own generation.

Those who would exclude musical instruments in the present day may feel very much alone in the modern Christian church. This brief look back assures them that they are not at all alone. In fact, they walk in the most solid traditions and the most blessed paths

---

257. Dabney, *Presbyterian Quarterly*, July 1889.

that the church has ever known. Girardeau wrote concerning the rise of musical instruments in the Presbyterian church in the late 19th century,

> Those of us who protest against this revolution in Pres-byterian worship are by some pitied, by others ridiculed, and by others still denounced as fanatics. If we are, we share the company of an innumerable host of fanatics extending from the day of Pentecost to the middle of the nineteenth century. We refuse not to be classed, although consciously unworthy of the honor, with apostles, martyrs, and reformers. But neither were they mad, nor are we. We speak words of truth and soberness.[258]

9) One of the most common concerns regarding the exclusion of musical instruments is the effect it will have upon singing. We have become so accustomed to the use of instruments that many believe singing cannot be done "decently and in order" without their aid. This assumes that the church has been offering indecent and disorderly praise for the greater part of its history. Those who believe that musical instruments are necessary in worship must wonder why the church for so many centuries never felt such a necessity. If they were not needed before, why are they needed now?

A cappella singing requires a minimum of musical skill and a heightened spiritual energy within the congregation. Everything rests upon the human voice, and there are no instruments to disguise the carelessness or the spiritual lethargy of the people. There seems to have been three difficulties with *a cappella* singing in the past: 1) the inability of the people to read each line of the hymn before singing, 2) the inability of the people to read musical notes, and 3) the difficulty of singing elaborate tunes. The first difficulty is almost non-existent today, while the second is only occasional. The third continues to be a concern because many of the tunes used

---

258. Girardeau, 208.

in our modern hymnbooks are complex and demand the use of instrumental accompaniment. This difficulty can be removed with the use of simple tunes that are easily sung by a congregation.

When these hindrances are removed, there are many who have testified throughout history to "the sweetness of the human voice" when unaccompanied by musical instruments. The English pastor and historian John Quick, in his *Synodicon in Gallia Reformata*, writes of the unaccompanied psalm-singing in France after the Reformation,

> Lewis Guadimel. . . . a most skillful master of music, set those sweet and melodious tunes unto which they are sung even unto this day. This holy ordinance charmed the ears, hearts and affections of court and city, town and country. They were sung in the Louvre, as well as in the Pres-des-Cleres, by ladies, princes, yea, and by Henry the Second himself. This one ordinance only contributed mightily to the downfall of Popery, and the propagation of the gospel. It took so much with the genius of the nation, that all ranks and degrees of men practiced it in the Temples and in their families. No gentleman professing the Reformed religion would sit down at his table without praising God by singing. Yea, it was a special part of their morning and evening worship in their several houses to sing God's praises. The Popish clergy raged . . . [259]

In 1646, Edward Winslow records the skillful singing of the Pilgrims before their departure from Holland,

> They . . . that stayed at Leyden feasted us that were to go at our pastor's house being large, where we refreshed ourselves after our tears, with singing of Psalms, making joyful melody in our hearts, as well as with the voyce, there being

---

259. John Quick, *Synodicon in Gallia Reformata,* (London: T. Parkhust and J. Robinson, 1692), Vol. 1, 5, *EEB* 1641–1700, Reel 473:2.

many of our congregation very expert in music; and indeed it was the sweetest melody that ever mine ears heard.[260]

William Rice writes on the American Puritans, "Musicologists are generally agreed that the early colonists not only delighted in their singing but sang quite well. Writers of the seventeenth century mention the presence of fine musicians during the early years. It is certain that they sang with vigor and had little patience with lethargic, mournful music. *The Ravenscoft* (1621) collection of 105 tunes was very popular among the Puritans."[261] The above testimonies are only a sampling of historical evidence that *a cappella* singing can be done with aesthetic beauty. This should be an encouragement to those willing to make this reformation in worship.

---

260. Edward Winslow, *Hypocrisie Unmasked,* (London: J. Bellamy, 1646), 90–91. *EEB*, 1641–1700, Reel 5.43.
261. Rice, 49

Chapter III

The Psychology of Music

A NOTHER important issue which must be considered is the powerful effect that music has upon the human emotions. Music is a direct appeal to the emotions. One of its secret powers is its effect upon human subconsciousness apart from our rational nature.[1] Every man knows from his own experience the powerful way music can stir the affections apart from any direct influence of the mind.

In this chapter we will briefly show that the powerful emotional effects of music have been known from the times of the early Greeks. We will then consider how this relates to the development of hymnody in the history of the church. The dangerously deceptive effects of music upon the human emotions, apart from the mind's being affected by the truth, have been known throughout Christian history. This chapter will close with some warnings from the history of the church to the harmful effects, not only of musical instruments, but also of sensual tunes in worship.

---

1. John Blanchard, *Pop Goes the Gospel,* (Hertfordshire, England: Evangelical Press, 1984), 72.

A Brief History

The ancient Greeks recognized the powerful impact of music upon the human emotional nature. They believed that music was first practiced by the gods before it was given as a divine gift to men. Music mysteriously penetrated the souls of men with a divine influence. Aristotle believed that music had the power to shape human character and affect behavior. Music that imitated certain emotions or states of the soul (such as gentleness, anger, or courage) would arouse the same emotion in the listener. Plato believed that the boy who listened to soft and indolent tunes would grow up to be effeminate, while the boy who listened to bold and energetic music would become a leader.[2] So powerful did Plato understand the effects of music to be on human behavior that he wrote, "Let me make the songs of a nation and I care not who makes its laws."[3] The constitutions of Athens and Sparta banned certain kinds of music as being harmful to the public welfare.

The power of music to manipulate certain responses is well known in our day, from Hollywood to advertising companies, and even to evangelistic crusades.[4] Modern dictators have used music as a tool of psychological manipulation.[5] Music is currently being used in psychotherapy.[6] Music has the most direct effects upon the functions of the human body as well, including digestion, internal secretions, respiration, and heart beat. David Tame writes in *The Secret Power of Music*, "There is scarcely a single function of the body which cannot be affected by musical tones."[7] The Bible gives its own testimony to the powerful effects of music upon the human psyche and behavior. When David played his harp, "Saul

2. Donald Jay Grout, Claude V. Palisca, *The History of Western Music*, (New York: W. W. Norton & Company), 6.
3. Quoted in Grout, 6.
4. Blanchard, 72.
5. Grout, 7.
6. Best & Huttar, 312.
7. David Tame, *The Secret Power of Music*, (New York: Destiny Books, 1984), 136.

would be refreshed and be well, and the evil spirit would depart from him" (1 Sam. 16:23).

Recent neurological studies have used positron emission tomography (PET) to analyze the response of the human brain to music.[8] These studies have shown that music can produce an intensely pleasurable, even euphoric, emotional response. The same areas of the brain influenced by euphoria-inducing stimuli such as food, sex, and drugs of abuse are activated by music. PET technology has shown that those brain regions involved in reasoning and decision making are deactivated in pianists when they perform their musical pieces.[9] While the effects of music remain a great mystery in many ways, no one can deny the tremendous power music has upon the subconscious and emotional nature of man.

The Struggle Between Words and Tunes

The powerful impact of music upon the human emotions has a direct bearing upon hymnody in the church. It is in this subtle and seductive power of music that lies its greatest danger to the intelligent worship of the gospel, which is to be "in spirit and truth."

In Christian worship, all things are to be done to edification, and our singing must engage all the faculties of the mind. As the apostle says, "Let the Word of Christ richly dwell within you, with all wisdom teaching and admonishing one another with psalms and hymns and spiritual songs, singing with thankfulness in your hearts to God" (Col. 3:16), and, "I will sing with the spirit and I will sing with the mind also" (1 Cor. 14:15). It is true that the emotions must be involved in worship, but it must be truth in the mind that leads the emotions. Anything that has the power to bypass the mind and directly affect the emotions must be handled

8. A.J. Blood & R.J. Zatorre, "Intensely pleasurable responses to music correlate with activity in brain regions implicated with reward and emotion," Proceedings of the National Academy of Sciences, 98 (2001): 11818–11823.

9. Lawrence Parsons, *Music of the Spheres,* BBC Music Magazine, November 2003, 36.

with the greatest care in the worship of God. Musical instruments, and even unaccompanied tunes, have this power. They can easily affect the emotions so as to divert the mind from the true objects of worship, which are spiritual and unseen. When this occurs, musical instruments come into direct conflict with the goals of spiritual worship.

Musicologists are well aware of the struggle that has persisted throughout history between the poet and the composer. The poets, or the ones who write the words of a hymn, have always been concerned that the minds of men are not carried away from their words by the tunes that composers apply to them. The poets have recognized this danger and have desired "to restrict music to its office of serving poetry" but have often been forced to admit that "the effect of tones is incomparably more powerful, more infallible, and quicker than that of words."[10] The composers, on the other hand, emphasize "feeling rather than logic"[11] and often desire that the words be subordinate to the music. As this battle between words and music has gone on throughout the centuries, the pendulum has swung back and forth between the ascendance of the poet and the composer.

Plato understood the danger of music's gaining the dominance over words. Music without the controlling influence of words is corrupt and would lead to confusion in the morals of society. Julius Portnoy states the views of Plato, "Music must, therefore, remain wedded to the text so that reason will prevail in music's appeal to us through the spoken word, otherwise music will become hopelessly irrational and base."[12] In other words with regard to Christian hymnody, the music must not be allowed to divert the mind from the text through its emotional appeal. If this is done, the entire

10. Julius Portnoy, *Music in the Life of Man,* (New York: Holt, Rinehart and Winston, 1963), 128.
11. Ibid., 129.
12. Ibid., 125.

purpose of intelligent worship with the mind is threatened. Portnoy summarizes the concerns of the poet or the hymn-writer,

> Music cannot express concepts, describe, or explain, and words do precisely this to fulfill their function in our exchange of ideas. With words we praise and blame, express admiration and disdain; with music we cannot be definite, but can only allude and suggest. Music cannot, as language can, convey specific ideas or detailed messages which are understood alike by all who hear them.[13]

Much more could be said upon this whole subject, but this very brief synopsis of the struggle between poet and composer has been given because it has the most direct bearing on singing in the worship of the Christian church. The words must have the ascendancy over the melody in singing "so that reason will prevail."[14] Worship must be in "spirit and truth," and the mind must be edified. As the apostle says, "I will sing with the spirit and I will sing with the mind also, . . . Brethren, do not be children in your thinking, . . . but in your thinking be mature, . . . Let all things be done to edification" (1 Cor. 14:15, 20, 26).

The Testimony of the Church Concerning This Struggle

The struggle over music's dominating the words has been deeply felt within the church in the development of hymnody. The power, not only of musical instruments but even of unaccompanied tunes to affect the emotions and lead the mind away from the truth, has been a concern throughout the centuries. We will now consider how this struggle has been expressed by Christian leaders throughout the history of the church.

William Rice, in *A Concise History of Church Music,* tells us that the early Church Fathers believed that "the ability of music

13. Ibid., 121.
14. Ibid., 125.

to affect the senses and arouse the emotions was a dangerous asset. Music could be used to draw the people away from paganism and into the church, but it could also arouse in them the same thoughts and actions upon which pagan beliefs were founded."[15] Many tunes that were, of course, without the accompaniment of musical instruments were forbidden because they were deemed too secular and sensual.[16] Only those tunes that possessed nobility and dignity were accepted for use in the church.

Clement of Alexandria, who believed in the use of unaccompanied hymns, wrote against the use "of sentimentality" and "over-colorful melodies." Clement stated, "We may indeed retain chaste harmonies, but not so those tearful songs which are too florid in the overdelicate modulation of the voice they require. These last must be proscribed and repudiated by those who would retain virility of mind, for their sentimentality and ribaldry degenerate the soul. There is nothing in common between restrained, chaste tunes and the licentiousness of intemperance. Therefore, over-colorful melodies are to be left to shameless carousals, and to the honeyed and garish music of the courtesan."[17]

Clement, who opposed the use of musical instruments because the instruments were often used in immoral parties, was well aware of their powerful effects upon the human emotions. He referred to musical instruments as "instruments of deception" and to music as "the licentious and mischievous art of music." "The exciting rhythm of flutes and harps, choruses and dances, Egyptian castanets and other entertainments get out of control and become indecent and burlesque, especially when they are re-enforced by cymbals and drums and accompanied by the noise of all these instruments of deception."[18] "Superfluous music is to be rejected, because it breaks and variously affects the mind, so that sometimes it is indeed

15. Rice, 12.
16. Lorenz, 219.
17. Quoted in Music, 37–38.
18. Ibid., 35.

mournful, sometimes unchaste and inciting to licentiousness, sometimes frenzied and insane."[19] "We must be on our guard against whatever pleasure titillates eye and ear, and effeminates. For the various spells of the broken strains and plaintive numbers of the Carian muse corrupt men's morals, drawing to perturbations of mind by the licentious and mischievous art of music."[20]

Clement goes on to say,

> In general, we must completely eliminate every such base sight or sound—in a word, everything immodest that strikes the senses (for this is an abuse of the senses)—if we would avoid pleasures that merely fascinate the eye or ear, and emasculate. Truly, the devious spells of syncopated tunes and of the plaintive rhythm of Carian music corrupt morals by their sensual and affected style, and insidiously inflame the passions.[21]

Athanasius sensed this problem of the tunes' carrying the mind away from the text and sought to avoid it by having the reader of the psalm use only a very slight inflection of the voice. The result was more like speaking or chanting than singing.[22]

Augustine confesses that he often felt his own mind drawn away from the words by the melody, which he calls "the delights of the ear."[23] He writes, "this sensual pleasure, to which the soul must not be delivered so as to be weakened, often leads me astray, when sense does not accompany reason in such wise as to follow patiently after it, but, having won admittance for reason's sake, even tries to run ahead and lead reason on. Thus in such things I unconsciously sin, but later I am conscious of it."[24] Augustine confesses, "Thus I

19. Quoted in Kurfees, 126.
20. Ibid., 128.
21. Quoted in Music, 36.
22. Augustine, *The Confessions of St. Augustine,* translated by John K. Ryan, (Garden City, New York: Image Books, 1960), 261.
23. Ibid.
24. Ibid.

do waver between the danger of sensual pleasure and wholesome experience."[25] His most famous statement in this regard is "When it so happens that I am moved more by the singing than by what is sung, I confess that I have sinned, in such wise as to deserve punishment, and at such times I should prefer not to listen to a singer."[26] At times the difficulty becomes so intense that he states, "I strongly desire that all melodies and sweet chants with which David's psalter is accompanied should be banished from my ears and from the church itself."[27] Augustine settles on a more reasonable solution and decides in favor of songs in the church provided "they are sung with clear voices and fitting modulation."[28]

This concern of the Church Fathers was felt all the way down to the development of the Gregorian chants at the end of the 6th century. In his book entitled *Church Music,* Edmund Lorenz writes,

> The stimulating, exciting character of the earlier pagan music was repudiated. . . lest they distract the attention from the spiritual purpose in view. . . . While there was a certain jubilance in the singing of such hymns as the "Te Deum," it was rendered with a noble restraint based on the awful presence of the Almighty.[29]

Edward Dickinson, in *Music in the History of the Western Church,* summarizes the views of the Church Fathers,

> The religious guides of the early Christians felt that there would be incongruity, and even profanity, in the use of the sensuous nerve-exciting effects of instrumental sound in their mystical, spiritual worship. Their high religious and moral enthusiasm needed no aid from external stimulus;

25. Ibid., 262.
26. Ibid.
27. Ibid., 261.
28. Ibid., 261–262.
29. Lorenz, 228–229.

the pure vocal utterance was the more proper expression of their faith.[30]

Joseph Bingham, in *Antiquities of the Christian Church,* writes that one of the vices that the early Church Fathers complained of was "regarding more the music of the words, and sweetness of the composure, than the sense and meaning of them; pleasing the ear, without raising the affections of the soul, which was the true reason for which psalmody and music was intended."[31]

In the late 1300s in England, John Wycliffe again faced the problem of church music's being aesthetically pleasing and luring the minds of the people away from the truth. We have already seen how he complained that the organ was used as one of the "sensuous preparations by which their other senses are moved, apart altogether from religious feeling."[32] Wycliffe strongly opposed the use of song to "stir to dancing" and to arouse the emotions in worship.[33] When he sent out his lollards to preach, they often quoted the statement of Augustine, "When it so happens that I am moved more by the singing than by what is sung, I confess that I have sinned."[34]

In the 1400s, John Hus complained as well of music in the churches of Bohemia that "incites to dance rather than piety."[35] We have seen previously that Huldriech Zwingli (1484–1531), the leader of the Swiss Reformation, was a highly skilled and accomplished musician. As a musician, Zwingli was convinced of the powerful psychological and emotional impact that music has over the human soul. To Zwingli, music has a unique power that demands an immediate emotional reaction. As soon as we hear music, we must respond to it, either by being soothed and calmed, or by being exhilarated and stimulated, depending on the type of

30. Dickinson, 55.
31. Bingham, Vol. 2, 685.
32. Quoted in Lechler, 326.
33. Masters, 26.
34. Victor Budgen, *On Fire for God: The Story of John Hus,* (Hertfordshire: Evangelical Press, 1983), 67.
35. Quoted by Spinka, 306.

music. This response is an unconscious and inescapable aspect of human nature. Zwingli argued that this emotional response was entirely a psychological phenomenon that had nothing to do with the true spiritual worship of God, and could easily be confused with it.[36] He warns that these psychological effects of music are powerfully experienced by all men, even though men do not understand how the effects are at work in them. He writes, "The ratio of no other discipline is so profoundly rooted and innate in the souls of men as that of music. For no men are so stupid that they are not captivated by it, even though they are entirely ignorant of its technique."[37] Zwingli helps us to understand how easily the emotional effects of music can be mistaken for spiritual worship, while in reality, they may have nothing to do with it. It is this confusing of the emotional effects of music with spiritual worship so prevalent in the churches of our own day.

In the middle 1500s, John Calvin wrestled with this issue of even unaccompanied tunes luring the mind away from the truth. Looking back to the struggles of Athanasius and Augustine before him, Calvin writes,

> And certainly if singing is tempered to a gravity befitting the presence of God and angels, it both gives dignity and grace to sacred actions, and has a very powerful tendency to stir up the mind to true zeal and ardor in prayer. We must, however, carefully beware, lest our ears be more intent on the music than our minds on the spiritual meaning of the words. Augustine confesses that the fear of this danger sometimes made him wish for the introduction of a practice observed by Athanasius, who ordered the reader to use only a gentle inflection of the voice, more akin to recitation than singing. But on again considering how many advantages were derived from singing, he inclined to the other side. If

36. Garside, *Zwingli and the Arts*, 73–75.
37. Quoted in Garside, 74.

this moderation be used, there cannot be a doubt that the practice is most sacred and salutary. On the other hand, songs composed merely to tickle and delight the ear are unbecoming the majesty of the church, and cannot but be most displeasing to God.[38]

Julius Portnoy writes, "Calvin admonished Protestants not to be misled by the false pleasures that music could bring by pleasing and delighting the senses. Music composed only for enjoyment 'is unbecoming the majesty of the church.' Grace will not come to those whose ears are 'more attentive to the modulation of the notes than the mind to the import of the words.'"[39]

Even the Roman Catholic theologian, Navarrus (1493–1586) recognized the effects of the organ in diverting the mind in worship,

Many organists frequently play profane, and even vain and sometimes evil songs in the church on the organ. . ., this is clearly sin. . ., because of the occasion it may present for diverting the mind's attention from divine and spiritual things and bending it to the temporal, vain, and evil.[40]

In Scotland, in 1531, the Augustinian priest, Robert Richardson, complained of the harmful effects of music in the churches,

The custom of singing and playing (instruments) in church was introduced for carnal (minds) therefore, not for spiritual (minds); so that since they were not counseled by words, they might be tickled by charm and sweetness of playing. . . By such very music which is now performed in almost the whole world, we charge that the souls of listeners are not excited to devotion but on the other hand are

---

38. John Calvin, *Calvin's Institutes,* Book Three, Chap. XX, 32, (Grand Rapids: Associated Publishers and Authors, Inc.), 475–476.
39. Portnoy, 126.
40. Quoted in Music, 67.

weakened by the frivolity, vanity and delight (of the music)
and turn away from devotion rather than are incited (to it)
by that contrivance.[41]

James Ramsey (1814–1871), an American minister, comments
on the deceptive influence music can have on true spiritual worship,

> By a skillful manipulation of the emotional and sensational
> nature of man, in the use of language, music, and ceremo-
> nies, individuals and assemblies may be galvanized into
> the highest excitement of feeling, which may be readily
> mistaken by the subject of it for the fervors of true worship.
> Instead of awakening profound and humbling views of the
> holiness and glory of God, they intoxicate the soul with
> a dizzy whirl of undefined emotions, of which self is the
> center and the end.[42]

Ramsey describes much of what we see today in the modern
evangelical church all around us. Music is used to draw the crowds
in and then manipulate their emotions. Vast numbers of unconverted sinners attend worship services simply because they enjoy
the emotional experience created by the music. And while they
remain unconverted, they are often led to believe they are Christians
because they take pleasure in a service that is called worship but is
dominated by music. At the same time, many true Christians are
deceived into believing that this emotionally charged atmosphere
is the presence of the Holy Spirit. Not a few professing Christians
have told me words to this effect, "when the music begins we can
feel the Holy Spirit come down." Such descriptions are testimony
to the deceptive power of music over the emotional nature.

---

41. Translated by Isobel Woods Preece, 91.
42. James Ramsey, *Revelation*, (Edinburgh; The Banner of Truth Trust, 1984), 277.

Robert L. Dabney analyzes how the emotions created by musical instruments can be mistaken for true religious affections and gives us a most powerful warning against it.

> Man's animal nature is sensitive, through the ear, to certain sensuous, aesthetic impressions from melody, harmony and rhythm. There is, on the one hand, a certain analogy between the sensuous excitements of the acoustic nerves and sensorium and the rational sensibilities of the soul. . . . Now, the critical points are these: That, while these sensuous excitements are purely animal and are no more essentially promotive of faith, holiness, or light in the conscience. . . . Sinful men, fallen and blinded, are ever ready to abuse this faint analogy by mistaking the sensuous impressions for, and confounding them with, spiritual affections. Blinded men are ever prone to imagine that they have religious feelings, because they have sensuous, animal feelings, in accidental juxtaposition with religious places, words, or sights. This is the pernicious mistake which has sealed up millions of self-deceived souls for hell. Rome encourages the delusion continually.[43]

If we placed four idols made of wood, silver, gold, and stone in front of a modern evangelical church, and then said that we were not going to bow down to them, but only use them as aids in worship, the people of God would become outraged. They would see this as a clear and blatant act of idolatry. But if those idols suddenly became living and animated beings and began to produce musical

---

43. Dabney, *Presbyterian Quarterly*, July 1889. James Henley Thornwell comments on the deceptiveness of such sensual worship in the Roman Catholic church, "The miserable votaries of Rome confound the emotions of mysterious awe produced by the solemnities of a sensual worship with reverence for God and the impressions of grace. Doomed to grope among the beggarly elements of earth, they regale the eye, the fancy and the ear, but the heart withers. . . . The gorgeous splendors of the liturgy, which famish the soul while they delight the sense, are sad memorials of religion 'lying in state surrounded with the silent pomp of death.' The Holy Ghost has been supplanted by charms, and physical causes have usurped the province of supernatural grace." Thornwell, Vol. 3, 319.

sounds that had the most direct and powerful influence upon the emotions, no one would have a problem. The emotional pleasure created by the music blinds men to the idolatry involved in the use of their musical instruments.

I will close this chapter with some further testimony concerning the distraction to true spiritual worship that musical instruments have caused in the history of the church down to the present time:

A controversy arose during the spiritual revivals of the early 1800s in the United States. The Calvinists were critical of the camp-meetings of the Methodists because they used the emotional effects of singing to secure evangelistic results. The Calvinists regarded such results as often false and spurious. Iain Murray comments on the Methodists, "Emotion engendered by numbers and mass singing, repeated over several days, was conducive to securing a response. Results could thus be multiplied, even guaranteed. Calvinists, using their Bibles rather than any knowledge of psychology, saw from the New Testament that no technique could produce conversions. On the contrary, the use of techniques was calculated to confuse the real meaning of conversion. Thus the opposition to the camp-meeting psychology was theological, and Richard M'Nemar was correct to identify Calvinism as the main hindrance to the type of meeting in which excitement was given full sway."[44]

J. Spencer Curwen, who favored the use of the organ in worship, still had concerns over its sensuality and harmful effects upon singing. Curwen writes on his visit to the Presbyterian Church at Regent Square in London, in the 1890s,

> I have always been in favor of organs, but a Sunday at Regent Square is enough to shake one's faith in them. The organ gives a great deal of pleasure, but, after all it is a sensuous pleasure. We worship when we send up aspirations

44. Iain Murray, *Revival & Revivalism*, (Edinburgh: The Banner of Truth Trust, 1994), 184.

and feelings of adoration, prayer, and joy to God. The organ can hardly do this, and, therefore can only be admitted as a helper to the voices. With this office about one organist in a hundred is at present content.[45]

Dr. Martyn Lloyd-Jones comments on the dangerous effects of music upon the mind, "We can become drunk with music—there is no question about that. Music can have the effect of creating an emotional state in which the mind is no longer functioning as it should be, and no longer discriminating. I have known people to sing themselves into a state of intoxication without realizing what they were doing. The important point is that we should realize that the effect produced in such a case in not produced by the Truth. . . ."[46]

Peter Masters, the current pastor of the Metropolitan Tabernacle in London, notes that the "contemporary worship" that is driven by musical instrumentation is a deviation from biblical principles. He calls it "ecstatic worship" as compared to the "rational worship" that is required in the New Testament. Masters writes,

The conscious, sound mind is the vital human organ of worship. . . Ecstatic worship is completely different. This aims at stirring the emotions to produce a simulated, exalted emotional state. Ecstatic worship takes place when the object of the exercise is to achieve a warm, happy feeling, perhaps excitement, and even a sense of God's presence through the earthly, physical aspects of worship such as music and movement. Among charismatics this is eagerly pursued, the programme being carefully engineered to bring worshippers to a high emotional pitch, and often to a mildly hypnotic state. In non-charismatic circles the objective is a little more modest, but essentially the same-to make an emotional impact. Worship leaders want to bypass

45. Curwen, 419.
46. Lloyd-Jones, 272.

the rationality and get the feelings going to other means. They want to stir up "sensations" in order to produce euphoria.[47]

Because of its emphasis on the emotions rather than intelligent worship through the truth, Dr. Masters goes on to warn us,

> Whether its advocates realize it or not, the contemporary worship movement is the instrument of the hour to pull down the doctrinal walls of Zion. How the arch-enemy of the churches of Christ and of human souls must be straining to bring about such a catastrophe! The new worship scene is undoubtedly our enemy, not our friend. If we give new worship the smallest foothold it will ruin the highest activity entrusted to us—the reverent, intelligent and joyful offering of spiritual praise. Those who begin by singing one new worship song at every service, will soon be singing two, then three, then adding the band, and so on. It is very noticeable that wherever new worship has been embraced by evangelicals, a perceptible loss of reverence, coupled with worldliness and shallowness, has set in.[48]

The testimony of the church is abundant and clear. Throughout church history, men have wrestled with the powerful effects that instrumental music and even unaccompanied tunes can have upon the emotions to divert the mind away from the truth. Even those who have approved the use of instruments have had to face the consequences of their own error and acknowledge the great harm they have brought upon the intelligent worship of the gospel.

In the light of the above testimony of the church, several questions must be asked. Why would any church desire the use of musical instruments when their dangers to Christian worship are so evident? Who is able to use musical instruments and avoid their

47. Masters, 23–24.
48. Ibid., 136.

subtle and yet powerful effects upon the human emotions? Who is able to bring them into church and prevent them from interfering with the intelligent nature of gospel worship? Even the slightest such effect should be unacceptable. What real and lasting spiritual profit can possibly come from them? Will they increase faith, or sanctify, or produce holiness? What real good to the souls of men, other than a fleeting emotional pleasure, will they bring?

The clear principles of Scripture set forth earlier in this book are sufficient to keep musical instruments out of the church. God's truth is all we need in this regard. The testimony of the church is added only to show the great problems that have taken place when men have deviated from God's Word.

Two Clarifications

It is important to clarify two points in regard to the above material on the powerful and dangerous effects of music upon the human emotions.

1) We are not saying that Christian singing should lack proper emotion. The singing of psalms, hymns, and spiritual songs should reflect the true affections of the heart, especially Christian joy and thankfulness for salvation through Jesus Christ. When we come to worship, we should "Serve the Lord with gladness; Come before Him with joyful singing" (Ps. 100:2). Christian joy in the singing of God's praise should be a matter of great concern to the church. Our need in this regard is not for musical instruments to create an elevated emotional atmosphere, but for the presence and power of the Holy Spirit. One of the marks of the Spirit's presence is joy (Luke 10:21; Gal. 5:22; Rom. 14:17, 15:13; Acts 13:48). If the Holy Spirit is present, there will be true spiritual joy in all of our worship, including our singing. But we must exercise extreme care that we do not create a false joy produced by the influence of music and mistake it for the joy of the Holy Spirit. The above quotations warn us that this danger is very real and has been recognized

throughout the history of the church. Musical instrumentation, and even the tunes themselves, can easily excite the emotions and carry the mind away from the truth of what is being sung.

Iain Murray comments on our need for the Spirit in this regard,

> Supremely, this whole subject is a reminder to us of our great need of the unction of the Holy Spirit. Why is worship not commonly more uplifting and transforming? Why has the expectation of God's felt presence become faint? The common diagnosis for the unhelpfulness of much contemporary worship is patently wrong. It is not changes in form that we need; not disorganized spontaneity in place of familiar structures; not professional musicians and all their instruments to ease the boredom. Such changes and others have been with us for years but what have they done to restore spiritual conditions? What have they done to inspire holy living and to restore eagerness for the Word of God?[49]

We are not saying that the tunes used should not reflect a spirit of Christian joy. We are not advocating a return to the very slight inflection of the voice under Athanasius or to monotone tunes. Whether a particular tune is appropriate to God's worship is admittedly a subjective issue upon which there will be differing opinions. On the one hand, we should not desire a dirge or melancholic tune that unnecessarily depresses the spirit in singing. On the other hand, we should not deliberately use tunes which create an elevated emotional state that is not the product of the truth alive in our hearts by the Holy Spirit. What we should desire is simplicity and ease of singing that allows our emotions to have their appropriate outlet under the influence of the Word and the Spirit alone. The Reformers emphasized simplicity of melody

---

49. Iain Murray, *To Glorify and Enjoy God*, 190–191.

and rhythm for the ease of the congregation in singing.[50] When Calvin instituted congregational psalm singing in Geneva, "only the simplest kind of harmony was permitted."[51] Beza used tunes that were "generally one note to a syllable, rhythmically simple, at a medium pitch, and narrow in vocal range."[52] One of the main reasons for this simplicity of tunes was so that the people could consider the words they sing and the truth could have its proper effect upon their hearts.

Perhaps one safe monitor of whether our joy in singing is true spiritual joy is whether we are experiencing a corresponding level of joy under the preaching of the Word of God. We often find joy experienced under preaching in the New Testament (Acts 2:46, 13:48, 13:52; 1 Thess. 1:6). But if we experience in singing joy that is not present to a similar degree in the preaching, then we may have reason to suspect that our emotions have been manipulated by the music. The question should be asked of many who claim to experience such high levels of joy in the music of the modern church: Do they experience the same joy under the preaching of the Word?

2) In light of the above material concerning the harmful effects of musical instruments upon intelligent and spiritual worship, someone may wonder why God commanded instruments at all in the Old Testament. The answer is that the worship of the Temple was never all that God intended worship to be. It was never true spiritual worship in its purity and simplicity which was ultimately God's desire for His people. Though there were spiritual aspects to that worship, they were covered over by a mass of external and carnal ordinances, musical instruments being one of them. All these carnal ordinances were destined to be removed by the coming of Christ, who was to institute a new worship in "spirit and truth." It was the simple worship of the gospel that God ultimately desired

50. Douglass, 39, 42.
51. Rice, 22.
52. Douglas, 45.

to be in His church. This is the apostle's meaning in Heb. 9:10, where he refers to the "carnal ordinances, imposed on them until the time of reformation" (KJV).

John Owen comments in regard to the Temple worship,

> All the laws concerning these things were carnal, "carnal ordinances;" such as, for the matter, manner of performance, and end of them, were carnal. This being their nature, it evidently follows that they were instituted only for a time, and were so far from being able themselves to perfect the state of the church, as that they were not consistent with that perfect state of spiritual things which God would introduce, and had promised so to do.[53]

Musical instrumentation, and even unaccompanied tunes, can have the most powerful effects upon the human emotions. By a direct appeal to the emotions, they can lead the mind astray from the truth of the words being sung and undermine the purpose of Christian worship, which is always edification through the Word of Christ (Col. 3:16, 1 Cor. 14:26). It is in this subtle and seductive power that music presents its greatest danger to the intelligent worship of the gospel. True emotion should be present in Christian worship, but this emotion must be produced by the Word of God applied to our hearts by the Holy Spirit, not through the manipulative use of music. This danger is very real and has abundant testimony throughout history of the Christian church. Great care must be exercised even in the choice of tunes so that the emotions are not inordinately affected. The words must dominate the tune so that the edification of God's people remains foremost in the singing.

---

53. Owen, Vol. 22, 252.

Chapter IV

Arguments in Favor of Instrumental Music

IN this chapter we will consider various arguments often made in favor of the use of musical instruments in the worship of the church. The two most prominent arguments are those concerning "circumstances of worship" and the word *psalmos* in Eph. 5:19. It is important to note that the historical material presented in Chapter II is vital to an understanding of what follows. Various other arguments will be considered at the end of the chapter.

The 1689 Baptist Confession and "Circumstances of Worship"

All who hold to the regulative principle of worship agree that Christ has commanded certain elements in His worship, which are 1) reading of the Scriptures, 2) preaching and hearing the Word of God, 3) singing with grace in our hearts to the Lord, 4) prayer with thanksgiving, 5) the administration of the sacraments, and 6) almsgiving. These are the elements of worship commanded by Christ as the Head of the Church, and no man can add to or take away from them. But there are "circumstances" that surround these commanded elements such as the place and time of the meeting, the order of the commanded elements, the number of hymns, the length of the sermon, the particular times during the service at which the people stand or sit, the use of chairs if desired, a hymn book, etc. Such "circumstances of worship" are not bound by the Word of God, as are the commanded elements, but are left to be determined by the authority of each individual church. Many assume that the use of musical instruments falls into this category of "circumstances of worship." They argue that musical instruments are only an aid to the commanded element of singing and therefore their use is not bound by the regulative principle of worship. Those who hold this view often take their support from the 1689 London Baptist Confession of Faith, or the Westminster Confession of Faith, Chapter 1, Paragraph 6, which states, "that there are some circumstances concerning the worship of God, and government of the church, common to human actions and societies, which are to be ordered by the light of nature and Christian prudence, according to the general rules of the Word, which are always to be observed." We agree that there are such "circumstances" which are not part of the commanded elements and which must be ordered by the church, but we do not believe that musical instruments are among them for the following reasons:

1) The view that musical instruments fall into the category of "circumstances of worship" as found in the Confession clearly contradicts the convictions and the intentions of its authors. The writers of the Confession were among the Puritans who rejected the use of musical instruments in Christian worship. The historical evidence is conclusive. We have heard the words of George Gillespie, Samuel Rutherford, and Thomas Goodwin, as leaders among the Westminster Assembly. We have also heard Benjamin Keach and Hanserd Knollys as leaders among the Particular Baptists who signed the 1689 London Baptist Confession of Faith. All of these men were decidedly against the use of musical instruments in Christian worship. Here is perhaps the simplest and most convincing argument that the "circumstances" of the Confession cannot include musical instruments. To use their term to include musical

instruments is to misuse and contradict the intentions of the men who wrote our Confession.

Girardeau comments on the Westminster Confession and its authors,

> To take the ground, then, that in the single clause in regard to "circumstances concerning worship of God. . .," they meant to include instrumental music, is to maintain that in that one utterance they contradicted and subverted their whole doctrine on the subject. . . The thing is preposterous. It cannot for a moment be supposed. One might close the argument here. . . . Whatever the Assembly meant to include in the category of circumstances falling under the direction of the church, it is absolutely certain that it was not intended to embrace in it instrumental music.[1]

2) The view that musical instruments are a circumstance of worship violates the limitations of the Word of God concerning such circumstances. The church's power to order its "circumstances of worship" finds its biblical support in 1 Cor. 14, where Paul tells the church, "Let all things be done for edification" (v. 26) and, "Let all things be done decently and in order" (v. 40). In this chapter, Paul is dealing with various indecencies and disorders that had entered into the life of the church, and he gives the church power to correct them. In the Corinthian church, the extraordinary gift of tongues was being used without any interpretation, and it appears that this was sometimes being done by two or three together at the same time (v. 27). The result was utter confusion and disorder in the church. The people of the church were nothing more than "barbarians" to one another, and the church had the appearance of being a "mad" house to unbelievers who entered. The whole worship of the church was turned on its head and became a mass of chaos with no one knowing what was being said or done. If the Corinthian church

---

1. Girardeau, 138.

did not exercise discretionary power to establish decency and order, it would prove fatal to the purpose of its gathering, which was for worship and edification.

It was in this context, to guard itself against such fatal disorders, that the apostle gave this discretionary power, "Let all things be done decently and in order." This is the biblical definition of "circumstances," and the church's power extends to such disorders and nothing further. It cannot possibly be argued that the use of musical instruments falls into this category. No one can claim that musical instruments are necessary or that their absence will prove fatal to the order and the worship of the church. This is what James Bannerman means when he says, "'Let all things be done decently and in order,' was a rule giving power to the Church in common with every civil society to guard itself against abuses that might be common to both and fatal to both, but nothing further."[2] It becomes clear from the context in which the apostle gave discretionary power to the church to order its "circumstances" so that the use of musical instruments does not fall among them.

3) A circumstance must be something that does not directly affect the commanded elements of worship. The church has the power to maintain decency and order so as to carry out the commanded elements, but she has no power to directly influence or affect those elements. The discretionary power given by the apostle, "Let all things be done decently and in order," was never meant to extend to the commanded elements of worship. Once the church begins to make additions that have a direct influence or effect on the commanded elements, in even the slightest manner, she has transgressed a boundary that belongs only to Christ. The Lord Jesus has commanded singing with the voice in His church, and for the church to make any additions to this element, such as the use of musical instruments, is to push her authority beyond the boundary given to her. There are circumstances such as the time and

2. Bannerman, *The Church of Christ*, Vol. 1, 352.

place where the church meets, the use of chairs or not, etc., which have no direct influence upon the commanded elements. The use of musical instruments clearly does not fall within this category. Musical instruments do have a direct and immediate influence upon the commanded element of singing and therefore cannot be considered a legitimate circumstance. Bannerman states,

> The power which the apostle gives to regulate such matters is no power to enter within the proper field of Divine worship, and to add to, or alter, or regulate its rites or ceremonies and institutions. . . nor . . .to interfere to the smallest extent with the rites, and observances, and ceremonies which have been positively prescribed and regulated by the express directory found in Scripture for worship.[3]

4) A circumstance must be something necessary (or essential) to the performance of the commanded element of worship. In other words, the circumstance must be of such a nature that if it is not carried out the element of worship cannot be performed. The use of musical instruments clearly does not fall within this category. Singing and playing musical instruments are two separate actions that can exist independent of each other. Musical instruments are not necessary or essential to the act of singing and therefore do not fall within the category of "circumstances." To add musical instruments to singing would be an unnecessary and unwarranted addition to the commanded element.

This understanding of "circumstances" as being necessary or essential to the commanded elements was recognized by the old writers. In discussing this very issue of "circumstances" from the Westminster Confession, James Henley Thornwell recognizes that the church can add only those circumstances essential to the performance of an action and without which the action cannot be performed. Thornwell writes, "We must carefully distinguish

3. Ibid., 358–359.

between those circumstances which attend actions as actions—that is, without which the actions could not be—and those circumstances which, though not essential, are added as appendages. These last do not fall within the jurisdiction of the Church. She has no right to appoint them."[4]

John Owen recognized the distinction between a circumstance necessary for an action to be performed and unnecessary appendages imposed upon an action.

> There are also some things which some men call circumstances also, that no way belong of themselves to the actions whereof they are said to be circumstances, nor do attend them, but are imposed on them, or annexed unto them, by the arbitrary authority of those who take upon them to give order and rules in such cases. . . These are not circumstances attending the nature of the thing itself, but are arbitrarily superadded to the things that they are appointed to accompany.[5]

Some will say that musical instruments are necessary to singing with decency and propriety. If this is true, then we must accuse the church throughout the greater part of its existence of singing without decency and propriety. Girardeau writes,

> This argument is conclusive, unless it can be shown that instrumental music is a circumstance necessary to the performance of the action—singing of praise. A simple and complete answer to this is, that for a thousand years the church sang praise without instrumental accompaniment. How then can its necessity to the singing of praise be maintained? Can a circumstance be necessary to the performance of an act, when the act has been performed

---

4. James Henley Thornwell, *The Collected Writings of James Henley Thornwell*, (Edinburgh: The Banner of Truth Trust, reprinted 1986), Vol. 4, 247.
5. Owen, Vol. 15, 35–36.

without it, and is now continually, Sabbath after Sabbath, performed without it? To say that instrumental music assists in the performance of the act is to shift the issue. The question is not, Is it helpful? but, Is it necessary?[6]

5) A circumstance must be limited to those things undetermined by the Word of God. Once an issue is determined by the Scripture, the Scripture alone has authority over it, and it can no longer be regarded as a "circumstance. . . . to be ordered by the light of nature and Christian prudence."

For example, the time and place of the meeting, whether seating will be used or not, etc., are matters undetermined by the Scripture and can be ordered by the church as circumstances. But when we come to the issue of musical instruments in worship, we have seen that God has clearly brought them under His authority in the Old Testament. It was only by divine command that any instruments were used in the Temple. With the coming of Christ, the Temple worship has been abolished, and His silence in the New Testament regarding musical instruments is the equivalent of a prohibition. The Scripture has determined that musical instruments are under God's authority, and without further evidence from them, we have no right to remove them from His authority by calling them "circumstances" so that we may do as we please. George Gillespie, a leading member of the Westminster Assembly who surely knew the intention of the authors of the Confession, tells us that circumstances "must be such as are not determinable by Scripture."[7] Girardeau adds,

> The Westminster Assembly intended to teach that instrumental music was not one of the circumstances indeterminable by Scripture and committed to the discretion of the church. . . . Instrumental music cannot, without

6. Girardeau, 140.
7. Quoted in Bannerman, Vol. 1, 356.

violence to the Confession, be placed in the category of circumstances determinable by the church.[8]

6) The view that musical instruments are only a circumstance of worship violates the limitations of the Confession itself. The Confession limits circumstances to those things "common to human actions and societies." When other human societies gather, such as political, scientific, literary, military, and academic societies, they must have a time and place and other such circumstances necessary for their meetings. The question is: Are musical instruments a necessary circumstance of such human societies? Would we expect upon entering such societies to find musical instruments being played? The answer is clearly no. Musical instruments are not "common to human actions and societies," and, therefore, do not fall into the category of circumstances as described by the Confession.

Professor Girardeau states,

Time and place, costume and posture, sitting or standing, and the like, are circumstances common to all societies, and therefore pertain to the church as a society. But will it be seriously maintained that instrumental music is such a circumstance? Is it common to human societies? These questions answer themselves. As instrumental music is not a circumstance common to all societies, it is not one of the circumstances specified by the Confession of Faith. It is excluded by the term which it uses.[9]

7) In the last place, we should consider that some of the great theologians of the church have believed in circumstances of worship that should be ordered by the church, but these very same men condemned the use of musical instruments as being among those circumstances. John Calvin believed that there were circumstances

8. Girardeau, 154.
9. Ibid., 139.

of worship that God had not explicitly commanded and that were left to the authority of the church. Calvin writes,

> But as in external discipline and ceremonies He has not been pleased to prescribe every particular that we ought to observe (he foresaw that this depended on the nature of the times, and that one form would not suit all ages), in them we must have recourse to the general rules which he has given, employing them to test whatever the necessity of the Church may require to be enjoined for order and decency.[10]

Calvin sounds as if he were throwing the door open to such things as musical instruments in worship, "He has not been pleased to prescribe every particular. . . . He foresaw that this depended on the nature of the times. . . whatever the necessity of the Church may require." What better justification could the advocates of instrumental music find than such words as these? But as we have seen, Calvin vehemently condemned the use of musical instruments in Christian worship. Calvin writes, "They are not now to be used in public thanksgiving. . . but they are banished out of the churches."[11] There can be no doubt that while he recognized there are circumstances of worship, he did not intend musical instruments to be among them.

Thornwell clearly believed in "circumstances" that attend the commanded elements of the worship of God. Thornwell writes,

> In public worship, indeed in all commanded external actions, there are two elements—a fixed and a variable. The fixed element, involving the essence of the thing, is beyond the discretion of the Church. The variable, involving only the circumstances of the action, its separable accidents, may be changed, modified, or altered, according to the

10. Calvin, *Calvin's Institutes*, Book Four, Chap. X, 30.
11. Calvin, Vol. 5, 98.

exigencies of the case. The rules of social intercourse and
of grave assemblies in different countries vary. The Church
accommodates her arrangements so as not to revolt the
public sense of propriety. Where people recline at their
meals, she would administer the Lord's Supper to com-
municants in a reclining attitude. Where they sit, she would
change the mode.[12]

A modern Christian could easily assume that these words concerning the variables or circumstances in worship should refer to the use
of musical instruments. Thornwell's words contain the very same
argument that many use to bring them into worship today: "the
circumstances. . . may be changed, modified, altered, according to
the exigencies of the case. The rules. . . in different countries vary.
The Church accommodates her arrangements. . ." But we have seen
that Thornwell strongly opposed musical instruments in worship
and he would protest his words' being used to justify their use.

Dr. Cunningham, the principal of the Free Church College at
Edinburgh, recognized that there is flexibility in the application of
the regulative principle of worship:

The principle must be interpreted and explained in the
exercise of common sense. One obvious modification
of it is suggested in the first chapter of the Westminster
Confession, where it is acknowledged "that there are some
circumstances, concerning the worship of God and government of the Church, common to human actions and
societies, which are to be ordered by the light of nature
and Christian prudence, according to the general rules
of the Word, which are always to be observed." But even
this distinction between things and circumstances cannot
always be applied very certainly; that is, cases have occurred

12. Thornwell, 248.

in which there might be room for a difference of opinion. . .
differences of opinion may arise about details.[13]

James Bannerman also understood there were "circumstances" of
worship under the discretion of the church and writes, "In what
belongs to the circumstances of worship necessary to its being
dispensed with propriety, and so as to avoid confusion, the Church
has authority to regulate them as nature and reason prescribe."[14]
No better words could the advocates of musical instruments find
than those given by these men: the use of musical instruments
is just "the exercise of common sense," they are among those
"differences of opinion" and are needed for "propriety," and we
should be able to use them as "nature and reason prescribe." But
these men were Scottish Presbyterians who strongly rejected the
use of musical instruments in worship. While they believed that
there are circumstance of worship and legitimate differences in the
application of the regulative principle, they would never have agreed
that musical instruments are found among them. George Gillespie
and John Owen are also among those who recognize legitimate
"circumstances of worship" but who would have excluded musical
instruments from them.

Many have assumed in our day that musical instruments fall
into the category described in the Confession as "circumstances. . . .
common to human actions and societies. . . . to be ordered by the
light of nature and Christian prudence." But we conclude that this
position cannot be maintained for all of the above reasons. Musical
instruments do not fall within the limits of the Confession as being
"common to human actions and societies." They are not among
those things left undetermined by Scripture. Musical instruments
are not necessary or essential to the commanded act of singing,
and are therefore an addition imposed upon the element which the
church has no authority to add. And finally, to use this statement

13. Cunningham, 32.
14. Bannerman, *The Church of Christ*, Vol. 1, 352.

in the Confession to justify the use of musical instruments would be to contradict the intentions of its authors and the understanding of many of the great theologians of the church who have dealt with this matter of circumstances of worship.

The Greek Verb "Psallo" and the Noun "Psalmos" in Ephesians 5:19

Another argument often used in favor of musical instruments in worship comes from the use of the Greek noun *psalmos*, translated "psalm," and from its verb form "*psallo*," translated "making melody," both of which are used in Eph. 5:19, "speaking to one another in psalms and hymns and spiritual songs, singing and making melody with your heart to the Lord."

The noun *psalmos* is used six other times in the New Testament. Three times it refers to the book of Psalms (Luke 20:42, 24:44; Acts 1:20); once it refers to the second psalm (Acts 13:33); once to a sacred song, either inspired or uninspired in 1 Cor. 14:26; and once in Col. 3:16 where it is used in the same manner as in Eph. 5:19. The verb form *psallo* appears four other times in the New Testament: once in Rom. 15:9 and twice in 1 Cor. 14:15 where it is translated "sing;" once in James 5:13 where it is translated "sing praises."

An early meaning of the verb *psallo* was "to play on a stringed instrument, to play the harp."[15] The original meaning of the noun *psalmos* was "a striking, twanging, specifically, a striking the chords of a musical instrument."[16] A psalm (*psalmos*) is defined as a sacred song originally designed to be sung with instrumental accompaniment.[17] From this single word (the verb and its noun form) and these definitions, some have concluded that the New Testament warrants the use of musical instruments. It will be shown in the

15. Joseph Henry Thayer, *The New Thayer's Greek–English Lexicon of the New Testament*, (Peabody: Hendrickson Publishers, 1981), 675.
16. Ibid.
17. Charles Hodge, *A Commentary on Ephesians*, (Edinburgh: The Banner of Truth Trust, reprinted 1991), 221.

following arguments that this position cannot be maintained. In our discussion, we will consider the verb *psallo* first and the noun *psalmos* second.

In the first place, the verb *psallo* cannot be used to support the use of musical instruments in Christian worship for the following reasons:

1) The Greek verb *psallo*, translated "making melody" in Eph. 5:19, passed through very clear changes in its meaning throughout the centuries of the Old Testament and up to the time of the apostles. These changes in meaning are witnessed by numerous lexicographers, some of whom we will sample below. The earliest meaning of this verb, about 900 B.C., had nothing to do with musical instruments and is given by Thayer as "to rub, wipe; to handle, touch," and "to pluck off, pull out."[18] Later, about the 5th century B.C., this verb came to mean "to cause to vibrate by touching, to twang . . . to touch or strike the chord, to twang the strings of a musical instrument so that they gently vibrate; and absolutely, to play on a stringed instrument, to play the harp, etc."[19] Our concern, however, is not with the earlier meanings of this verb but with its meaning as it was used in the New Testament. The question is what did the apostle Paul mean when he used it? By the time of the Septuagint, which was written in the third century B.C., the most common use of *psallo* was "to sing to the music of the harp."[20] In other words, *psallo* no longer meant exclusively to play on a musical instrument, but it also included singing. This development in its meaning continued until the time of the New Testament, when it came to mean to sing with the voice exclusively without reference to instrumental accompaniment. Thayer states that its meaning is "in the New Testament, to sing a hymn, to celebrate the praises of God in song, James 5:13 (R.V. sing praise)."[21] The

18. Thayer, 675.
19. Ibid.
20. Ibid.
21. Ibid.

apostles used the verb *psallo* to refer to singing exclusively, and because of this it is never translated in the New Testament as "to play on a stringed instrument." In Eph. 5:19 it is used figuratively and translated as "making melody," and in every other passage in the New Testament it is translated as "singing" with no reference to musical instruments.

Other lexicographers confirm that by the time of the New Testament, this verb had come to refer exclusively to singing without musical accompaniment. W. E. Vine notes this change in meaning over the centuries, "*psallo*, primarily 'to twitch, to twang,' then, 'to play a stringed instrument with the fingers,' and hence, in the Sept., 'to sing with a harp, sing psalms,' denotes in the NT, 'to sing a hymn, sing praise,' in Eph. 5:19, 'making melody.'"[22] Harold K. Moulton, in *The Analytical Greek Lexicon Revised*, defines *psallo* as originally "to move by a touch, to twitch; to touch, strike the strings or chords of an instrument; absolutely, to play on a stringed instrument; to sing to music; in New Testament, to sing praises (Rom. 15:9, 1 Cor. 14:15, Eph. 5:19, et al)."[23] E. A. Sophocles, Professor of Greek at Harvard University for 38 years, states in his lexicon, which covers the period from 146 B.C. to A.D. 1100, that the only meaning of *psallo* is "to chant, sing religious hymns."[24] According to Sophocles, by 146 B.C. this verb had already lost its association with musical instruments and from that time forward referred only to the human voice. Other lexicographers could be multiplied who state the same things.[25]

---

22. W. E. Vine, Merrill F. Unger, William White, Jr., eds., *Vine's Complete Expository Dictionary of Old and New Testament Words*, (New York: Thomas Nelson Publishers, 1985), 402.

23. Harold K. Moulton, *The Analytical Greek Lexicon Revised*, (Grand Rapids: Zondervan Publishing House, 1978), 441.

24. E. A. Sophocles, *Greek Lexicon of the Roman and Byzantine Periods*, (Leipzig: Harvard University Press, 1914), 1178.

25. I will include the following lexicographers: (1) James Hope Moulton and George Milligan state the meaning of *psallo* as "'play on a harp,' but in the New Testament, as in James 5:13, 'sing a hymn.'" *The Vocabulary of the Greek Testament*, (London: Hodder and Stoughton, 1929), 697; (2) The *Theological Dictionary of the New Testament* gives the

The development of *psallo* over the centuries is very clear. Among its most ancient meanings was to play on a stringed instrument. By the time of the Septuagint, it meant to play on a stringed instrument along with singing. Finally, by the time of the New Testament, its association with musical instruments had faded away, and it referred exclusively to singing with the human voice. The lexicographers indicate that this was the meaning of the verb as the apostles used it. It is unsound exegesis to reach back into the etymology of a word and bring forward an antiquated meaning that is not the intention of the authors who used it. The argument that by the use of this verb Paul is authorizing the use of musical instruments in Christian worship cannot be sustained based upon

original meaning of this verb as "to touch, then it takes on the sense 'to pluck' (a string), and finally it means 'to play' (an instrument)." But by the time of the New Testament, in regard to Eph. 5:19, this dictionary states, "*psallontes* does not now denote literally playing on a stringed instrument." Gerhard Kittel and Gerhard Friedrich, eds., *Theological Dictionary of the New Testament*, abridged in one volume, (Grand Rapids: William B. Eerdmans Publishing Company, 1985), 1225–1226; (3) The ten-volume edition of the *Theological Dictionary of the New Testament* gives the original meaning of this verb as "'to touch,' then 'to pluck' the string . . . , 'to play a stringed instrument.'" In the Septuagint, the verb came to be associated with singing as well as playing a stringed instrument. When we come to the New Testament, its literal association with musical instruments has fallen away. In regard to Eph. 5:19, this dictionary states, "The literal sense 'by or with the playing of strings,' still found in the LXX, is now employed figuratively." Gerhard Friedrich, *Theological Dictionary of the New Testament*, 10 Vols., (Grand Rapids: William B. Eerdmans Publishing Company, 1985), Vol. 8, 490, 493–494, 499; (4) K.H. Bartels states that *psallo* in the New Testament means "to sing a spiritual or sacred song." Colin Brown, ed. *The New International Dictionary of New Testament Theology*, (Grand Rapids: Zondervan, 1929), Vol. 3, 671; (5) G. Abbot-Smith gives the meaning of *psallo* as "1. to pull, twitch, twang (as a bowstring, etc. . .), hence, 2. absolutely, (a) to play a stringed instrument with the fingers. . .; (b) later, to sing to a harp, sing psalms (LXX); in New Testament, to sing a hymn, sing praise." G. Abbot-Smith, *A Manual of Greek Lexicon of the New Testament*, (New York: Charles Scribner's Sons, 1952), 487; (6) Arndt and Gingrich comment on the meaning of *psallo* in Eph. 5:19, "The original meaning of *psallo* was 'pluck' or 'play' (a stringed instrument); this persisted at least to the time of Lucian. In the LXX, *psallo* frequently means 'sing,' whether to the accompaniment of a harp or (as usually) not (Ps. 7:18, 9:12, 107:4 al.). This process continued until *psallo* in Modern Greek means 'sing' exclusively; cf. *psaltas* means singer, chanter, with no reference to instrumental accompaniment. Although the NT does not voice opposition to instrumental music, in view of Christian resistance to mystery cults, as well as Pharisaic aversion to musical instruments in worship. . . . it is likely that some such sense as 'make melody' is best here. Those who favor 'play'. . . . may be relying too much on the earliest meaning of *psallo*."

the historical development of its meaning. When the apostle instructed believers to be "making melody with your hearts," he was referring to the sincere manner in which their hearts should be engaged while singing.

2) The meaning of *psallo* must ultimately be determined from its usage in the New Testament. When we consider how this verb is used in other passages of the New Testament, it becomes clear that its meaning must be "to sing" and not "to play on a stringed instrument." If we take the earlier meaning of *psallo*, "to play on a

Arndt and Gingrich agree with the other lexicographers that there was a "process" by which the verb *psallo* came to mean singing without musical instruments. By the time of the Septuagint, it was already undergoing this transition so that it "usually" referred to singing without the accompaniment of a harp. By the time of the New Testament, Arndt and Gingrich note that the historical facts of the rejection of musical instruments in both the synagogue ("Pharisaic aversion") and by the Church Fathers ("resistance to mystery cults") shed light on the meaning of this verb in the New Testament. Based upon these historical realities, they cannot support the view that its original meaning of "to play a stringed instrument" continues in the New Testament. The meaning has changed, and in Eph. 5:19, they translate the verb as "make melody" which avoids any necessary implication of the use of musical instruments. Those who would use it to refer to musical instruments "may be relying too much on the earliest meaning of *psallo*." While the conclusion of Arndt and Gingrich is consistent with the other lexicographers, they do mention Lucian of Samosata (ca. 125–180) as evidence that *psallo* continued to mean to "play a stringed instrument" into the 2nd century. Several things should be noted about this reference to Lucian: 1) It involves only a single quotation in Parasite 17 in which Lucian writes, "It is impossible to pipe (*aulein*) without a pipe or to strum (*psallein*) without a lyre or to ride with a horse." 2) The New Testament was written in Koine Greek (the common language of the people) while Lucian was educated and wrote in Pre-Biblical Attic Greek (the language of the literary and educated classes) from about 400 years before the apostle Paul. While *psallo* may have "persisted" in its earlier meaning in the Attic Greek, this does not prevent it from referring to singing exclusively in the Koine Greek of the New Testament. 3) Lucian was a satirist (or comedian) and not a Christian, and therefore, he was not writing as a biblical exegete to explain the meaning of *psallo* as used by the apostles. 4) Lucian often described the instrumental music of the pagan cultic rituals and this surely influenced his use of *psallo*. 5) Considering the author, his educational background, the purpose of his writing, and the fact that this involves a single quotation, it would be extremely tenuous to assume that this determines the meaning of the verb as used by the apostles in the New Testament. Arndt and Gingrich make it clear that Lucian does not alter the meaning of *psallo* in Eph 5:19 and it should be translated as "making melody." William F Arndt and F. Wilbur Gingrich, *A Greek–English Lexicon of the New Testament*, 2nd ed., (Chicago: The University of Chicago Press, 1979), 891; (7) It should be noted that in his shorter lexicon, F. Wilbur Gingrich gives the meaning of *psallo* for the New Testament only as "sing, sing praise." F. Wilbur Gingrich, *Shorter Lexicon of the Greek New Testament*, (Chicago: The University of Chicago Press, 1957), 238.

stringed instrument," and place it in the verses where this verb is used, we begin to see that this cannot be its New Testament meaning. For example, Eph. 5:19 becomes "speaking to one another in psalms and hymns and spiritual songs, singing and playing on a stringed instrument with your heart to the Lord." 1 Cor. 14:15 becomes "What is the outcome then? I shall pray with the spirit and I shall pray with the mind also; I shall play on a stringed instrument with the spirit and I shall play on a stringed instrument with the mind also." James 5:13 becomes "Is anyone among you suffering? Let him pray. Is anyone cheerful? Let him play on a stringed instrument." We see what absurdities this leads us into. We cannot imagine the apostles exhorting us "to play on a stringed instrument with the heart" and to "play on a stringed instrument with the spirit" and "with the mind." The use of this verb in other passages shows clearly that the only reasonable meaning of it in the New Testament is to sing, without reference to musical instruments. All English Bibles translate *psallo* in all other passages as "to sing." James 5:13 reads, "Is anyone cheerful? Let him sing praises," 1 Cor. 14:15 reads, "I will sing with the spirit and I shall sing with the mind also," and Rom 15:9 reads, "I will sing to Thy name."

3) It is an historic fact that the Church Fathers vehemently rejected the use of musical instruments in the worship of the church. These same men were also masters of the Greek language, many of them speaking and writing fluently in it, since it was the language of their day. Surely they knew the meaning of the verb *psallo* and its noun form *psalmos* better than any modern lexicographer. It is clear by their own example that they did not understand this word to refer to musical instruments, but to singing with the voice alone. If they had understood the word to include musical instruments, surely they would have brought them into the church. We cannot, nearly two thousand years later, question the understanding of the Church Fathers and give this word a meaning they never used. Jerome (ca. 340–420), a most distinguished Greek scholar who

translated the Greek New Testament into Latin, comments on Eph. 5:19,

> Let young men hear this, let those hear it who have the office of singing in the church, that they sing not with their voice, but with their heart to the Lord; not like tragedians, physically preparing their throat and mouth, that they may sing after the fashion of the theatre in the church. He that has but an ill voice, if he has good works, is a sweet singer before God.[26]

We should remember, as we have already seen in Chapter II, that Jerome rejected the use of musical instruments in worship, and in regard to our verse in question, the only "instrument" he mentions is the human voice.[27]

4) In Eph. 5:19, the participial form of the verb *psallo* retains the imperative character of the main verb, "be filled with the Spirit," in verse 18. This means that it carries the force of an apostolic command.[28] The duty involved is not a matter of liberty or personal preference, but one that must be performed. If this verb means "to play on a musical instrument," then Paul is commanding the use

26. Quoted in Bingham, Vol. 2, 685.

27. Quotations showing that the Church Fathers understood *psallo* to refer to vocal singing could be multiplied. When the classical meaning of *psallo* was preserved, it refered to musical instruments only in a metaphorical sense. See Everett Ferguson, *A Cappella Music in the Public Worship of the Church*, (Abilene, Texas: Biblical Research Press, 1972), 18–27.

28. It is a feature of New Testament Greek that a participle can be used as a imperative. While *psallo* is a participle, it carries the force of the imperative "be filled" from v18. This is why the lexicographers list it as "participle (imperative sense)." See Barbara & Timothy Friberg, *Analytical Greek New Testament*, (Grand Rapids: Baker Book House, 1975), 598. H. E. Dana & Julius R. Mantey, *A Manual of Grammar of the Greek New Testament*, (New York: MacMillan Publishing Co., Inc., 1955), 229. A. T. Robertson, *A Grammar of the Greek New Testament in the Light of Historical Research*, (Nashville: Broadman Press, 1934), 945–946. A similar example of this is found in the parallel passage, Col. 3:16, where "let dwell" is an imperative, while "teaching," "admonishing," and "singing" are participles. These participles are obviously used as imperatives in the context. Another example is found in Matt. 28:19–20. The only imperative is "make disciples." The verbs "Go," "baptizing," and "teaching" are all participles. But we would understand these participles in this context to carry the force of the imperative and therefore to be the equivalent of commands of Christ.

of musical instruments in the churches. And if the apostles commanded and used musical instruments in the churches, then it is certain this practice would have been carried on during the time of the Church Fathers. But this we know did not happen. Musical instruments had no place in Christian worship during the time of the Church Fathers. How can we account for this fact, other than to assume that the Church Fathers completely revolted against an apostolic command and practice? And this was done, not by one or two of them, but by all of them in unison, and without a single voice raised in their defense. The thought is preposterous. The only explanation for the absence of musical instruments in the days of the Church Fathers is that this verb was never understood, either by the apostles or by them, to be a command for the use of musical instruments.

5) If we accept that this verb means "to play on a musical instrument," let us consider what this would actually mean in the worship of the church. All three verbs in Eph 5:19, "speaking," "singing," and "making melody," are participles that carry the force of the imperative, as stated above. This means they are commands that must be performed. What is also clear is that all three commands are given to all believers in the church. The entire congregation must obey all three of these commands. This would mean that every believer must not only speak to one another in psalms, hymns, and spiritual songs, and sing, but every believer must also play on his musical instrument with his heart. There is not the slightest indication that only a select group within the church is to obey the last command to play on a musical instrument. Can we imagine what would happen if this command were actually carried out? Every member of the congregation would come to worship with his own musical instrument and play it as if Christian worship were some kind of an orchestral performance. Can we really envision such a scene taking place in an apostolic church? It cannot be. We can envision the entire congregation singing with their voices, but we

cannot possibly imagine the entire congregation playing on musical instruments.

6) A comparison should be made between Eph. 5:19 and its parallel passage in Col. 3:16. In these two passages the apostle is giving essentially the same exhortation concerning the singing of praise. The participle translated "singing" (*adontes*) in Eph. 5:19 is derived from the verb *ado*, which means to sing with the voice and has no reference to musical instruments. This same participle, "singing" (*adontes*), is also used in the parallel passage in Col. 3:16, "Let the Word of Christ richly dwell within you, with all wisdom teaching and admonishing one another with psalms and hymns and spiritual songs, singing with thankfulness in your hearts to God." It is clear that Paul commands the Colossians to use only their voice in singing with no reference to musical instruments. The verb *psallo* is not used in Col. 3:16, and this further confirms that its use in Eph. 5:19 has reference to singing alone. How could Paul command the Colossians to sing with the voice only and then command the Ephesians to sing with musical instruments? Did he command the use of musical instruments in some churches and not in others? It cannot be. Surely Paul meant to command all the churches to sing with the voice only.

7) The history of translation confirms that *psallo* in the New Testament means "to sing" without musical accompaniment. This verb has been translated "to sing" by the vast majority of translators since the Reformation.[29] In Eph. 5:19, *psallo* is an explanation of the verb "speaking" and another way in which the apostle expresses the command of "singing." When Paul says we are to be "singing and making melody with our hearts to the Lord," he means we are to sing not just outwardly with the lips, but inwardly, with the full faculties of our inner man. The meaning of the apostle clearly has reference to how Christians are to sing and not to the use of musical instruments.

29. Girardeau, 119.

8) We should understand that there may be a contrast, throughout this whole passage in Eph. 5:18–19, between the sensual worship of the pagan cults and the spiritual worship of Christians. The apostle is exhorting believers that when they gather, their enjoyment should not be in the fullness of wine, but in the fullness of the Spirit; their singing should not be in the profane drinking songs of the heathen, but in psalms, hymns, and spiritual songs; the accompaniment of their singing is not to be in the music of the lyre and other instruments as the pagans, but in the inward melody of the heart; and their praise is not to be directed to the false gods, but to the Lord Jesus Christ. It is a well known fact that the mystery cults used musical instruments in their worship. Paul is instructing believers that the contrast between Christian worship and that of the cults is to extend even to the use of musical instruments. They play on their instruments, but the believers are to make their melody in a different way, with their hearts.

9) If the verb *psallo* warrants musical instruments, then the Holy Spirit has entirely changed His method of authorizing their use in the New Testament. Throughout the Old Testament, the Spirit was clear and explicit in the musical instruments that He commanded in the Temple worship. He spoke abundantly and gave numerous examples of the use of instruments. If the Holy Spirit desires instruments in the church today, why does He not speak to us clearly? Why does He now communicate in such a veiled and concealed manner as in this verb *psallo*?

10) Finally, those who would argue that Eph. 5:19 warrants the use of musical instruments must acknowledge that their entire argument rests upon a single word of Scripture (*psallo*). They should also recognize that the issue they are dealing with is nothing less than the proper worship of God, perhaps the most crucial issue in the life of the Christian church. There is nothing about which we should be more certain than the will of God in His worship. The Bible itself warns us that to bring unauthorized things into God's

worship is a most dangerous venture. There should be a deep sense of fear and trembling as we handle this aspect of the life of the church; to base a practice in worship upon a single word of Scripture is most precarious and foolish. The scriptural arguments presented earlier in this book have clearly and convincingly demonstrated that musical instruments are to have no part in Christian worship. If these arguments have any weight at all, they cannot be overturned by a single word. No doctrine or principle of the Bible that rests upon numerous clear passages should ever be overturned by a single word. Those who believe that this word authorizes instruments should confirm their view with support from the rest of the New Testament. They are under a most solemn obligation to do so before they proceed with confidence. And when they search for such support, what do they find? They find none. There is no command nor any example of musical instruments ever being used in the apostolic churches. If this word really does authorize musical instruments, we should surely expect to find confirmation of it somewhere in the rest of the New Testament. And we do not. There can be no reasonable doubt, from all of the above arguments, that there is no support for musical instruments in Christian worship from the verb *psallo* in Eph. 5:19.

We come now to the noun *psalmos*, translated "psalm" in Eph. 5:19, "speaking to one another in psalms, hymns, and spiritual songs," and in Col. 3:16, "teaching and admonishing one another with psalms, hymns, and spiritual songs." From its original meaning, "the touch of the chords of a stringed instrument," some have concluded that instruments are warranted in Christian worship. This conclusion cannot be supported for the following reasons:

a) The noun *psalmos* underwent a similar etymological development over time as did its verb form, as noted above. Harold K. Moulton gives the meaning of the noun as an "impulse, touch, of the chords of a stringed instrument; in New Testament, a sacred song, psalm, 1 Cor. 14:26, Eph. 5:19."[30] The ancient meaning was "to touch the chords of a stringed instrument." But by the time of the New Testament, this sense has fallen away, and it refers only to "a sacred song, psalm," without reference to a musical instrument. The same process of development that took place in the meaning of the verb also took place in the meaning of this noun. While its original meaning had reference to musical instruments, by the time of the New Testament, it referred only to singing with the voice.

b) This etymological development of this noun is consistent with the historic facts, seen earlier in this book, that the psalms had been sung without musical accompaniment in the synagogues for hundreds of years before the New Testament. Over the centuries, this noun came to be associated with the practice that the Jews were most accustomed to, namely, the unaccompanied singing of the psalms each Sabbath in the synagogue. The worship of the Christian church was derived from the worship of the synagogue. So when the apostle commands Christians to sing psalms, he is telling them to continue the practice of the synagogues, which was the unaccompanied singing of psalms. To assume that Paul's command to sing psalms included the use of musical instruments would be to assume that he was reintroducing the Temple worship rather than continuing the synagogue worship. This violates all known historical facts and cannot possibly be his thought.

c) We would only remind the reader of the argument presented above concerning the Church Fathers. Surely these men, who were masters of the Greek language, knew the meaning of the noun *psalmos*. And yet it is clear, from their own example and writings, that they never understood it to refer to the use of musical instruments in Christian worship. The worship of the early church contained the singing of the lyrics of the Psalms without the musical instruments. The practice of the Church Fathers confirms the true meaning of the apostle in using this noun.

30. Harold K. Moulton, 441.

d) Some argue that, because the Psalms mention the use of musical instruments, the apostle's command in Eph. 5:19 to sing psalms warrants their use. If this is true, then everything else mentioned in the psalms must be brought into the church as well: "a two-edge sword in their hand, to execute vengeance on the nations" (Ps. 149:6), and they must "go to the altar of God" (Ps. 43:4), and "bind the festival sacrifice with cords to the horns of the altar" (Ps. 118:17), and "bow down toward Thy holy temple" (Ps. 138:2), etc. We recognize that, while the psalms should still be sung in the New Testament church, all of these ceremonial aspects of worship, including the musical instruments, are part of that Old Covenant temple worship that has passed away. It should also be noted that under the Old Covenant, God gave explicit commands both to sing psalms and use the instruments. Under the New Covenant, it is only the command to sing that continues.

e) Both Eph. 5:19 and Col. 3:16 command the use of "psalms, hymns, and spiritual songs." Those who would argue that the word "psalms" implies the use of musical instruments must admit that the words "hymns and spiritual songs" do not. The words "hymns and spiritual songs" carry no reference to musical instruments. This would bring about the inconsistency that some parts of the apostolic worship were accompanied by musical instruments and some were not.

We are forced to conclude, from all the above arguments, that Paul's use of the verb *psallo* and its noun *psalmos* in Eph 5:19 has no reference to musical instrumentation, but to the vocal singing of praise only.

Other Arguments in Favor of Instrumental Music

In this section we will briefly consider various other arguments often made in favor of instrumental music in the church.

1) Many say that musical instruments assist the devotion of the people of God. They are emotionally "uplifting," and they tend to stimulate and elevate religious affections.

There is an assumption in this argument that the emotions produced by musical instruments are true religious affections simply because they may be connected to religious words or a place of worship. This may not be the case at all. This argument does not take into account the deceptive effects music can have upon our emotions as a result of our fallen and depraved nature. It is a well-established fact of the psychology of music that musical instruments can have a most direct and powerful effect upon the human emotions apart from any truth in the mind. Such sensuous emotions in themselves are not to be trusted and are no valid argument for the use of instruments in the worship of God. The deceptive nature of the such temporary emotions has been more fully discussed in Chapter III.

In a similar argument, others say that musical instruments add an attractiveness to the services of the church and impart a dignity and elegance to Christian worship. But all such arguments are entirely subjective to each individual and are based upon human expediency and preference alone. Acceptable worship is to be determined not by what is deemed to enhance dignity and elegance, but by God's command alone. These arguments of assisting the devotion of the people and adding an attractiveness to the services of the church were the very same arguments used by the Roman Catholic church to bring in all its unbiblical ceremonies and rituals in the dark ages, including its musical instruments. These same arguments can be applied to Christian paintings and sculpture and all other forms of art. Such arguments will lead the church directly back to the sensuality of Medieval worship. We must look to the Word of God alone for our warrant for any aspect of worship. What is needed to assist our devotion and bring a true glory to our services is not the use of musical instruments, but the power of the Holy Spirit in our hearts as we use the commanded elements alone.

2) Others argue that musical instruments in public worship were approved by God under the Old Testament and, therefore, they must continue to be approved in the New Testament church as well. Once God has sanctioned musical instruments in His worship, it must remain the same for all time, and no man ever has the right to condemn them.

This argument fails to understand that God has the prerogative to alter His worship when He pleases and He has done so in the transition from the Old to the New Covenant. All would agree that many of God's positive commands under the Old Covenant such as circumcision, the Passover, the bloody sacrifices, and other ceremonies of the Temple have been abolished under the New Covenant. He has the right to alter these elements of His worship when He desires, and He has done so. God's right to alter His worship extends to the use of musical instruments as well. Musical instruments are one of those positive enactments of the Temple worship that He has been pleased to abolish with the coming of Christ. This argument was more fully addressed in Chapter I.

3) Another argument in favor of musical instruments is based on a supposed parallel between the Temple as a building of worship and musical instruments. The Temple was clearly commanded by God and under His authority as the building of worship in the Old Testament. In the New Testament, however, the building in which we worship has become a circumstance or a matter of liberty. The same holds in regard to musical instruments. They were commanded by God and under His authority in the Old Testament, but they are now a circumstance or a matter of liberty.

This argument is not valid for the following three reasons. First, we have explicit statements in the New Testament that the place of worship is now a matter of indifference. In John 4:21, Jesus said to the woman at the well, "Believe Me, an hour is coming when neither in this mountain, nor in Jerusalem, shall you worship the Father." (See also 1 Cor. 1:2 and 1 Tim. 2:8.) While the place of worship is explicitly stated to be a matter of indifference, we find no such statement in the New Testament regarding musical instruments. The argument that instruments are now a matter of indifference is an assumption that has no support in Scripture.

Second, there is not a true parallel between buildings and musical instruments in the New Testament. We find examples of various buildings being used as places of worship in the New Testament. The early church gathered in the portico of Solomon, houses, synagogues, and a school. It is clear by apostolic example that the meeting place is a matter of indifference. The apostles state no preference of one place over the other. If there were a parallel between buildings and musical instruments, then we would expect to find various instruments used in different churches just as various buildings were used. We would expect the apostles to use different instruments and to have no preference for one over the other. But we find no evidence to this effect. No musical instrument is ever used in the worship of any church. The fact that the building is now a matter of indifference cannot be used to justify the use of musical instruments.

Third, a true circumstance of worship can have no direct or immediate effect upon the commanded elements of worship. This is true of a building. The building of worship does not directly affect or alter the elements of worship. But the same cannot be said of musical instruments. They do have a direct and immediate effect on the element of singing and therefore cannot be considered a true circumstance of worship. The issue of circumstances of worship has been more thoroughly discussed earlier in this chapter. Once again, the silence of the New Testament on the use of any musical instrument can be interpreted only to mean that musical instruments were not present in the apostolic churches.

4) Some say that harps are used in the worship of heaven (Rev. 5:8, 14:2, 15:2) and therefore musical instruments should be used in the church as well.

This argument must be rejected for several reasons. First, Revelation's description of the worship of heaven with its harps also has a "Temple" (15:5) with "golden bowls full of incense" (5:8, 15:7) and a "golden altar which was before the throne" (8:3) and the twenty-four elders "clothed in white garments, and golden crowns on their heads" (4:4). The same argument that would bring the harps into the church must also bring all these other aspects of worship as well. The apostle John is speaking figuratively of heaven's worship under the image of the Old Testament Temple.

Second, the book of Revelation is filled with figurative language. We would not understand the harps to be literal instruments any more than we would understand that there are literal "bowls of the wrath of God" (16:1) or "a gold cup full of abominations" (17:4) and many other such things. We have seen in Chapter 2 that the Puritans often interpreted these harps as being the hearts of the saints filled with the Holy Spirit

Third, even if we believe that the harps are actual instruments in heaven, this argument still fails to justify their use in the church. What the saints may do in their perfectly sanctified state in heaven is no rule for what we may do in our state of remaining sin on earth. We must obey the clear commands and examples of His Word for worship on earth. If there are changes in the worship of heaven, we must wait for those to come. There are many things that will change with our entrance into heaven. For example, we will "neither marry nor be given in marriage." If this example of heaven becomes our rule on earth, then we would cease to exist after one generation.

5) Others claim that musical instruments are not forbidden in the New Testament and therefore their use is acceptable.

In the first place, this is a misunderstanding of the regulative principle of worship, which has been cherished by the Reformed churches throughout the centuries. The Bible affirms that worship is always a matter of what God commands, never a matter of what He has not forbidden. It is not enough to show that musical instrument are not forbidden; it must be shown that God has positively commanded them.

In the second place, we may compare this to the Lord's Supper. In the same way that He has not forbidden the use of musical instruments in the New Testament, He has not forbidden the eating of meat at His Supper. All would agree that to eat meat at the Lord's Supper would be a presumptuous addition to His will. But if we use the rule that what is not forbidden is acceptable, then to eat meat at the Lord's Supper must be admissible. Why should the addition of musical instruments in His worship be viewed any differently than the addition of eating of meat at His Supper? The argument that because musical instruments are not forbidden in the New Testament and, therefore, their use is acceptable must be dismissed.

6) Some have said that because music has been created by God and He has obviously made us creatures who take pleasure in music, it should be brought into worship.

The fact that God has created something can surely be no rule for what may be done in worship. There is an infinite number of other created things that we may take pleasure in and that may be good in themselves, but we would never bring them into worship. We can only imagine what chaos and confusion would result if our pleasures became the guide of worship. This argument is a direct denial of *sola scriptura* and the regulative principle of worship. The Scriptures, not the creation, are to be the final guide in matters of worship. God has declared His will for worship, not through natural revelation, but special revelation. Within special revelation He has restricted His worship to only what He commands. This is what our Confession states in Chapter 1, Paragraph 1, "The Holy Scripture is the only sufficient, certain, and infallible rule of all saving knowledge, faith and obedience, although the light of nature and the works of creation and providence do so far manifest the goodness, wisdom and power of God, as to leave men inexcusable, yet are they not sufficient to give that knowledge of God and his will which is necessary unto salvation." Chapter 1, Paragraph 6, states, "The whole counsel of God concerning all things necessary for his own glory, man's salvation, faith and life, is either expressly set down or necessarily contained in the Holy Scripture. . . ."

7) Others have argued that God has gifted His people with all kinds of talents, including musical gifts. We are not to squander our gifts but to use them for the glory of God, and, therefore, the use of musical instruments is justified in the church.

There are a great number of natural gifts that God has entrusted to His people, and every Christian should use them fully to God's glory, but this does not mean they are to be brought into public worship. It is not natural gifts such as those of husbandry and metalworking that are to be used in worship, but spiritual gifts for the edification of God's people. We have already noted that musical talents are not among those spiritual gifts given in the New Testament and therefore they are not to be a part of God's worship. Girardeau writes,

> This argument is also futile, because it proves too much. It would prove that the sculptor should install his statues in the sanctuary, that the painter should hang his pictures upon its walls, that the mechanic should contribute the products of his skill as "object lessons" for the elucidation of gospel truths, and that the architect should, by massive piles, express the greatness of God, and by the multiplicity of their minute details the manifoldness of his works. Avaunt! The argument is suited only to a Papist.[31]

31. Girardeau, 186.

We may add that this same reasoning has brought in the talents of drama and dancing, etc. into the modern church in our day and all these things should be rejected from the worship of God for the same reasons as stated above.

8) Some argue that musical instruments are among things indifferent, and therefore Christian liberty allows their use.

The Christian is surely free to use musical instruments in private, but once he enters into the presence of other brethren, he is bound by the higher law of love. The same argument that the apostle uses in the eating of meat sacrificed to idols should be applied to the use of musical instruments in worship. "Therefore, if food causes my brother to stumble, I will never eat meat again, so that I will not cause my brother to stumble" (1 Cor. 8:13). Christian love demands that we do not institute anything into worship unless it is explicitly commanded by God so as not to offend our brethren. Furthermore, Christian liberty in private is never a justification for bringing our own desires and preferences into the public worship of God. As we have stressed throughout this book, the regulative principle of worship demands that worship be according to God's commands alone, not according to our perceived liberty.

9) Some have rightly observed that the New Testament is less detailed in its prescriptions for worship than was the Old Testament. The advocates of musical instruments argue from this that the reason for God's silence in the New Testament regarding musical instruments is not that He prohibits them but that the gospel is universal and inclusive. Under the Old Testament, God dealt with one nation, one culture, and one people, and therefore He regulated the use of musical instruments. However, now under the gospel He deals with many nations, many cultures, and many peoples with many different musical styles and instruments, and therefore He has given men liberty to use whatever musical instruments they desire.

This argument assumes that God once held musical instruments under His authority in the Old Testament but now has completely relinquished His authority in the New Testament. This must be proven by clear and convincing evidence from the Scripture and not just assumed. We agree that there is less detailed prescription for worship in the New Testament. But we also believe that the elements of worship are clearly commanded and the lack of prescription can be no valid argument for making unwarranted additions or alterations, in the least degree, to those commanded elements.

Furthermore, we can only imagine the confusion and disorder in the worship of Christ as worshippers use every musical instrument from every nation and culture, from every musical style and preference, and from one generation to the next. When this resulting chaos is considered, it seems that this argument that Christ now deals with many nations, cultures, and musical styles is better suited for the exclusion of instruments. It seems reasonable that God commanded and controlled them under the Old Testament when He dealt with only one nation and culture, but now, to keep order in His worship, He has abolished them when He deals with many nations and cultures.

10) Some argue that a pitch-pipe, which is sometimes used by those who do not use musical instruments, is really an instrument itself. If a pitch-pipe can be used, why not any other musical instrument?

The differences between a pitch-pipe and a musical instrument are quite apparent and should hardly need to be mentioned. The pitch-pipe is used before the hymn actually begins, and it remains silent throughout the entire act of singing. Once the singing begins, not another sound is made from it, and only the human voice is heard. There can be no reasonable comparison between this and the use of a musical instrument that continues to sound its own notes with every note of singing throughout the entire hymn. If a musical instrument is used for the same purpose as the pitch-pipe, namely, to set the pitch with a single note before the hymn begins, we will have no objection to its use.

Every argument commonly used to justify the use of musical instruments in Christian worship has been effectively dismissed. There really is no reasoning that can be legitimately used to bring musical instruments into the worship of the Christian church.

I must confess that in all of the above discussion I have written as if the burden of proof were on those who would exclude the use of musical instruments from Christian worship. We must prove why they should be removed. However, a proper view of the regulative principle places the burden of proof upon those who would bring them in. The regulative principle demands that those who would bring additions or innovations into God's worship prove scriptural warrant for doing so. They must demonstrate, by clear and convincing evidence from the New Testament, that such a practice is appointed and required in worship. The reality is that, when the New Testament Scriptures are examined, there is no evidence that demands the use of musical instruments in worship.

The burden of proof becomes even greater when the advocates of musical instruments face the overwhelming testimony of church history, which we have already seen. They must come forward with convincing proof as to why we must overturn the convictions and practices of the greatest theologians whom Christ has ever given to His church. When all of this is honestly faced, the burden seems insurmountable.

Practical Considerations

In this section we will briefly consider several practical considerations that mitigate against the use of musical instruments.

1) It should be recognized that even the use of a single musical instrument in worship is a violation of the regulative principle of worship and can easily lead to the introduction of various other instruments along with it. There is a natural progression from the

use of a single instrument to the use of many. This has been clearly demonstrated in the history of the church, and this is the very problem being experienced in many modern churches today. The piano or the organ has been brought into worship and has been used for many years without any scriptural warrant. A biblical principle has been violated in its introduction, and the arbitrariness of its use eventually becomes evident to all. Everyone begins to realize that there is no scriptural authority in its use. Sooner or later, questions begin to arise as to why the piano is used to the exclusion of other instruments, and the elders find themselves with no convincing biblical answer. The use of a single instrument has been based upon human reasoning and preference alone, and the congregation knows it. It is only a matter of time before men will demand that this inconsistency be brought to its next logical step, which is the use of various other musical instruments. The piano is like the hole in the dike. The elders may be able to plug the hole for a while, but the next generation will come, the dike will break open, and the flood will come.

The Synod of Zeland during the Protestant Reformation recognized that even the smallest addition to pure worship, no matter how insignificant it may seem, has the power to grow and corrupt the entire worship. "Long experience hath taught us, that there is in such rites, a secret and wonderful power to defile, if but the smallest part thereof be admitted, it will not long continue so, but speedily like a gangrene it will begin to spread, while at last it corrupt the whole worship, having lost the simplicity and purity of Christ's institutions."[32]

2) If musical instruments are brought into worship, the question must be answered, which ones will be used? Under the Old Covenant, as we have seen, the specific musical instruments were commanded, and there could be no question as to which ones God approved. But now, without any divine command, whose

32. Synod of Zeland, 16.

instruments will prevail? The individual members of a church may have any number of different musical preferences and tastes. Whose musical instruments will be used in the worship? Will it be the violin and the cello of the older members or the guitars and drums of the young? Will it be the instruments of the elders or the deacons? Once the door has been opened, the preference of one instrument over another becomes entirely subjective, and no one can stand on any solid biblical authority. And without biblical authority, the church is ripe for division and strife over these matters. Some will trust in the rule of the elders and "Christian prudence" to settle these matters. But elder rule and Christian prudence will eventually not be able to hold back the pressure and demand for every kind of musical instrument.

Dabney comments on how musical instruments are often the source of conflicts within the church,

> Again, instruments in churches are integral parts of a system which is fruitful of choir quarrels and church feuds. How many pastoral relations have they helped to disrupt? They tend usually to choke congregational singing, and thus to rob the body of God's people of their God-given right to praise him in his sanctuary.[33]

3) To whatever extent musical instruments are used in public worship, the atmosphere of human performance will also enter with them. The one cannot be separated from the other. Once the atmosphere of human performance enters, the full communion of the soul must be lost to some degree. This is especially true of the instrumentalists. It is psychologically impossible for the instrumentalists to play their instruments and to be fully engaged in worship at the same time. They are distracted by their activity of playing their instruments. The question must be asked: What justification

---

33. Dabney, *Presbyterian Quarterly*, July 1889.

can be found for any group of believers to be so distracted from the worship of God in the New Testament?

Martyn Lloyd Jones comments on how music easily distracts from worship and leads to entertainment in the church, "Music in its various forms raises the whole problem of the element of entertainment insinuating itself and leading people to come to the services to listen to the music rather than to worship."[34]

34. Lloyd-Jones, 267

Chapter V

The True Glory of Gospel Worship

THE eyes of men have never seen a more glorious worship than that of Solomon's Temple: all the splendor of the Temple and its surrounding buildings; the interior made of the most intricately carved cedar wood overlaid with gold; all the gold and silver furnishings, the priests dressed in their bright blue and white garments with their shining breastplates, the smoke of the sacrifices ascending, the Levites with their silver trumpets, the choir singing, and all the musical instruments being played; many thousands gathered for the joyful scene; the *shekinah* glory descending and filling the house of the Lord so that the priests could not stand to minister. The outward sight and sounds of such a worship would stir all the human senses and emotions. Never have the eyes of men seen a more glorious and majestic worship than that of Solomon's Temple.

But as glorious as the Temple worship was, it has been replaced by a far more glorious worship in the gospel. We now enter, not into an earthly Temple but into the holy place, the heavenly sanctuary itself. We come not through the blood of bulls and goats, but through the blood of the Son of God Himself. We have full and free access into the presence of God through faith in Jesus Christ and by the Holy Spirit (Eph. 2:18). We have communion with all three Persons of the Trinity (2 Cor. 13:14). "We have a great high priest who has passed through the heavens," and we "draw near with confidence to the throne of grace" (Heb. 4:14–16). We are led into the throne room of God our Father as blood-washed souls by our elder brother, Jesus Christ. And when we worship, "we all with unveiled face, beholding as in a mirror the glory of the Lord, are being transformed into the same image from glory unto glory, just as from the Lord, the Spirit" (2 Cor. 3:18). There is nothing more glorious or excellent in all the earth than the worship of the gospel. No greater privilege could men on earth ever have than this worship. All the glory of Solomon's Temple simply fades away when compared with the glory of gospel worship. "For indeed what had glory, in this case has no glory because of the glory that surpasses it" (2 Cor. 3:10).

But all of this glory of gospel worship is spiritual and unseen. All of these glorious realities are invisible to human eyes and cannot be known by the outward senses. We enter into this worship, not by any outward sights or sounds, not by earthly or material aids, but only by faith in Jesus Christ and by the presence of the Holy Spirit. This glory is completely hidden and indiscernible to the natural minds of men; it cannot be seen with human eyes; it cannot be touched with human hands; it cannot be heard with human ears. The glory of gospel worship can be known and experienced only by those who have the Spirit. The excellence of our worship is found in the inward and spiritual realities that take place between our souls and the God of heaven.

The outward and carnal ordinances of the Temple worship are contrary to the inward and spiritual realities of gospel worship. Jesus and His apostles always saw a contrast between the earthly worship of the Temple and the spiritual worship of the gospel (John 4:21–23; 2 Cor. 3; Eph. 2:14–22). The two were inconsistent with each another. Owen says that they were "so inconsistent as that no man could at once serve two masters."[1] All that outward

---

1. Owen, Vol. 21, 429.

worship of the Temple, including its musical instruments, had to be abolished in order to bring in the spiritual worship of the gospel. All the musical instruments of the Temple can never add a single ounce to the glory of gospel worship. However pleasant musical instruments may seem to be, however appealing to the emotions and stirring to the affections, they can never add any power to the true spiritual worship of Christ. They may give a sensual pleasure and be attractive to the ears, they may leave us with very grand and elevated impressions, but they can never aid in drawing near by faith into the holy place of heaven. They cannot sanctify our hearts and bring us more under the power of the truth. They can never show us more of the glory of God in the face of Christ. Musical instruments, and all other sensual elements of worship, can only distract the mind from the true and heavenly objects of worship.

John Owen writes of additions to pure gospel worship, "Yea, and it cannot be but that attendance unto them and their effects must needs divert the mind from those proper spiritual actings of faith and grace which is its duty to attend unto."[2] The Puritan George Hutcheson recognized that even though the ordinances of the Temple worship were divinely given, they still took the minds of the people away from true worship.

> If being God's own ordinance, yet did take up worshippers so (through their own weakness) as ofttimes to keep them from minding this spiritual worship, how much more may it be expected that the more external pomp there be of men's devising there will be the less spiritual truth.[3]

The ordinances of New Testament worship are marked by their bare simplicity and plainness. It is this bare simplicity and plainness alone that is consistent with the spiritual nature of gospel worship. Spiritual worship, by its very nature, demands simplicity. Simplicity is the best friend to spiritual worship. To whatever extent men

2. Ibid., Vol. 15, 468.
3. Hutcheson, 65.

depart from the simplicity of gospel worship, they must also depart from its true spiritual nature. Any additions to the simplicity of gospel worship, including musical instruments, can tend only to undermine its spiritual ends.

Lloyd-Jones writes on the dangers of musical instruments in worship,

> I contend that we can lay it down as a fairly general rule that the greater the amount of attention that has been paid to this aspect of worship—namely the type of building, and the ceremonial, and the singing, and the music—the greater the emphasis on that, the less spirituality you are likely to have; and a lower spiritual temperature and spiritual understanding and desire can be expected.[4]

The unconverted man and much of the modern professing church will enter a gospel worship service containing nothing more than the simple ordinances of the New Testament and declare it all dull and uninteresting. They will have contempt upon its simplicity and plainness. But they disdain such services only because they cannot discern the glorious spiritual realities that are taking place by faith. We must not be troubled or perplexed by this. We must not be ashamed of the simplicity of our worship because carnal men cannot see its true glory. Men will never find the simplicity of gospel worship attractive apart from the power of the Holy Spirit in their hearts. "Men of unspiritual minds cannot delight in spiritual worship."[5]

It is when men fail to see the inward and spiritual glory of gospel worship that they forsake its simplicity and add outward devices to make it more attractive to the senses. This is what has happened throughout the history of the church and again in much of the modern church through its use of music. When the power of the Holy Spirit is no longer present in the simple ordinances

4. Lloyd-Jones, 267.
5. Owen, Vol. 21, 420.

of the gospel, men become discontent and substitute things that can be seen and touched and heard. Unable to discern the unseen realities of the Spirit, they cry out for something tangible to human sense. By the addition of musical instruments, they forsake the simplicity of true gospel worship. They may have made it more attractive to the emotions and the outward senses, but they have only diminished its true glory.

Owen writes,

> It is almost incredible how the vain mind of man is addicted unto an outward beauty and splendor in religious worship.[6] Hence the generality of men, although professing the Christian religion, are quickly weary of evangelical worship, and do find out endless inventions of their own, wherewith they are better satisfied, in their divine services. Therefore have they multiplied ceremonies, fond superstitions, and downright idolatries, which they prefer before the purity and simplicity of the worship of the gospel.[7]

Owen refers to the external splendor of Solomon's Temple "with all the most solemn musical instruments that David found out" and concludes, "yet that it was no way comparable to the beauty and glory of this spiritual worship of the New Testament, yea, had no glory in comparison of it."[8] He goes on to contrast the glory of the Temple worship with that of the church and states, "The Lord Jesus sees more beauty and glory in the weakest assemblies of his saints, . . .than ever was in all the worship of Solomon's Temple when it was in its glory."[9]

B. L. Manning writes,

> To call on the name of God, to claim the presence of the Son of God, if men truly know and mean what they

6. Ibid., Vol. 22, 22.
7. Ibid., Vol. 21, 420.
8. Ibid., Vol. 9, 81.
9. Ibid., 83.

are doing, is in itself an act so tremendous and so full of comfort that any sensuous or artistic heightening of the effect is not so much a painting of the lily as a varnishing of sunlight.[10]

What is the glory that Christ sees in His church when He looks down from heaven? He sees faith in the hearts of His people, faith in Himself as the Savior, and faith in the Word of God. He sees His people entering by faith into the presence of God and beholding His glory with unveiled face as in a mirror. He sees the work of His Spirit sanctifying their hearts by the Word. He sees Himself in the midst of His people by the Spirit. This is the invisible glory of His worship. And what can men on earth ever add to this glory by playing on their musical instruments?

10. B.L. Manning, in *Christian Worship*, quoted in Horton Davies, in *The Worship of the English Puritans,* (New York: Soli Deo Gloria Publications, 1997), 270.

CHAPTER VI

The Exalted Place of Singing in the Church

SINGING began in eternity with the songs of the angels as they sang of God's holiness and glory (Isa. 6; Job 38:7). It was God's intention in the creation that the voices of men and women on earth would join the chorus of the angels above. As the image bearers of God, we were made to contemplate God's glory and to sing His praise. One of the greatest distinctions between us and all other creatures is our power of speech. And there is no higher or more noble use of our tongues than to bless and honor the name of God in singing. "With it we bless our Lord and Father" (James 3:9). "I will bless the LORD at all times; His praise shall continually be in my mouth" (Ps. 34:1).

Singing is the natural, spontaneous expression of the wonder of the human soul in the contemplation of God. It is when we see the excellencies of God's character and the glory of His works that the soul becomes filled with a sense of awe that must find its natural expression in singing. The thought of God is to produce a joyful celebration in the heart that must flow upward and find its legitimate outlet in the lifting of the voice in praise. Mere words in normal, subdued speech would be insufficient and would place too much restraint upon the emotions. The heart would feel too confined and restricted. There must be a fuller opening of the soul and a freer venting of the affections, and this can come only through the voice in singing. In singing, the soul is carried upwards toward its object of praise in the living and true God. The Puritan John Wells writes,

> When we sing psalms, there is more than ordinary raising and lifting up of the soul, there is an elevation to a higher degree of communion with God. It is the soul's high mount toward heaven; the saint flies higher toward the element and sphere of joy.[1]

God made man so that His praise would be heard throughout the world. But the singing of God's praise, which is due to Him as Creator, was lost by the fall into sin. No longer is the natural man able to recognize the glory of God and joyfully sing His praise. The voices of adoration that were to join the angels above have been silenced by the power of sin. But what was lost by sin is now being restored to an even higher place by the salvation of Jesus Christ. Not only can we contemplate the glory of God in His Person and works, but we can also see His glory as manifested in the life and death of His Son, Jesus Christ. The truths set before us in the gospel should raise our souls to the highest possible level of praise. Those of us who have been redeemed from our sin by the blood of Jesus have all the more reason to sing to the glory of God.

All the various emotions of soul can be expressed in singing. We exult in the glory of God and we are filled with thankfulness for His goodness and kindness; we stand in awe of His power and have reverence before His judgments; we have faith and confidence when we meditate on His promises. In this present world, there are also songs of lamentation and grief over sin and its effects upon the world around us. All these various emotions can find their free and true expression in singing.

---

1. John Wells, "How We May Make Melody in Our Hearts to God in Singing of Psalms," in *Puritan Sermons,* Vol. 2, (Richard Owens Roberts Publishers: Wheaton, IL, 1981), 76.

But the main theme of singing for those who know salvation through Jesus Christ is joy and thankfulness. The New Testament tells us of the spiritual experiences of those who have come under the blessings of the gospel. The apostle Paul states that in our regeneration, "God, who said, 'Light shall shine out of darkness,' is the One who has shone in our hearts to give the light of the knowledge of the glory of God in the face of Christ" (2 Cor. 4:6). "The love of God has been poured out within our hearts through the Holy Spirit who was given to us" (Rom. 5:5). Paul prays, "that Christ may dwell in your hearts through faith; and that you, being rooted and grounded in love, may be able to comprehend with all the saints what is the breadth and length and height and depth, and to know the love of Christ which surpasses knowledge, that you may be filled up to all the fullness of God" (Eph. 3:17–19). And Peter writes, "though you have not seen Him, you love Him, and though you do not see Him now, but believe in Him, you greatly rejoice with joy inexpressible and full of glory" (1 Pet. 1:8). We do not always live in the felt experience of these realities, but these are true Christian experiences and they should be present in the life of every believer to one extent or another. When they are, they should be expressed in joyful singing. The soul pours out its affection, and the voice cannot be imprisoned.

The psalmist often declared how the joyful emotions of his soul had to find their expression in the singing of praise. "My soul is satisfied as with marrow and fatness, And my mouth offers praises with joyful lips" (Ps. 63:5), "My heart is steadfast, O God; I will sing, I will sing praises, even with my soul" (Ps. 108:1). If the psalmist had such joy in singing in a day of limited revelation and restrained influences of the Spirit, how much more joy should we have under the light of Christ in the gospel and the fullness of the Spirit's grace in the New Covenant!

There are five ways in which the Lord Jesus has exalted the ordinance of singing among His people:

1) By His Own Example. After completing His Upper Room discourse and offering His high priestly prayer in John 17, Jesus sang a hymn with His disciples. Matthew records, "After singing a hymn, they went out to the Mount of Olives" (Matt. 26:30). It is most likely that Jesus and His disciples sang what was called "the great Hallel," comprised of Psalms 115 to 118, as this was the Jewish custom at the paschal meal. These Psalms are hymns of praise, thanksgiving, and trust in God. It was fitting that the Lord Jesus should sing such hymns to strengthen and encourage His heart before the sufferings of the cross. But our Lord no doubt also sang with joy and thanksgiving as He viewed the glory that was set before Him (John 16:28, 17:1). What a remarkable scene it must have been to see incarnate deity lifting His voice in praise with His small band of disciples. A higher honor could not be placed upon the ordinance of singing than for the Son of God Himself to come down from heaven and bless it by His own example. One of the most exalted purposes of our existence is here seen in the perfect Man, Jesus Christ. In all our singing we should be conscious that we are following in the ways of our Savior.

2) By His Singing With Us in the Church. In Rom. 15, Paul exhorts the church at Rome, made up of Jews and Gentiles, to live in peace and unity. This peace and unity was to be manifested in their singing of praise together, "so that with one accord you may with one voice glorify the God and Father of our Lord Jesus Christ" (v. 6). In verses 9 through 12, the apostle quotes various Old Testament passages to prove that it had always been God's plan to bring salvation to the Gentiles. But what is striking about these passages is that they are focused on the act of singing. In other words, Paul not only proves that salvation would go to the Gentiles, he also shows what its manifestation would be among them. It would be in their joyful singing. For the first time since the creation, the singing of praise will rise to God from all the nations of the earth. "Rejoice, O Gentiles, with His people, And again, Praise the Lord

all you Gentiles, And let all the peoples praise Him" (vv. 10–11). This is the glory of the church that the prophets looked forward to, that men from every tribe and tongue and nation would glorify God in their singing.

But when we look at this passage more closely, Paul tells us a most astonishing truth in verse 9. Quoting from Ps. 18:49, he tells us that it was Christ who spoke through David, "Therefore I will give praise to Thee among the Gentiles, And I will sing to Thy name." Jesus prophesied not only that His salvation would spread to the Gentiles, but that when it did, He Himself would actually be among them, singing the praises of God. The Lord Jesus has promised His presence by His Spirit to all His churches, "For where two or three have gathered together in My name, there I am in their midst" (Matt. 18:20). Here we see one of His great works among His churches, that He is present with them to sing God's praises. When we stand to sing in the church, we are not alone. The Lord Jesus is present and is singing with us and through us. He desires His heavenly Father to be praised among all the nations of the earth, and we become His mouth pieces by which He sings the glory of God. No higher glory could be placed upon the singing of the church than to have Christ present, singing the praises of God through us. "Therefore I will give praise to Thee among the Gentiles, And I will sing to Thy name."

We find the same truth in Heb. 2:10–12. Jesus is the sanctifier of His people, and because He has sanctified us, He is not ashamed to call us His brethren. He was not ashamed to call us His brethren in His incarnation and in His death upon the cross. He is still not ashamed to call us His brethren now that He is exalted to the right hand of God. When we come to worship, Christ condescends to meet with us by His Spirit. He takes us by the hand and ushers us into the presence of God. He confesses before the Father that we are His brethren, purchased and sanctified by His own blood. And when He is present among us, we find one of His great works, "I will declare Thy name unto my brethren, in the midst of the church will I sing praise unto Thee (v. 12, KJV)." Once again, it is Christ Himself who is present to sing the Father's praise in His church. This quotation is from Ps. 22:22, and its context in that psalm is of special importance. The entire psalm is Messianic, and the first section describes the humiliation and the sufferings of Christ on the cross. Suddenly, at verse 22 the psalm takes a dramatic change in tone and begins to celebrate the victories of Christ over His enemies. Jesus has passed through His death and sufferings and has now entered into His triumph. It is the ascended and exalted Christ who speaks, and it is as if singing the praise of His Father through His church is the first work He desires to do as He takes His place on the throne of heaven. This is part of the joy that was set before Him, "In the midst of the church will I sing praise unto Thee."

3) By Making Singing a Teaching Ministry. We see both the high demands placed upon us and the benefits of singing in Paul's words in Col. 3:16, "Let the word of Christ richly dwell within you, with all wisdom teaching and admonishing one another with psalms and hymns and spiritual songs, singing with thankfulness in your hearts to God." The first thing the apostle commands is that the Word of Christ must richly dwell within us, ruling over our minds and hearts. Apart from this duty, singing cannot be what it ought to be. Singing must rise from the Word of Christ, and the solid theological content of that Word must be reflected in the psalms, and hymns, and spiritual songs that we sing. When this takes place, our singing actually becomes a "teaching and admonishing" ministry of the church. In Col. 1:28, the apostle speaks of his own "teaching and admonishing" ministry. Here he uses the same words to describe the "teaching and admonishing" ministry of the entire church through its singing. Just as there is teaching and admonishing in the preaching, so there is teaching and admonishing in the singing.

Singing is not a secondary or inconsequential ordinance of worship that carries no edifying benefit in itself. Christ has given singing a most vital role in the instruction of His church. It is a ministry that He has entrusted to the entire congregation. Whenever we stand to sing, we must be conscious that we are fulfilling a teaching ministry of the Lord Jesus to His church. We are teaching and admonishing ourselves and our brethren by the Word of Christ that we sing.

We should not underestimate the doctrinal influence singing will have on believers. Throughout history men have recognized the tremendous impact singing can have on the theology of the church. The hymns we sing can have such power in teaching that they can actually mold the theology of the church. Albert Barnes comments,

> He who is permitted to make the hymns of a church need care little who preaches, or who makes the creed. He will more effectually mold the sentiments of a church than they who preach or make creeds or confessions. Hence, it is indispensable, in order to the preservation of the truth, that the sacred songs of the church should be imbued with sound evangelical sentiment.[2]

4) By the Power He has Sent Upon His Singing People. The Lord shows the honor He has placed upon this ordinance by His response to His people when they sing. In 2 Chron. 20, the nation of Judah is threatened with invasion by three enemy armies. King Jehoshaphat gathers the people for fasting and prayer. He states the nation's helplessness before the invaders, "O our God, wilt Thou not judge them? For we are powerless before this great multitude who are coming against us; nor do we know what to do, but our eyes are on Thee" (v. 12). The Spirit of the Lord then comes upon the prophet Jahaziel, who promises Judah victory the following

---

2. Barnes, Vol. 12, 279.

day. On the next morning, when Jehoshaphat sends out his army, he appoints singers to go before them, saying, "Give thanks to the Lord, for His lovingkindness is everlasting" (v. 21). Rather than ensuring that his army is equipped with the best of weaponry, Jehoshaphat is concerned that they go out with faith and that God is honored by the singing of praise. No stranger advance of an army into battle has ever been seen. As they enter the field of conflict, we read, "When they began singing and praising, the Lord set ambushes against the sons of Ammon, Moab and Mount Sier, who had come against Judah; so they were routed" (v. 22). There is an immediate connection between their singing and their deliverance. It is when the voices of the singers ascend to heaven that the power of God comes down and gives them the great victory.

We find a similar event in the New Testament. In Acts 16, Paul and Silas are arrested in Philippi and thrown into the inner prison with their feet fastened in stocks. They follow the example of the apostles on a previous occasion, "rejoicing that they had been considered worthy to suffer shame for His name" (Acts 5:41). When they begin to express this joy in the singing of hymns, we see what happens: "But about midnight Paul and Silas were praying and singing hymns of praise to God, and the prisoners were listening to them; and suddenly there came a great earthquake, so that the foundations of the prison house were shaken; and immediately all the doors were opened, and everyone's chains were unfastened" (v. 25–26).

On both of these occasions, it is when the singing ascends into God's ears that He sends down His power of deliverance. We see the peculiar dignity He has placed upon this ordinance. The singing of His praise is something in which the Lord takes special delight and pleasure. At times, He responds with mighty works of His power when He hears the singing of His people on earth.

5) By Making Singing a Foretaste of Heaven. The worship of heaven is filled with songs of praise for salvation, "And they sang

the song of Moses, the bond-servant of God, and the song of the Lamb" (Rev. 15:3). The apostle tells us that the church on earth has already entered into the worship of heaven, "You have come to Mount Zion and to the city of the living God, the heavenly Jerusalem, and to myriads of angels. . . . and to God, the Judge of all, and to the spirits of righteous men made perfect, and to Jesus, the mediator of a new covenant" (Heb. 12:22–24). What higher privilege and blessing could belong to men on earth than to be part of the worship of heaven? The joyful singing of heaven should be reflected in the joyful singing of the church on earth. We are not yet in heaven, and so there are psalms of lamentation and hymns of repentance that must still be sung here below. But surely, in light of the great salvation that Jesus Christ has accomplished for us, the overall characteristic of the Christian singing should be joy and thanksgiving (Heb. 13:15).

It is in singing that our worship on earth comes closest to that of heaven. We enter into the work of angels. John Wells expressed the Puritan view of singing when he wrote, "There is not a great resemblance of heaven upon earth than a company of God's people singing a psalm together."[3] "In singing of psalms the gracious heart takes wings and mounts up to God to join with the celestial choir."[4] Singing is the only ordinance of the church that shall continue for eternity in heaven. When we see Him face to face, preaching, prayer, and the sacraments shall all be done away with. But singing is an eternal ordinance and shall continue forever. Our singing now is just the tuning of our hearts and the beginning of our singing the everlasting songs of heaven.

All that we have considered above should encourage us to make our singing all that it ought to be. The Lord Jesus has not only commanded us to sing, but He has exalted this ordinance to a most noble place in the worship of His church. We are under the

3. *Puritan Sermons*, Vol. 2, 76.
4. Ibid., 73.

highest obligations to give Him the singing He so earnestly desires. True singing is a labor that involves the exertion of spiritual energy on the part of every member of the congregation. Indolence and carelessness is unacceptable, and we should spare no pain to insure that Christ is honored in His ordinance.

Singing involves both the inward realities of our hearts and the outward use of our voices in singing. In the first place, we should consider our hearts. Paul commands us in Eph. 5:18, "And do not get drunk with wine, for that is dissipation, but be filled with the Spirit." It is the ongoing duty of every Christian to be continuously living under the grace and power of the Holy Spirit. It is remarkable that just after commanding us to be "filled with the Spirit," the very first thing the apostle mentions is singing, "speaking to one another in psalms and hymns and spiritual songs, singing and making melody in your hearts to the Lord" (v. 19). There is an immediate connection between the two. It is as if the first effect of the Spirit's work in our hearts is singing. True spiritual singing begins with a "melody in the heart" that rises to Christ. It must be a melody of faith and love to God and a melody of joy and purity and fervency. There can be no such melody without our hearts' being filled with the Spirit. If our words are only outward on our lips and do not rise from the melody of our hearts, then we fall under our Lord's condemnation of hypocrisy, "this people honors Me with their lips, but their hearts are far away from Me" (Matt. 15:8).

Singing is not something we can do in our own strength. We must see our complete dependence upon the Spirit. No ordinance of worship has life in itself without the power of the Spirit. Jesus said, "It is the Spirit who gives life; the flesh profits nothing" (John 6:63). We expect the preaching and prayers of the church to be done in the power of the Spirit. We should expect nothing less with singing. We often pray for the presence of the Spirit in the preaching of the word. We should pray for the presence of the Spirit in the singing as well. Without the aid of the Holy Spirit, singing will never accomplish the exalted purposes Christ intends. This places the highest demands upon every member, and this involves the labor of prayer. Every member must earnestly pray for the presence of the Holy Spirit before worship. And every member must come "filled with the Spirit" with a melody in his heart rising upward to the Lord. Only then will singing be what Christ desires. It is when we gather with other believers who are also filled with the Spirit that there is a mutual stirring up of one another in the singing of praise. Each believer brings the coals of his own heart and builds the spiritual fire of the church. So pleasant was the corporate singing of the church to the Puritans that Thomas Manton wrote,

> All the pleasures of the carnal life are not comparable to it. Surely, if there be anything pleasant in the world to a gracious heart, it is the praises of God that flow from a believing and loving soul. . . The unanimous conjunction of such souls in praising God in their assemblies is the heaven that we have upon earth.[5]

Singing involves, in the second place, the outward use of the voice (Heb. 13:15). We have in our voices the most wonderful God-given instrument on earth, and yet most of us are unfamiliar with even the basic principles of its use. Singing is almost a lost art in our generation. In many modern evangelical churches, great attention is paid to the skillful use of musical instruments, while the art of singing is completely neglected. If Christ is to be honored in our praise, we must not be insensitive to the aesthetic beauty of our singing. "Whatever your hand finds to do, verily, do it with all your might" (Eccl. 9:10). Those who have never learned the fundamentals of proper singing should seriously consider making such an effort. We learn how to use our physical bodies to perform almost every other task. We learn how to use our feet to walk and our hand to write and our eyes to read. We learn various sports and

5. Manton, Vol. 19, 414.

other skills that require physical dexterity, and we are often willing to do so at great pains. But far too often we fail to make any serious effort in learning how to perform one of the highest purposes for which we were created and saved, to sing God's praise.

If singing is the noble work we have seen it to be, then this exhortation applies to all believers, whether they use a musical instrument in worship or not. It is the singing of the human voice that Christ desires from His church. Is not the singing in many churches so poor because we have become dependent upon the musical instruments? We fail to cultivate our singing as we should and engage in it with all of our hearts because the instruments have made such labor unnecessary. Rather than aiding our singing, as many claim they do, musical instruments have become the mask that conceals our spiritual lethargy and our inability to sing. The use of instruments is often a positive hindrance to the development of singing skills.

Some believe that without musical instruments worship will be "dreary, dry, and joyless." Rather than being a justification for the use of instruments, such statements expose the deficiencies of our singing. Take away musical instruments, and the deadness and dreariness of the singing will be seen for what it truly is. And if our singing is dead and dreary, is the use of musical instruments really the way to resolve this problem? Should we not deal with the problem at its root, which is our lack of spiritual zeal and ability to sing?

Let us labor that in His church Christ may have the singing of human voices that He desires, both inwardly and outwardly. Let us take whatever pains necessary to insure that singing truly is the exalted ordinance Christ intends. May He be pleased to fill us with the Spirit and be present in our worship to sing the praise of the Father through us.

Chapter VII

Conclusion

WE must always remember that the God we worship in the church is a God of holiness. He is "sitting on a throne, lofty and exalted," and He is a God who regards the worship of His creatures as a most serious and solemn matter. God alone has the right to determine what is pleasing to Him in His worship. He alone has the wisdom to know by what elements He is glorified and His people edified and sanctified. He has not left sinful man in the darkness and ignorance of his own mind as to what He requires in worship. He has given light and truth in the Scripture.

The regulation of God's worship according to His Word is one of the greatest tasks of the Christian church. It is a matter of the highest importance. Great care must be taken in all we do in worship. For man to bring his own inventions into the church is false worship and idolatry. Dangers abound, and eternal consequences lie before us if mistakes are made in this area of the church's life. False worship brings God's judgment (Lev. 10:1–3), and the apostle warns us that idolaters shall not inherit the kingdom of God (Gal. 5:20–21).

We have seen that every aspect of God's worship throughout the Old Covenant was under divine command, even in regard to the use of musical instruments. No musical instrument was ever to be used in the public worship of God apart from an explicit divine command. The regulative principle of worship applies to musical instruments just as it does to every other aspect of God's worship. Even the specific instruments to be used were commanded by Him, and gifts of the Holy Spirit were given to men for their invention. Just as all the furnishings and utensils of the Tabernacle and Temple worship were sanctified and set apart for God's worship, so also were the musical instruments.

We have seen from the Old Testament Scripture that God has established His authority over musical instruments in public worship. This principle has been clearly set forth: by explicit divine commands through which alone musical instruments were introduced into worship; by numerous examples of the men of God looking only to His command for their use in worship; and by God's giving gifts of the Spirit for their invention. In all these ways, the Lord has made His mind known, that musical instruments are under His authority in public worship. Those who assume that they are a matter of liberty have adopted a view that is contrary to the Scripture and finds no support in the Word of God. Those who believe that God no longer holds musical instruments under His authority today must prove their case from the Scripture. They must demonstrate from the New Testament that He has relinquished His control and given muscial instruments over to the liberty of men to use them as they please in His worship. Apart from clear and convincing evidence, we must leave them where He has placed them, under His control.

The issue before us is nothing less than a matter of *sola scriptura*. Will we look to the Scripture alone to govern our thinking in regard to musical instruments in worship, or will we look to human reasoning? Will we leave this issue where God has left it, or will we add our own thoughts to His Word? The principle of *sola scriptura* demands that once God has made His mind known on any subject in the Scripture, we have no right to think otherwise apart from further evidence from those Scriptures. Once the truth has been established that He has placed musical instruments under His control, without further light from the Scripture we have no right to alter this perspective.

When we come to the New Testament, we see that the Temple worship in all of its outward ceremonies and rituals is completely abolished by the coming of Christ. We can no longer look to the ceremonies or rituals of the Temple for any of the elements of worship in the church. We must look to Christ and His apostles in the New Testament Scripture alone. With musical instruments continuing under His authority, we see that Christ has issued no command, given no example, and provided no indication whatsoever, that He desires them to be used in His worship. The silence of Christ in the New Testament in regard to the use of musical instruments is the expression of His will that they are to have no place in His church. If it had been His mind to institute musical instruments in gospel worship, He surely would have given the command, just as He had done in the Temple. The elements of worship commanded in the gospel are the reading and preaching of the Word, prayer, vocal singing, the sacraments, and the giving of alms.

We must reaffirm our commitment to the regulative principle of worship. This principle must be used with Christian prudence, wisdom, and toleration. While we must hold firmly to it, we must also understand that legitimate differences will exist among churches with respect to its specific application. Men who hold equally to this principle will differ in the arrangement or implementation of the details and legitimate circumstances of worship. When such differences exist, we must avoid the arrogance which believes that those who differ in circumstances are violating the regulative principle.

While we should allow for differences in the circumstances of worship, we cannot see how the use of musical instruments is among them. If the Word of God alone is our guide in this matter, we cannot escape the conclusion that musical instruments in Christian worship are a violation of the regulative principle. To bring them into the church is to transgress the authority of Christ in His worship.

In addition to the theological arguments regarding the regulative principle, we have also seen abundant historical evidence confirming a no-instrument position in Christian worship. We should remember the two historical facts that provide a most powerful aid in interpreting the silence of the New Testament on musical instruments. First, the worship of the early church was derived, not from the Temple, but from the worship of the Jewish synagogue, which was unaccompanied in the singing of psalms. Second, the post-apostolic church rejected the use of musical instruments in worship for many centuries. These historic realities, both immediately before and after the time of the apostles, are convincing evidence that the silence of the New Testament must be interpreted to mean that musical instruments had no place in the worship of the apostolic church. Should we not follow the example of the apostles and the churches of their day? If musical instruments were not present in the apostolic church, then why should they be present in the church of the 21st century?

We have also seen the overwhelming testimony throughout the history of the Christian church. The Church Fathers were unanimous and vehement in their rejection of musical instruments in worship. For well over a thousand years, musical instruments were virtually unknown in the worship of the church. It was only during the dark age of Roman Catholicism, in the 14th and 15th centuries, that they became more prominent. One of the great works of the Protestant Reformation was to banish their use from worship. And this policy was continued by the English and American Puritans, the Presbyterian and Baptist churches of Ireland, Scotland, and America, and many others, for centuries following the Reformation. The greatest theologians throughout the history of the church have been convinced that musical instruments are to have no place in Christian worship. What can we say to this massive evidence from church history on this issue? Do we believe that we have more light than did the Reformers and the Puritans and so many others who have followed in their steps? Are we willing to oppose the collective testimony of the brightest lights that Christ has ever given to His church?

We have also seen the effects of musical instruments over the human emotions and how they can easily undermine the intelligent worship of the gospel. One of the central purposes of Christian worship, which is edification, is threatened by their use. We have seen that this danger is very real, and we have heard the strong warnings of the church throughout its history in this regard. Why would any church be willing to face such dangers to true worship for the sake of some passing pleasure created by musical instruments? What possible benefits can they bring that make them worthy of such a great risk?

We bring all of this together—the theological arguments from the Scripture concerning the regulative principle, the abundant historical evidence of the rejection of musical instruments by the church, and the testimony of their harmful effects upon gospel worship — and we ask the reader: what other conclusion can we come to than that musical instruments should have no place in Christian worship? Can clearer and more convincing light from the Word of God be presented to overturn the scriptural arguments before us? Can biblical evidence be presented to convince us to abandon the convictions of our Reformed heritage and those of such vast segments of the Christian church throughout its history?

We have seen that a no-instrument position has been the classic Reformed practice throughout the centuries. This historical evidence is a challenge to us, as Reformed Christians today, to reconsider the use of even a single musical instrument such as the piano in worship. Do we really have any scriptural authority for its use? Have we come to accept a man-made tradition that is inconsistent with the regulative principle of worship and with our Reformed heritage? And finally, whatever perceived benefit it may bring, does it really make our worship more pleasing in the eyes of Christ, and is it worth the risk of violating His will? These are the kinds of questions that we are led to consider.

As this study is brought to a conclusion, the seriousness of the issue compels us to consider the warnings of several men from the past. If we use musical instruments in worship because of their emotional effect, let us remember the warning of James Ramsey,

> Such influences can never touch the spiritual life but benumb it. They divert the mind from the only object of spiritual worship. The impressions they make are danger-ously deceptive, just in the proportion to their power over the emotional nature.[1]

John Owen warns us that many have "fallen away from the gospel with respect to its worship, . . .by rejecting its simplicity and pure institutions." He states that this falling away does not happen all at once, but "there are various degrees of declension from the purity of gospel worship, according as men forsake any part of it, or make any additions of their own to it,"[2] and this declension can come by "insensible degrees and in a long tract of time."[3]

Perhaps the words of Professor Girardeau, which express God's jealousy over His worship, are a fitting conclusion to all we have considered.

> He himself stands guard over his own sanctuary, and armed with bolts of vengeance, threatens with condign punishment the invaders of his prerogative, the usurpers of his rights. We have seen how awfully this lesson was enforced under the old dispensation, how swiftly, like

1. Ramsey, 276–277.
2. Owen, Vol. 7, 221.
3. Ibid., 222.

lightning, his judgments flashed against rash and insolent assertors of their own will in regard to the mode in which he was to be worshipped, and how severely he dealt with his own choicest and holiest servants for departures from his prescriptions in this matter. This vehement zeal and jealously of God for the purity of his worship should deter us from venturing one step beyond the directions of his Word. Who, for the sake of the ornaments of art and the suggestions of fancy, would unnecessarily challenge the visitations of his wrath? In this dispensation he is patient and forbearing, but who will coolly elect to go, with the unexpunged guilt of encroaching upon the sovereignty of God over the worship of his house, to the tremendous bar of last accounts?[4]

4. Girardeau, 126–127.

Appendix A

An Exhortation to Unity

THERE are perhaps few issues in our generation that tend more toward divisions among Christians than those involving the worship of God and, in particular, the role and use of musical instruments. Those who have been convinced of the need for reformation in this area of worship should also take seriously their solemn duty to guard the unity of the church. The unity of the church should be among the highest concerns of every Christian. The Lord Jesus prays for the unity of His church (John 17:20–23), the apostles give many exhortations to unity (1 Cor. 1:10; 2 Cor. 13:11; Phil. 1:27, 2:1–4; 1 Thess. 5:12; James 3:13–18; 1 Pet. 3:8–9), and unity is the responsibility of every member of the church (1 Cor. 12:25).

Those who desire the exclusion of musical instruments should be sensitive to the peculiar difficulties that such reformation may present to many in our generation. We live at a time when it is assumed by the vast majority of Christians that musical instruments are to be present in the worship of the church. As a result, reformation in this area of worship often seems radical, and it may take much time and patience for a biblical theology of music in worship to be absorbed and developed into convictions.

Three different situations are envisioned in the following exhortation to unity. In each situation, it is assumed that all who are involved share a high regard for the regulative principle of worship and its practical application. The potential division envisioned is between those who continue to use a single musical instrument as a subordinate accompaniment in singing and those who desire its exclusion. The underlying principle in each of these situations is that the unity of the church is a higher concern than the use or non-use of a single musical instrument. Disunity over the use of a single musical instrument would be a more serious breach of Christ's will than the use of the instrument itself. The application of the regulative principle to this area of worship is of great importance, but the use of a single instrument to accompany singing should not be seen as a violation of such gravity that it should disrupt the peace or the unity of any church.

1) Unity Between Pastors and People. Pastors who are convinced that reformation is necessary should proceed "with great patience and instruction" in leading their congregations. The minds and consciences of the people must be fully persuaded before any changes can be made. The pastors should proceed slowly and with care, always seeking to guard the unity of the church throughout the entire process of reformation.

It may be helpful to envision a scenario in which this reformation proceeds in a most judicious manner. The pastors are the first to become convinced of the exclusion of musical instruments from Christian worship. They then provide the necessary reading materials to the members of their church, encouraging them to respond with their thoughts and concerns. As the people read and respond, the pastors get a feel for the pulse of the congregation. During regular oversight meetings, they may continue to receive input concerning this issue. This process may go on for many months before the pastors believe there is sufficient unity to proceed to public instruction of the entire church. If they do not believe that this unity is present, they should wait and graciously try to persuade those who may be opposed as they have opportunity. The hope is that the church will be able to make this reformation with one mind and heart. In this way, the pastors move carefully and slowly, seeking to guard the unity of the church throughout the reformation process.

We should remember an historical model in this matter of patience in reformation. In the late 1600s, the Particular Baptists in England did not believe that singing was an ordinance of New Testament worship. When Benjamin Keach came to the conviction that it was, he gave instruction to his congregation. But Keach was willing to wait patiently for seventeen years before his church was fully convinced and finally received singing as a part of their worship.

2) Unity Within the Congregation. In this situation, we envision an individual member who has become convinced that musical instruments should be excluded from New Testament worship. Before this individual speaks with other members of his church over this issue, he should first humbly bring his concern before his elders. He should prayerfully and patiently wait upon their response. Under no circumstances should he seek to stir up a faction within the membership of his church or cause any disruption of its peace over this issue. If the elders do not come to share the same convictions, the individual member should continue to diligently maintain "the unity of the Spirit in the bond of peace." He should understand that his church may have a high regard for the regulative principle of worship, while not being convinced of this particular issue. The concern over the use or nonuse of a single musical instruments is not of such importance that any member should absent himself from the assembly of the church or in any other way disturb its peace.

The London Baptist Confession of Faith gives a helpful admonition regarding unity in the church. Although the admonition regards issues of discipline, the principle still applies, "No church members, upon any offense taken by them, having performed their duty required of them towards the person they are offended at, ought to disturb any church order, or absent themselves from the assemblies of the church, or administration of any ordinances, upon the account of such offense at any of their fellow members, but to wait upon Christ, in the further proceeding of the church."[1]

3) *Unity Between Churches.* Every church should desire to maintain communion with other like-minded churches that hold to the same confessional standards. Divisions that separate churches from one another are as grievous as those that split individual congregations. Churches that exclude musical instruments from worship should continue to have high esteem for other churches that differ from them on this issue. Once again, the concern of unity is of greater importance than this particular issue of reformation. Those churches that reform should remember that this particular aspect of reformation does not guarantee that their worship is all that Christ desires it to be. A church may exclude the use of musical instruments and still fall short of the biblical standard in other areas of worship. "Therefore let him who thinks he stands take heed lest he fall" (1 Cor. 10:12).

---

1. London Baptist Confession of 1689, Chapter 26, Paragraph 13.

APPENDIX B

Suggestions for Reformation

THE following are some brief suggestions that may be helpful for those who desire to make this reformation to *a cappella* singing. These suggestions are based upon both the recommendations of others and the experience of our own church in making this change. Every congregation will mark out its own path that seems most appropriate based upon its own circumstances.

1) Congregational Instruction. Instruction from the Word of God must always precede reformation. It is assumed that the congregation has been instructed and convinced that the singing of the church should be composed of human voices without the accompaniment of musical instruments. Instruction should also be given regarding the exalted place Christ has given to singing in His church. The people must understand the benefits and the blessings of singing if they are to engage in it with all their hearts. If singing is to be what Christ desires, there must first be a zeal for it among the members of the church.

2) Identifying and Using Simple Tunes. Many of the tunes found in modern hymnbooks were written in the 19th century when the organ was increasing in use among Protestant churches. These tunes were often written more for the enjoyment of the organist than for the ease of congregational singing. The result is that many tunes are beyond the musical ability of the average congregation.

Each congregation must assess its own singing talent and identify those tunes it knows and sings well. In our church, we were able to identify more than 150 tunes acceptable for *a cappella* singing. These tunes are used on Sunday mornings. On Sunday evenings and Wednesday prayer meetings, we use other tunes, and when we have learned them well, they are added to the Sunday morning list. By interchanging tunes with the same meter, we are able to sing the majority of hymns in our book.

3) Beginning the Hymn. Some have a concern over how the congregation can begin a hymn when there is no instrumental accompaniment. The solution is quite simple. One man who can hit the proper pitch and whose voice can be sufficiently heard can begin the hymn. The congregation should then quickly follow along with him. This is the method used by Spurgeon and many other churches.

4) Learning of New Tunes. A church should never stagnate in the number of tunes it knows but should be encouraged to periodically learn new tunes appropriate for congregational singing. An effort to learn one new tune a month will add up quickly over time. Simple tunes that may be learned relatively easily may be found in many hymnbooks and other resources. Louis Bourgeois wrote the majority of the tunes used by John Calvin in Geneva during the Protestant Reformation. His tunes, such as the Old Hundredth, used in the doxology, were simple and became the standard for the Reformed churches of Europe and England for hundreds of years. At a time other than Sunday worship services, simple tunes such as these or others can be introduced to the congregation by those who are musically talented. The experts tell us that a new tune can be learned by listening to another's voice even more easily than with a musical instrument. James Sydnor states, "The conductor's voice is a better teaching medium than playing the tune on the organ."[1]

---

1. James Rawlings Sydnor, *Hymns & Their Uses,* (Carol Stream, IL: Agape, 1982),

When a satisfactory level of singing proficiency is achieved, these new tunes can then be used in the Lord's Day services.

5) Good Singing Begins at Home. When a congregation gathers for worship, it is really made up of a collection of families. The public singing of the church is a reflection of the singing of the families throughout the week. The hymns sung in family worship should be the same as those sung in the public worship of the church. If families sing these hymns well at home, they will do even better when they gather for corporate worship. The fathers should take the lead and encourage their children in singing both in the home and in the church. During the Reformation, John Calvin had his psalter published in pocket size so that the people could bring it home and use it in singing with their families.

6) Proper Use of Singing Skills. Every church has a number of members who possess a higher-than-average level of singing talent. Such members may want to place themselves in different locations throughout the congregation in order to help guide and carry the rest of the people in singing. The musically talented members of the church may want to give some simple instruction in the basic principles of singing. The duty of singing rests not upon a trained group within the church, but on the entire congregation. Every member should be encouraged to develop whatever gift of singing he possesses to the best of his ability. The purpose here is not to turn the church into a choral society, but to increase confidence so that all the members can fulfill Christ's command to sing. In this way, a church makes the most use of the talents God has given to it. In a smaller congregation, the people may want to sit closer together so that their voices can be better heard by one another.

John Wesley gave the following points of practical advice in regard to singing:

> 1. Sing all. See that you join with the congregation as frequently as you can. Let not a slight degree of weakness

126.

or weariness hinder you. If it is a cross to you, take it up, and you will find a blessing.

2. Sing lustily, and with a good courage. Beware of singing as if you are half-dead or half-asleep; but lift up your voice with strength.

3. Sing modestly. Do not bawl, so as to be heard above or distinct from the rest of the congregation—that you may not destroy the harmony—but strive to unite your voices together so as to make one clear melodious sound.

4. Sing in time. Whatever time is sung, be sure to keep with it. Do not run before nor stay behind it; but attend close to the leading voices, and move therewith as exactly as you can; and take care not to sing too slow.

5. Above all sing spiritually. Have an eye to God in every word you sing. Aim at pleasing him more than yourself, or any other creature. In order to do this attend strictly to the sense of what you sing, and see that your heart is not carried away with the sound, but offered to God continually; so shall your singing be such as the Lord will approve here, and reward you when He cometh in the clouds of heaven.[2]

7) Acoustics. The experts all agree that the acoustical surroundings in the church building will have the most important and direct effect upon the sound of singing voices.[3] A plain tile floor with a relatively low non-absorbent ceiling and walls allows the sound of the voices to carry throughout the room. What is desired is a proper acoustical reverberation without an echo. In existing buildings,

2. John Wesley, *The Works of John Wesley,* (Grand Rapids, Zondervan Publishing House, 1958), Vol 14, 346.
3. James Rawlings Sydnor, *Hymns & Their Uses,* 137–139. William J. Reynolds, *Congregational Singing,* (Nashville: Convention Press, 1975), 41–48. Hopson, *100+ Ways to Improve Hymnsinging.*

some relatively inexpensive corrective measures may be taken. An acoustics engineer should be consulted.

8) Commitment and Perseverance. A cappella singing will not be done well without effort and labor on the part of the entire church. The church must remember that it has embarked upon this path as a matter of scriptural principle, and there must be a determination to make progress. There should be a long range view, realizing that good congregational singing will be a gradual process. We should not expect to sing as well today as we will several years from now. The church should be encouraged that with perseverance, *a cappella* singing can be accomplished with a high degree of aesthetic beauty. Such has been the case throughout the history of the church, and it continues to be so in many churches today.

Index of Names[*]

THE CHURCH FATHERS

THE REFORMERS

*Men or groups in agreement with the conclusions set forth in this study

Bibliography

Abbot-Smith, G. *A Manual of Greek Lexicon of the New Testament*. New York: Charles Scribner's Sons, 1952.

Ainsworth, Henry. *The Old Orthodox Foundation of Religion: Left for a Pattern to a New Reformation*. London: E. Cotes, 1653. Early English Books, 1641–1700. Ann Arbor, MI: University Microfilm International, 1961—.

———. *An Arrow Against Idolatrie,* 1640. Early English Books, 1475–1640. Ann Arbor, MI: University Microfilm International, 1937—.

Ames, William. *A Fresh Suit Against Human Ceremonies in God's Worship.* Gregg International Publishers Limited, reprinted, 1971.

Augustine. *Expositions of the Book of Psalms.* Oxford: James Parker and Co. and Rivingtons, 1877.

———. *The Confessions of St. Augustine.* Translated by John K. Ryan, Garden City, New York: Image Books, 1960.

Arndt, William F. and Gingrich, F. Wilbur, *A Greek–English Lexicon of the New Testament.* Chicago: The University of Chicago Press, 1979.

Baird, Charles W. *The Presbyterian Liturgies.* Grand Rapids: Baker Book House, 1957.

Barnes, Albert. *Barnes Notes.* London: Blackie & Son, 1884-1885; Reprint, Grand Rapids: Baker Book House, reprinted 1987.

Bannerman, Douglas D. *The Scripture Doctrine of the Church.* Grand Rapids: Baker Book House, 1976.

Bannerman, James. *The Church of Christ.* 1868. USA: Still Waters Revival Books. n.d.

Baxter, Richard. *The Practical Works of Richard Baxter.* Ligonier, PA: Soli Deo Gloria Publications, reprinted 1990.

Benedict, David. *Fifty Years Among the Baptists.* New York: Sheldon & Company, 1860.

Best. H.M., Hutter, D. Music; Musical Instruments, *The Zondervan Pictorial Encyclopedia of the Bible.* Grand Rapids: The Zondervan Corporation, 1976.

Bingham, Joseph. *The Antiquities of the Christian Church.* 2nd ed. London: Simpkin, Marshall, and Co., 1870.

Blanchard, John. *Pop Goes the Gospel.* Hertfordshire, England: Evangelical Press, 1984.

Blood, A.J. & Zatorre, R.J. 2001. Intensely pleasurable responses to music correlate with activity in brain regions implicated with reward and emotion, *Proceedings of the National Academy of Sciences* 98.

Boer, Harry R. *A Short History of the Early Church.* Grand Rapids: Eerdmans Publishing Company, 1976.

Breward, Ian. *The Works of William Perkins.* Berkshire: The Sutton Courtenay Press, 1970.

Brown, Colin. ed. *The New International Dictionary of New Testament Theology.* Grand Rapids: Zondervan, 1929.

Brown, Francis. *The New Brown–Driver–Briggs–Gesenius Hebrew and English Lexicon.* Peabody: Hendrickson Publishers, 1979.

Budgen, Victor. *On Fire for God.* Hertfordshire: Evangelical Press, 1983.

Bunyan, John. *The Works of John Bunyan.* Edinburgh: The Banner of Truth Trust, reprinted 1991.

Calderwood, David. *The Pastor and the Prelate.* Edinburgh: Alexander Henderson, 1692.

Calvin, John. *Calvin's Commentary.* 22 Vol., Grand Rapids: Baker Book House Company, Reprinted 1984.

Calvin, John. *Calvin's Institutes.* ca. 1559. Grand Rapids: Associated Publishers and Authors, Inc. n.d.

———. *The Necessity of Reforming the Church.* Edinburgh: Calvin Translation Society, 1844; Reprint, Dallas: Protestant Heritage Press, 1995.

Carson, D. A., ed. *Worship by the Book.* Grand Rapids, Zondervan, 2002.

Carson, John L. and David W. Hall, eds. *To Glorify And Enjoy God.* Edinburgh: The Banner of Truth Trust, 1994.

Clement of Alexandria. *Christ the Educator.* Translated by Simon P. Wood. New York: Fathers of the Church, Inc., 1954.

Coleman, Lyman. *The Antiquities of the Christian Church.* Andover: Gould, Newman & Saxton, 1841.

Cotton, John. *Singing of Psalmes: A Gospel Ordinance.* London: Sunne and Fountaine in Pauls-Churchyard, 1650. Thomason Tracts, Ann Arbor, MI: University Microflim International, 1977–1981.

Cross, F. L. ed., E. A. Livingstone, ed., 3rd edition. *The Oxford Dictionary of the Christian Church.* Oxford: Oxford University Press, 1997.

Cunningham, William. *The Reformers and the Theology of the Reformation.* Edinburgh: The Banner of Truth Trust, reprinted, 2000.

Curwen, J. Spencer. *Studies in Worship Music.* London: J. Curwen & Sons, 1890.

Dabney, Robert L. *The Presbyterian Quarterly.* July 1889. http://www.naphtali.com/dabney's_review_of_girardeau.htm (accessed March 24, 2004).

Dagg, John L. *Manual of Theology.* Harrisonburg, VA: Gano Books, 1982.

d'Aubigne, J.H. Merle. *History of the Reformation of the Sixteenth Century.* Grand Rapids: Baker Book House, Reprinted 1987.

Dana, H. E. & Julius R. Mantey. *A Manual of Grammar of the Greek New Testament.* New York: MacMillan Publishing Co., Inc., 1955.

Davies, Horton. *Christian Worship, Its History and Meaning.* New York: Abingdon Press, 1957.

———. *The Worship of the American Puritans.* New York: Peter Lang Publishing, Inc., 1990; Reprint, New York: Soli Deo Gloria Publications, 1999.

———. *The Worship of the English Puritans.* New York: Soli Deo Gloria Publications, 1997.

Dickinson, Edward. *Music in the History of the Western Church.* New York: Charles Scribner's Sons, 1902.

Dickson, David. *A Commentary on the Psalms.* Edinburgh: The Banner of Truth Trust, reprinted 1985.

Douglass, Robert. *Church Music Through the Ages.* Nashville: Convention Press, 1967.

Edersheim, Alfred. *The Temple.* Peabody: Hendrickson Publishers, 1994.

Eire, Carlos M. N. *War Against Idols.* Cambridge: Cambridge University Press, 1986.

Ferguson, Everett. *A Cappella Music in the Public Worship of the Church.* Abilene, TX: Biblical Research Press, 1972.

Fleming, David Hay. *The Reformation in Scotland.* London: Hodder and Stoughton, 1910.

Foote, Henry Wilder. *Three Centuries of American Hymnody.* Cambridge, MA: Harvard University Press, 1940.

Friberg, Barbara & Timothy. *Analytical Greek New Testament.* Grand Rapids: Baker Book House, 1975.

Froude, J. A. *Life and Letters of Erasmus.* New York: Charles Scribner's Sons, 1894.

Fuller, Andrew. *The Complete Works of Andrew Fuller.* London: Arthur Hall, Virtue, And Co., 1851.

Friedrich, Gerhard. *Theological Dictionary of the New Testament.* 10 Vols., Grand Rapids: William B. Eerdmans Publishing Company, 1985.

Garside, Charles Jr. *Zwingli and the Arts.* New Haven: Yale University Press, 1966.

———. *The Origins of Calvin's Theology of Music.* 1536–1543. Philadelphia: The American Philosophical Society, 1979.

Gelineau, Joseph. *Voices and Instruments in Christian Worship.* Collegeville, MN: The Liturgical Press.

George, Timothy. *Theology of the Reformers.* Nashville: Broadman Press, 1988.

Gill, John. *Gill's Commentary.* London: William Hill, 1852-1854; Reprint, Grand Rapids: Baker Book House, 1980.

Gingrich, F. Wilbur. *Shorter Lexicon of the Greek New Testament.* Chicago: The University of Chicago Press, 1957.

Girardeau, John L. *Instrumental Music in the Public Worship of the Church.* Richmond: Whittet & Shepperson, Printers, 1888.

Goodwin, Thomas. *The Works of Thomas Goodwin.* Edinburgh: James Nichol, 1861.

Grout, Donald Jay; Palisca, Claude V. *The History of Western Music.* New York: W. W. Norton & Company.

Harris, R. Laird, ed. *Theological Wordbook of the Old Testament.* 2 Vols. Chicago: Moody Press, 1980.

Hart D. G. and John R. Muether. *With Reverence and Awe.* Phillipsburg, NJ: P&R Publishing, 2002.

Haykin, Michael A. G. *Kiffin, Knollys and Keach.* Leeds: Reformation Today Trust, 1996.

Henry, Matthew. *Matthew Henry's Commentary on the Whole Bible.* Old Tappen, NJ: Fleming H. Revell Company, n.d.

Hill, Samuel, S. ed., *Encyclopedia of Religion in the South.* Mercer University Press, 1984.

Hirst, Thomas. *The Music of the Church.* London: Whittaker, & Co.; Simpkin, Marshall, & Co., 1841.

Hodge, Charles. *A Commentary on Ephesians.* Edinburgh: The Banner of Truth Trust, reprinted 1991.

Hopson, Hal H. *100+ Ways to Improve Hymnsinging.* Carol Stream, IL: Hope Publishing Company, 2002.

Hutcheson, George. *The Gospel of John.* Edinburgh: The Banner of Truth Trust, reprinted 1985.

Josephus. *Josephus Complete Works.* Grand Rapids: Kregel Publications, 1981.

Keach, Benjamin. *The Breach Repaired in God's Worship.* London: John Marshall, 1700. Early English Books, 1641-1700. Ann Arbor, MI: University Microfilm International, 1961—.

Keil, C. F. and Delitzsch, F. *Commentary on the Old Testament.* Peabody: Hendrickson Publishers, 1989.

Kittel, Gerhard and Gerhard Friedrich, eds. *Theological Dictionary of the New Testament.* Grand Rapids: William B. Eerdmans Publishing Company, 1985.

Knollys, Hanserd. *An Exposition of the Whole Book of the Revelation.* London: Newgate Street, 1688. Early English Books, 1641–1700, Ann Arbor, MI: University Microfilm International, 1961—.

Kurfees, M. C. *Instrumental Music in the Worship.* Nashville: Gospel Advocate Co., 1950.

Lechler, Professor. *John Wycliffe and His English Precursors.* London: The Religious Tract Society, 1904.

Lippy, Charles H. and Peter W. Williams, eds. *Encyclopedia of the American Religious Experience.* New York: Charles Scribner's Sons, 1988.

Lloyd-Jones, D. Martyn. *Preaching & Preachers.* Grand Rapids: Zondervan Publishing House, 1996.

Lorenz, Edmund. *Church Music.* New York: Fleming H. Revell Company, 1923.

Luther, Martin. *Luther's Works.* Philadelphia: Muhlenberg Press, 1959.

MacCulloch, Diarmaid. *The Reformation.* New York: Viking, 2003.

MacMillan, William. *The Worship of the Scottish Reformed Church 1550–1638.* London: The Lassodie Press, Ltd., 1930.

Manton, Thomas. *The Complete Works of Thomas Manton.* Worthington, PA: Maranatha Publications, n.d.

Martin, Ralph P. *Worship in the Early Church.* Grand Rapids: Eerdmans, 1974.

Masters, Peter. *Worship in the Melting Pot.* London: The Wakeman Trust, 2002.

Mather, Cotton. *The Great Works of Christ in America.* London: 1702; Reprint, Hartford: Silas Andrus and Son, 1853; Reprint, Edinburgh: The Banner of Truth Trust, reprinted 1979.

Mather, Samuel. *The Figures or Types of the Old Testament.* New York: Johnson Reprint Corporation, 1969.

Maxwell, William D. *An Outline of Christian Worship.* London: Oxford University Press, 1955.

McClintock, John and James Strong. *Cyclopedia of Biblical, Theological and Ecclesiastical Literature.* New York: Harper & Brothers, Publishers, 1879.

McKee, Elsie Anne. "Reformed Worship in the Sixteenth Century," *Christian Worship in Reformed Churches Past and Present.* ed. Lukas Vischer. Grand Rapids: Eerdmans Publishing Company, 2003.

McKinnon, James. *The Church Fathers and Musical Instruments.* Ann Arbor: University Microfilms, Inc., 1965.

———. *Music in Early Christian Literature.* Cambridge: Cambridge University Press, 1987.

———. *The Temple, the Church Fathers and Early Western Chant.* Brookfield: Ashgate Publishing Company, 1998.

Morecraft, Joe. *How God Wants Us to Worship Him.* San Antonio: The Vision Forum, Inc., 2001.

Moulton, Harold K. *The Analytical Greek Lexicon Revised.* Grand Rapids: Zondervan Publishing House, 1978.

Moulton, James Hope and George Milligan. *The Vocabulary of the Greek Testament.* London: Hodder and Stoughton, 1929.

Murray, Iain. *Revival & Revivalism.* Edinburgh: The Banner of Truth Trust, 1994.

Music, David W. *Instruments in Church.* Lanham, Maryland, and London: The Scarecrow Press, Inc., 1998.

Nichols, James Hastings. *Corporate Worship in the Reformed Tradition.* Philadelphia: The Westminster Press, 1984.

Old, Hughes Oliphant. *The Patristic Roots of Reformed Worship.* Zurich: Theologischer Verlag, 1975.

————. *Worship That Is Reformed According to Scripture.* Atlanta: John Knox Press, 1984.

Owen, John. *The Works of John Owen.* Vols. 1-16 Johnstone & Hunter, 1850-1853; Reprint, Edinburgh: The Banner of Truth Trust, 1979.

————. *The Works of John Owen.* Vols.17-23. Johnstone & Hunter, 1854-1855; Reprint, Edinburgh: The Banner of Truth Trust, 1991.

Parsons, Lawrence. *Music of the Spheres.* BBC Music Magazine, November 2003.

Perkins, William. *A Golden Chain.* London: John Legatt, 1621. Early English Books, 1475–1640. Ann Arbor, MI: University Microfilm International.

Portnoy, Julius. *Music in the Life of Man.* New York: Holt, Rinehart and Winston, 1963.

Preece, Isobel Woods. *Music in the Scottish Church up to 1603.* Glasgow: The Universities of Glasgow and Aberdeen, 2000.

Pratt, Waldo Selden. *The Music of the French Psalter of 1562.* New York: Columbia University Press, 1939.

Preus, James S. *Carlstadt's Ordinaciones and Luther's Liberty.* Cambridge: Harvard University Press, 1974.

Puritan Sermons. Wheaton, IL: Richard Owen Roberts, Publishers, 1982.

Quick, John. *Synodicon in Gallia Reformata.* London: T. Parkhust and J. Robinson, 1692. Early English Books, 1641–1700. Ann Arbor, MI: University Microfilm International, 1961—.

Ramsey, James. *Revelation.* Edinburgh: The Banner of Truth Trust, 1984.

Reese, Gustave. *Music in the Renaissance.* New York: W. W. Norton & Company, Inc., 1959.

Reid, W. Stanford. *Trumpeter of God.* Grand Rapids: Baker Book House, 1982.

Reisinger, Ernest C. and D. Matthew Allen. *Worship.* Cape Coral: Founders Press, 2001.

Reynolds, William J. *Congregational Singing.* Nashville: Convention Press, 1975.

Rice, Howard L. and James C. Huffstutler. *Reformed Worship.* Louisville, KY: Geneva Press, 2001.

Rice, William C. *A Concise History of Church Music.* New York: Abingdon Press, 1964.

Ridgeley, Thomas. *A Body of Divinity.* Edinburgh: A. Fullarton and Co., 1844.

Roberts, Alexander and James Donaldson, eds. *The Ante-Nicene Fathers.* Buffalo: The Christian Literature Publishing Company, 1885.

Robertson, A. T. *A Grammar of the Greek New Testament in the Light of Historical Research.* Nashville: Broadman Press, 1934.

Ryken, Philip Graham, Derek W.H. Thomas, J. Ligon Duncan, eds. *Give Praise to God.* Phillipsburg, NJ: P&R Publishing, 2003.

Sadie, Stanley, ed. *The New Grove Dictionary of Music and Musicians.* New York: MacMillan Publishers Limited, 1980, Vol. 1.

Schaff, Philip. *History of the Christian Church.* New York: Charles Scribner's Sons, 1910: reprint ed., Vol. 1, Grand Rapids: Eerdmans, 1985.

Scholes, Percy A. *The Puritans and Music.* London: Oxford University Press, 1934.

Simons, Menno. *The Complete Writings of Menno Simons.* Scottdale, PA: Herald Press, 1956.

Spinka, Matthew. *John Hus' Concept of the Church.* Princeton: Princeton University Press, 1966.

Sophocles, E. A. *Greek Lexicon of the Roman and Byzantine Periods.* Leipzig: Harvard University Press, 1914.

Spurgeon, Charles. *The Autobiography of Charles H. Spurgeon,* New York: Fleming H. Revell Company, 1899, Vol. 3, 256.

————. *Metropolitan Tabernacle Pulpit.* Rio, WI: Ages Digital Library, Ages Software Inc., 2000.

————. "How Shall We Sing?" *The Sword and the Trowel,* June 1, 1870. Reprinted in *C. H.*

Spurgeon's Works as Published in His Monthly Magazine The Sword and the Trowel. Vol. 2, Years 1868, 1869, 1870. Pasadena, Texas: Pilgrim Publications, 1975.

———. *The Treasury of David.* McLean, VA: MacDonald Publishing Company.

Steinmetz, David C. *Reformers in the Wings.* 2nd. Ed. Oxford: Oxford University Press, 2001.

Stiles, Ezra. *The Literary Diary of Ezra Stiles,* ed. Franklin Bowditch Dexter. New York: Charles Scribner's Sons, 1901.

Sydnor, James Rawlings. *Hymns and Their Use.* Carol Stream, IL: Agape, 1982.

Tame, David. *The Secret Power of Music.* New York: Destiny Books, 1984.

Thayer, Joseph Henry. *The New Thayer's Greek–English Lexicon of the New Testament.* Peabody: Hendrickson Publishers, 1981.

The Acts of the General Assemblies of the Church of Scotland, 1638–1649. Edinburgh: George Mosman, 1691. Early English Books, 1641–1700. Ann Arbor, MI: University Microfilm International, 1961—.

The Treasury of Scripture Knowledge. McLean, VA: MacDonald Publishing Company, Inc., 1982.

Thornwell, James Henley. *The Collected Writings of James Henley Thornwell.* Edinburgh: The Banner of Truth Trust, reprinted 1986.

Vine, W. E.; Merrill F. Unger, ; William White, Jr., eds. *Vine's Complete Expository Dictionary of Old and New Testament Words.* New York: Thomas Nelson Publishers, 1985.

Waldron, Samuel. *The Regulative Principle of the Church.* Quezon City: Wisdom Publications, 1995.

Walker, Williston. *A History of the Christian Church.* New York: Charles Scribner's Sons, 1985.

Watts, Isaac. *The Works of Isaac Watts.* 6 Vols. London: John Barfield, Wardour Street, 1810.

Wesley, John. *The Works of John Wesley.* Grand Rapids: Zondervan Publishing House, 1958.

Wilson-Dickson, Andrew. *The Story of Christian Music.* Minneapolis: Fortress Press, 1996.

Winslow, Edward. *Hypocrisie Unmasked.* London: J. Bellamy, 1646. Early English Books, 1641–1700, Ann Arbor, MI: University Microfilm International, 1961—.

Zeland, Synod of. *A Letter from the Synod of Zeland to the Commissioners of the General Assembly of the Kirk of Scotland.* Edinburgh: Evan Tyler, 1643. Thomason Tracts. Ann Arbor, MI: University Microflim International, 1977–1981.

Old Light on New Worship
Cover Designed by Benjamin W. Geist
Printed by Bookmasters, Inc.

SIMPSON
PUBLISHING COMPANY

The righteous are bold as a lion-Proverbs 28:1